Power and Agency in the Lives of
Contemporary Tibetan Nuns

The Study of Religion in a Global Context

Series editors

Satoko Fujiwara	Katja Triplett	Alexandra Grieser
Executive Editor	Series Editor	Managing Editor
University of Tokyo	Leipzig University	Trinity College Dublin

The series, published in association with the International Association for the History of Religions, encourages work that is innovative in the study of religions, whether of an empirical, theoretical or methodological nature. This includes multi- or inter-disciplinary studies involving anthropology, philosophy, psychology, sociology and political studies. Volumes will examine the continuing influence of postcolonial, decolonial and intercultural dynamics, as well as contemporary responses from intersectional studies. They will also address the relevance and application of more recent approaches such as cognitivist, as well as ones concerned with aesthetic culture – art, architecture, media, performance and sound.

Published

Global Phenomenologies of Religion
An Oral History in Interviews
Edited by Satoko Fujiwara, David Thurfjel and Steven Engler

Philosophy and the End of Sacrifice
Disengaging Ritual in Ancient India, Greece and Beyond
Edited by Peter Jackson and Anna-Pya Sjödin

Religion as Relation
Studying Religion in Context
Edited by Peter Berger, Marjo Buitelaar and Kim Knibbe

The Relational Dynamics of Enchantment and Sacralization
Changing the Terms of the Religion Versus Secularity Debate
Edited by Peik Ingman, Terhi Utriainen, Tuija Hovi and Måns Broo

Translocal Lives and Religion
Connections between Asia and Europe in the Late Modern World
Edited by Philippe Bornet

Power and Agency in the Lives of Contemporary Tibetan Nuns
An Intersectional Study

Mitra Härkönen

SHEFFIELD UK   BRISTOL CT

Published by Equinox Publishing Ltd.

UK: Office 415, The Workstation, 15 Paternoster Row, Sheffield, South Yorkshire S1 2BX

USA: ISD, 70 Enterprise Drive, Bristol, CT 06010

www.equinoxpub.com

First published 2023

© Mitra Härkönen 2023

All rights reserved. No part of this publication may be reproduced or transmitted in any form or by any means, electronic or mechanical, including photocopying, recording or any information storage or retrieval system, without prior permission in writing from the publishers.

ISBN-13 978 1 80050 300 7 (hardback)
978 1 80050 301 4 (paperback)
978 1 80050 302 1 (ePDF)

British Library Cataloguing-in-Publication Data

A catalogue record for this book is available from the British Library.

Library of Congress Cataloging-in-Publication Data

Names: Härkönen, Mitra, author.
Title: Power and agency in the lives of contemporary Tibetan nuns : an intersectional study / Mitra Härkönen.
Description: Sheffield, South Yorkshire ; Bristol, CT : Equinox Publishing Ltd., 2023. | Series: The study of religion in a global context | Includes bibliographical references and index. | Summary: "This book examines the lived experiences of oppression and opportunities encountered by contemporary Tibetan Buddhist nuns living in the People's Republic of China and the Tibetan exile community in India. It investigates how the intersections of the nuns' female gender, their Buddhist religion and their Tibetan nationality on the one hand produce subordination and an unequal distribution of power but, on the other, provide the nuns with opportunities and agency"—Provided by publisher.
Identifiers: LCCN 2022041312 (print) | LCCN 2022041313 (ebook) | ISBN 9781800503007 (hardback) | ISBN 9781800503014 (paperback) | ISBN 9781800503021 (pdf)
Subjects: LCSH: Buddhist nuns—China—Tibet Autonomous Region. | Monastic and religious life of women—China—Tibet Autonomous Region. | Buddhist nuns—Religious life.
Classification: LCC BQ6160.C2 H37 2023 (print) | LCC BQ6160.C2 (ebook) | DDC 294.3/657082--dc23/eng/20221013
LC record available at https://lccn.loc.gov/2022041312
LC ebook record available at https://lccn.loc.gov/2022041313

Typeset by JS Typesetting Ltd, Porthcawl, Mid Glamorgan

For all brave Tibetans

Contents

Note on Non-English Terms	ix

Part I Introduction

1	Tibetan Women: "Extraordinarily Liberated" or "Shockingly Oppressed"?	3
2	Intersectionality: A Theory and a Method	18
3	Doing Research in the Contested Tibetan Field	25

Part II From Laity to Monastic Life

4	The Idea of Nunhood Matures	47
5	Donning the Robes	71
6	Finding a Place to Stay	85
7	Life as a Nun	101

Part III Tibetan Nuns in Domains of Power

8	Oppressive Social Institutions of Tibet under Chinese Rule	131
9	Internalized and Forced Discipline	146
10	Hegemonic Ideologies and Doctrines	153
11	Domination in Everyday Practices	169

Part IV Opportunities in Monastic Life

12	Freedom in Monasticism	173
13	Agency as Resistance and Cultural Maintenance	178
14	Compassionate Agency	186
15	Increasing Opportunities	193

Part V Conclusion

16	Between Oppression and Opportunities	201

Appendix: Short Biographies of the Nuns	209
References	214
Index	231

Note on Non-English Terms

This research contains Tibetan, Sanskrit and some Chinese terms. I have applied the Wylie transliteration scheme to transliterate some Tibetan names and especially the Buddhist concepts I use. Wylie transliteration has become a standard transliteration system in Tibetan studies. It does not give the correct pronunciation of a Tibetan word, but is used to transcribe Tibetan script as it is written. For Buddhist terms and some central figures of Buddhism, Sanskrit is also used. For Chinese terms, pinyin romanization is used.

Part I

INTRODUCTION

Tibetan Women

"Extraordinarily Liberated" or "Shockingly Oppressed"?

The decision to become a nun was apparently taken by me. I didn't have to go far to see the suffering of *saṃsāra*. The life I led with my family gave me a vivid picture of what my future would be like. What we were doing was only filling our stomachs. From a tender age, I wanted to become a nun so that I could get a good education and help other people more efficiently in the future. But, due to lots of circumstances, I just left it aside – especially because I knew that my help was crucial to my mother to raise our family since our dad was not able to do anything.

One day I met three girls from our village. They were going to Lhasa to become nuns. This event made my heart jump to the stars. I told myself how happy I would be if I was one of them. Ultimately, it was the right time for me to join them; I knew I had earned enough money for my family and I didn't see them facing any financial problems in the future. Thus, I started my journey to Lhasa without disclosing my secret to my family.

But it didn't take long for all the beautiful things to deteriorate. The Chinese began to send troops to our nunnery whenever there was unrest in Lhasa. Slowly, they set up a program purposely to brainwash the nuns into thinking that the Communist party is good and His Holiness the Dalai Lama is bad. And every day we were compelled to read their small pamphlets, which stated colossal accusations toward outside Tibetans. We also had to carry them to our home and explain them to every family member. I was not that good at enduring all this and started to feel suffocated to live in my own country. Later, without telling my parents, I fled to India.

Ani Sherab[1]

---

1. Ani Sherab is a pseudonym. In Tibetan, nuns are usually referred as ani (*a ni*) or chomo (*jo mo*). Chöla (*chos lags*) is a polite way to refer to a nun, and it is used especially in Central Tibet and among exiled Tibetans. Tsunma (*btsun ma*), which is also a proper and polite way to address nuns, is becoming more common.

Introduction

Setting the Stage

The scholar whose research relates to women or gender is often asked about the "status" or the "position" of women, for example, in particular religious doctrines or practices, or in a certain culture and society. As a scholar of gender in Tibetan Buddhism, I have repeatedly been asked about the status of the female in Buddhism, about the position of Tibetan women and especially about the status of Tibetan nuns.

These questions are important because they show that people are not indifferent when it comes to gender. We also need to ask these questions to understand gender inequality and in order to change the prevailing state of affairs.[2] If my academic interest has from the beginning focused on the life and the status of the Tibetan nuns, why is it so hard to offer nothing but vague statements concerning their position?

Many tensions and conflicting views prevail when the "status" of Tibetan women is at stake. First, there is an often repeated – but equally as often challenged – assumption about the "high" status of Tibetan women. Second, empirical observations have shown that Tibetan women's status as religious practitioners, especially in Tibetan monasticism, is "low." Nevertheless, previous studies of Tibetan nuns imply that despite their "lower" status, life as a nun is also seen as providing women with opportunities and offering them more freedom, compared to the life of a laywoman. This suggests that there are a variety of factors that simultaneously draw women to monasticism and draw them away from lay life.

Almost thirty years ago, Hanna Havnevik, who was among the first to write about contemporary Tibetan nuns, argued that they are subjected to a threefold subordination. According to Havnevik, "first, they are discriminated against by the Chinese; second, they are women within a patriarchal society; and third, they have to adjust to a monastic structure made by monks for monks" (Havnevik 1994, 266). What Havnevik wished to describe, however, was not only the subordination faced by Tibetan nuns. Her aim was also to demonstrate that their active participation in the Tibetan nationalist struggle had improved their standing as nuns. The notion of the simultaneous subordination and agency of the nuns has served as a starting point for my research on Tibetan nuns and led me to apply *intersectionality* in approaching, analyzing and understanding their various and often contradictory positions.

---

2. Gender is undeniably important. Jill Dubisch (2016) asks if there can be religion without gender. The answer is no because as long as gender is part of the world in which we live, it will also be part of religion in one way or another.

In the feminist research tradition, intersectionality refers to a critical theory that describes and analyzes the ways in which different oppressive institutions are interconnected. These intersecting institutions are seen to shape systems with an uneven distribution of power. The unequal circulation of power means that individuals occupy multiple and often contradictory status positions that simultaneously advantage and disadvantage them. Thus, according to the intersectionality approach, a person or a group can be subordinated and privileged at the same time (e.g., Collins 2000; Pelak 2007).

Research founded on intersectionality often takes as its research subject a particular social group or individuals at multiple points of different intersections. It focuses on the ignored knowledge systems of the marginalized groups and allows people to speak for themselves. This is also an ethical stance taken by intersectionality. However, since the personal and political spheres are connected, it is necessary to relate micro-level individual experiences to the macro-level structures.

The aim of the book is mainly twofold. The first goal is to provide a voice to a largely marginalized group of Tibetan Buddhist nuns – such as Ani Sherab quoted above.[3] This is done by giving plenty of space for their reflections on their experiences and perceptions. The second goal is to analyze these reflections in order to extract different dimensions of disadvantages and opportunities in the intersection of their female *gender*, *religion* and *nationality*. By taking gender, religion and nationality as the main focus of my analysis, I am not claiming that there are no other important dimensions where power is unevenly distributed.[4]

---

3. I am well aware of the dispute over the question of "giving voice" to subordinated groups. According to Saresma (2010, 61), for example, "giving voice" is a recent fashion phrase, which means that a researcher tries to minimize power imbalance between herself and the research subjects but which also implies that she only organizes and describes her research material and refrains from any theoretical analysis. I have sought to minimize the potential power imbalance between the nuns and myself by trying to be faithful to their stories and by giving space for their experiences. Nevertheless, I have also taken a theoretical stand but this discussion comes only later.

4. Early African American feminists saw gender, class and race in particular as the stronghold for unequal power relations (e.g., Crenshaw 1991; Collins 2000). According to Fjeld, the organization of the pre-Communist Tibetan social system in the areas of Central Tibet, for example, included different social strata: the clergy, householders or commoners (*mi ser*), those regarded as being "inferior types" (*smad rigs*), and those considered noble (*sku drag*). In the Tibetan ethnographic region in general, certain people are categorized as being an "unclean kind" (*rigs btsog pa* or *rigs ngan*). These people are workers in traditional occupations, such as blacksmiths, butchers, corpse-cutters and beggars, or the kin of such workers (Fjeld 2008, 113, 116).

Introduction

Nevertheless, based on my research material and analysis, I argue that in the context of Tibet under Chinese rule, power is most clearly interwoven in the intersection of these three. The questions I wish to answer in this book are as follows:

1. What kinds of dimensions of oppression[5] and of unequal distribution of power are experienced by the nuns in the intersection of their female gender, their Buddhist religion and their Tibetan nationality?
2. How are the dimensions of oppression constructed and maintained from structural, disciplinary, hegemonic and interpersonal forces?
3. What kinds of opportunities[6] and agencies[7] do the intersections of gender, religion and nationality offer to the nuns?

Just like the nuns I studied, my research itself stands at the intersection of various disciplines and fields of research. I began my university studies in what was then called Comparative Religion, but ended up earning my master's degree in Social and Cultural Anthropology. After graduation, I returned to my roots and began my doctoral studies in the Study of Religions. Already during my undergraduate studies, my interest in gender issues and the religions of Indian origin brought me to India, where I met Tibetan nuns for the first time. My encounter with the nuns finally brought me to the field of Tibetan studies and Tibetology.

The research thus touches upon and engages different fields of study, the most important of which are the study of religions, feminist studies, Buddhist studies, modern Tibetan studies and ethnography, and its value should be estimated from this point of view. First, the book takes part in the discussion on gender and religion, and it aims at surmounting the tension that has been noted to prevail between feminist approaches and religious women. This is done by applying the intersectionality framework which is still used mainly in the contexts of American and European societies. Moreover, while there are various studies of intersectionality

---

5. According to the *Oxford English Dictionary*, oppression is "prolonged cruel or unjust treatment or exercise of authority." Nevertheless, I employ the concept as used by Patricia Hill Collins. According to her, oppression is an unjust situation, where one group systematically and over a long period of time denies another group access to the resources of society (Collins 2000, 320).
6. Opportunity is a time or set of circumstances that makes it possible to do something.
7. In short, agency is the capability, the power, to be the source and originator of acts. Collins defines it as "an individual or social group's will to be self-defining and self-determining" (2000, 319).

as a theory and a method, it seems that there are still few that actually apply intersectionality.⁸ My book is aimed at taking up the challenge.

Second, the book continues the ethnographic study of religion by contributing to the study of women and religion in particular. Third, my ethnographic work contributes especially to the research on contemporary Tibetans. Ethnographic research in the People's Republic of China (PRC) became somewhat possible for non-Chinese scholars only in the 1980s. The "Tibet question" (i.e., the unsettled political status of Tibetan regions in China) has been the main reason for the lack of ethnographic studies of Tibet, particularly those on monasticism. Doing fieldwork in the Tibetan regions in China is, from the point of view of the PRC, still highly suspicious.

Last, because ethnographic studies of Tibetan women living in China are still few in number, I find my contribution important in filling this particular gap. The world has become "smaller," and it is nearly impossible to find a place that has not been touched by global progress. It would thus be an exaggeration to claim that we do not know anything about the realities of Tibetan women in contemporary China or in exile. Today we have more than imaginings.⁹ And yet, there is much we do not know when it comes to the everyday life, religion, ideas and concerns of Tibetan women. Even though my research cannot be generalized to concern all Tibetan nuns and women, it tells a story of some of them. For me, this is the most important contribution of this book.

The Status of Women in Historical Tibet

For a long time, the information on Tibetan women and Tibetan studies in general relied mainly on written sources and on the accounts of early

---

8. When writing about the theoretical perspectives that since the 1990s have increasingly attempted to recognize "multiple lines of differences", Wiesner-Hanks (2002, 611) writes: "Those of us who attempt to keep all these categories in mind are sometimes wistful of the time when only race, class, and gender mattered, and think often on the aphorism, 'In heaven you get to think about only one thing at a time.'" There is, of course, a large body of research that takes two differences, such as religion and gender, under investigation, and the number of studies considering three differences are growing in number. Nevertheless, recognizing multiple lines of differences empirically is challenging because crossing of differences produces countless individual realities, which are difficult to cover in one study.
9. The Western imaginations of Tibet have been forcefully criticized by some Tibetologists. In particular, the idea of a religious (premodern) Tibet has been dismissed as nothing more than a Western projection (e.g., Lopez 1998; Adams 1996; see also Dreyfus 2003).

Introduction

missionaries and exiled Tibetans. The first time foreign scholars were able to travel to the Tibetan regions of China as tourists was in the early 1980s (Barnett 2008, xiii; Huber 2002, xi). According to Robert Barnett, the late arrival of international scholars was partly due to ideology: it was believed either that China had destroyed Tibetan society as a distinctive entity or that Tibetan culture was a social relic which had been rendered irrelevant by Chinese modernity (Barnett 2008, xiii).

The literature existing before the 1950s already tended to emphasize the relatively influential position of Tibetan laywomen. According to Charlene Makley, the Chinese and Western observers who visited Tibetan regions prior to 1949, before the Chinese invasion, found the greater visibility and noticeable freedom of movement of Tibetan women striking. They remarked that practices for controlling women's bodies and sexuality, such as the foot-binding and *purdah* practiced among the neighboring Han Chinese and Hui Muslim communities, were absent among the Tibetans (Makley 2002b, 582, 619). Charles Bell, a British political officer stationed in Sikkim, Bhutan, and Tibet in the early part of the twentieth century, described the status of Tibetan women in this way:

> Those who have studied domestic life in Tibet can hardly fail to agree that the position of women in Tibetan society is remarkably good... When a traveler enters Tibet from the neighboring nations in China or India, few things impress him more vigorously or more deeply than the position of the Tibetan women. They are not kept in seclusion as are Indian women. [...] They are at ease with men, and can hold their own as well as any women in the world.
> (Bell 1968 [1928], 147, 156)

The notion of the high status of Tibetan women and their perceived physical and sexual freedom is widely repeated today among Tibetans – and among many Westerners. In fact, it has become an important theme in the nationalistic discourse adopted by the Tibetans, as will be discussed later (e.g., Butler 2003; Thonsur 2003).

Makley has criticized the literature which refers to the status of Tibetan women prior to the Chinese occupation, but which has been written and published since the invasion (Makley 1997, 67). Alex Butler (2003), however, has noted that the undeniably scarce literature which existed prior to the invasion also presented Tibetan women as enjoying a relatively high status. According to Butler, insofar as there is a problem with presenting women in historical Tibet, it is related to the tendency to generalize on the basis of particular observed cases. Based on the evidence available, Butler finds it reasonable to conclude that women in "premodern" Tibet experienced a quite broad range of freedoms.

However, there were also restrictions related to female gender and these varied according to region, occupation and class (Butler 2003, 14–15, 17).

As noted also by Janet Gyatso and Hanna Havnevik (2005), any generalizations about "women" involve the risk of essentializing. They remind that the women of traditional Tibet did not comprise a homogeneous group, but they were individuals whose lives, positions and experiences varied from one another. Nevertheless, according to Gyatso and Havnevik, generalizations are not necessarily essentializing if they are descriptive rather than normative, and if tendencies are not seen as being innate but as the products of particular socio-economic conditions (Gyatso & Havnevik 2005, 5).

Havnevik (1989) has also noted that scholars writing about Tibetan culture often refer to Tibetan women as having "high status," without specifying what the term "status" implies. Yet, as she argues, women's status varies depending on different areas of life; thus, it can be "lower" or equal when compared to men, but also exceed the status of men in certain spheres (Havnevik 1989, 127).

There are unquestionably many difficulties in evaluating the position of women in historical Tibet because relatively little is known about the actual situation and experience of Tibetan women in traditional Tibet (Gyatso and Havnevik 2005, 1). Nonetheless, based on observations such as those mentioned above, it has been assumed that, generally speaking, Tibetan women did enjoy many privileges denied to neighboring Chinese, Indian and Muslim women. It seems to be true that women in traditional Tibet were endowed with a relatively high amount of prestige and freedom in nomadic pastoralism, agricultural life and trade. Women also enjoyed certain freedoms in marriage and community life, and they could divorce and remarry, inherit property, and manage business and estates (see Thonsur 2003; Tsomo 1999a; Hyytiäinen 2008).

Yet, despite the comparatively high range of opportunities for Tibetan women, men were still considered as the heads of the household, and from a young age girls were taught to respect men. The main responsibility for women of all classes was – and still is – the well-being of the family. Responsibility for the family is often cited as the main reason for ordinary Tibetan women not being educated. With some exceptions of girls from aristocratic and rich families, girls were rarely sent to school in traditional Tibet (Butler 2003, 16–17, 83; Thonsur 2003, 324, 327; Havnevik 1989, 50).

Moreover, many observers of Tibetan culture have noted the vast discrepancy that equally exists in many other Buddhist societies – namely, that despite their considerable social and spatial freedom, laywomen

Introduction

still have fewer opportunities to devote themselves to religious life.[10] Bell also noted the different positions of monks and nuns in the Tibetan monastic institution. He wrote:

> In some measure Buddhism may have helped the Tibetan women, strong, intelligent, capable, to maintain their position; but it does not give them such power in religious affairs as it does to the men. And perhaps they do not want it. They are religious up to a point, more so than the men. But it is a part only of their daily life, along with the home, the family, the friends. They are not willing, to the extent that the men are willing, to renounce all in the quest of the great deliverance. For every nun there are thirty or forty monks.
>
> (Bell 1968 [1928], 163–164)

Compared with what has been written about monks and *yogīs*, there exist very few records of the lives of nuns and other female religious practitioners in Tibet. As an example, Dan Martin estimates that, in overall, women comprise about one or two percent of the sum total of the available biographical information of the eleventh and twelfth centuries (2005, 50-51), and according to Kurtis Schaeffer, out of over 150 Tibetan autobiographies currently known, only three or four are by women (2005, 83). Furthermore, it is noticed that no indigenous Tibetan literature of any historical period focuses upon nuns. This is probably partly due to the fact that few Tibetan women were educated and could write about their lives.[11] (Havnevik 1989, 65; Willis 1987, 98-99).

According to Karma Lekshe Tsomo, there is presently no historical evidence that the *bhikṣuṇī* ordination was transmitted from India to Tibet at all. Apparently, the difficulty of the journey across the high Himalayas was an important factor that prevented the *bhikṣuṇī saṅgha* from being established in Tibet (Tsomo 1996, viii). While Janice Willis states that she has been unable to find a single reference to the earliest ordination of Tibetan nuns (Willis 1987, 104), according to Kim Gutschow literary evidence shows that there were fully ordained nuns in the Indo-Tibetan borderlands east of Kashmir Valley until at least the eleventh century. She suggests that individual nuns may have traveled between Kashmir and Tibet, but there is no record of a minimum number of nuns required to establish a formal monastic order in Tibet (Gutschow 2004, 93). The evidence gathered by Martin (2005) on the full ordination for women at

---

10. On the status of Thai women and nuns, see van Esterik (1982) and Bunnag (1973); on Burmese women and nuns, see Spiro (1970). For a general discussion, see Karma Lekshe Tsomo (1988, 1999b).
11. See however Schaeffer's book (2004) about Orgyan Chokyi (1675-1729), whose story is the oldest known autobiography by a Tibetan nun.

various historical periods suggests that the lineage was not completely absent in Tibet after all. He notes that when reading the English translation of the Blue Annals, it is important to note that the translation "nun" is used to cover a number of Tibetan terms, including *chomo* (*jo mo*), *majo* (*ma jo*), and *tsunma* (*btsun ma*). It is likely that in most cases these terms refer to ordained women, but not necessarily to full ordination (Martin 2005, 72–73).

While the ordination status of the nuns remains somewhat unclear, there were nuns and nunneries in historical Tibet. According to Havnevik, statistics based on the Council for Religious and Cultural Affairs of H.H. the Dalai Lama suggest that there were 818 nunneries and 27,180 nuns before 1959[12] (Havnevik 1989, 37–38). Not all nuns lived in nunneries but led a wandering life, observed their vows in their birth home or lived with their relatives. There were also nuns who stayed in retreat communities or in caves with one or two nuns (Tsomo 1987, 119). One possibility for nuns was to attach themselves to a monastery (Havnevik 1989, 38; Willis 1987, 102).

Nevertheless, the number of nuns and nunneries was clearly smaller than the number of monks and monasteries at that time.[13] Studies of Tibet have traditionally assumed that a very high proportion of the male population were monks before 1959. In addition to their spiritual, ritual and educational functions, monasteries were central in Tibetan socio-political and socio-economic life. Compared with monasteries, nunneries were often poor, had fewer educational opportunities and were, in general, considered as rather insignificant institutions. There are various reasons for the lower number of nuns as well as their inferior religious and social prestige. Besides their gender, the inferior status of nuns in historical Tibet can at least partly be explained by the close connection between Tibetan political and religious life, in which nuns and nunneries did not hold a notable position. This situation appeared to change with the rise of modern Tibetan nationalism in the twentieth century, as will be discussed later.

---

12. By contrast, citing statistics given by the former Tibetan government official and historian Shakabpa, Janice Willis estimates that there were up to 120,000 nuns, comprising 11% of the monastic population and 2% of the total Tibetan population before 1959 (Willis 1987, 100).
13. Powers (1995) estimates that monks comprised about 25 percent of the male population just before 1959, while Dreyfus (2003) gives the estimate of 20 percent and Willis (1987) 18 percent. According to Samuel, however, the size of the male monastic population seemed to generally be 10–12 percent in the centralized agricultural areas and significantly lower elsewhere (Samuel 1993, 578, 582).

Introduction

Studies on Contemporary Tibetan Nuns

Perhaps the first most extensive ethnographic research on Tibetan nuns in contemporary China was conducted by the anthropologist Charlene Makley in the 1990s. Her doctoral dissertation *Embodying the Sacred: Gender and Monastic Revitalization in China's Tibet* (1999) is based on long-term fieldwork in the Tibetan Buddhist monastery town of Labrang (*bla brang*) in Xiahe County in southwest Gansu Province. In various articles (1997, 2002a, 2002b) mainly based on her dissertation, Makley discusses the questions of gender, sexuality, Tibetan Buddhist monasticism and their relationship to the Chinese state. Of her papers, "The Body of a Nun" (2005) concentrates specifically on nuns living in the Amdo region of China. Among the questions Makley tackles are the revitalizing of the lay-monastic relationship among Tibetans in Labrang, the ways in which these relationships are gendered, and the changes in these relationships in the transformed context of the modern Chinese state. Makley notices that at the time of her study, nuns' bodies were the objects of intense denial and the nuns were severely denigrated. She claims that this was because the body of a nun had become more visible and the nuns were seen as challenging the gender ideals of the community (Makley 1999).[14]

In a more recent ethnographic study on Tibetan nuns living in Yachen Gar,[15] a massive religious encampment five hours south by car from Garze town in Sichuan, Yasmin Cho (2015) claims that in order to understand the lives of the nuns in Yachen, we should focus on mobility, materiality, and sensory experiences. According to Cho, Yachen Gar gives rural Tibetan girls, "the most underrepresented group in Chinese society," exceptional opportunities when it comes, for example, to education and social status. Importantly, as she points out, Yachen Gar has largely come into being thanks to labor, mobility and daily material activities of the nuns. In their paper, Padma'tso (Baimacuo) and Sarah Jacoby (2020) focus on a group of nuns living in another dharma camp, the largest Buddhist monastery in the world, Larung Gar Five Sciences Buddhist Academy, in

---

14. Makley is particularly interested in the question of the essential performativity of gender – the approach most impressively outlined by Judith Butler (1999). Following Butler, Makley argues that gender is not a fixed and internal mental state. Rather, it is "an unstable surface politics of the body in which actors in their everyday lives are both forced to reiterate conventional meanings concerning sex and sexuality and able to reinterpret or manipulate them in potentially innovative ways" (Makley 1999, 25). See *Gender Trouble: Feminism and the Subversion of Identity* (1999) by Butler.
15. *ya chen sgar* is located in Baiyu County in the Garze Tibetan Autonomous Prefecture in Sichuan Province.

the Serta region of Garze.[16] Interestingly they claim that even though the nuns they studied did not identify themselves as feminists in the "liberal rights-based terms," they still found themselves actively working to dismantle the view that men are superior to women.

Other studies of Tibetan nuns living in contemporary China are articles focusing on the nationalist struggle of nuns in central Tibet (TAR) (Young 2000; Barnett 2005; Havnevik 1994). The point of departure of these contributions is the fact that in most of the demonstrations that have taken place in Tibet since the autumn of 1987, nuns have been very active. Havnevik (1994), for example, discusses the role of nuns in contemporary China and comes to the conclusion that, in addition to being an expression of religious motivation, monastic life is also a commitment to the survival of the Tibetan people and culture.

The other ethnographic studies of Tibetan nuns, or studies that mention nuns, have been conducted in the Tibetan communities in India[17] and among the Tibetan Buddhist Sherpas and refugees in Nepal.[18] In her pioneering work on Tibetan nuns living in Tibetan refugee settlements in northern India, Havnevik (1989) explores how predominant attitudes and norms found in Buddhist literature and in Tibetan culture relate to the actual situation of female religious specialists, particularly nuns. Havnevik argues that Tibetan nuns continue to find themselves at the bottom of the religious hierarchy. This is mainly because sexist norms are acquired from a male-dominated society and applied to the organizational structure of monasticism. Nevertheless, she also suggests that while attempting to fulfill their spiritual and more mundane goals, Buddhist nuns do not merely adjust to religious norms but also maintain and change them (Havnevik 1989, 17, 143).

More recent studies on Tibetan communities in India concentrate especially on the changing status of the nuns in exile and especially on their increasing opportunities for education (Mann 2009; LeClear 2013). According to Judy Tobler (2006), for instance, the Tibetan Buddhist nuns

---

16. Serthang Larung Ngarig Nangten Lobling (*gser thang bla rung lnga rig nang bstan slob gling*) is located about 25 km southeast of Serta or Serthar (*gser thar*) County, situated in the northern part of Garze Tibetan Autonomous Prefecture. It is a massive religious encampment and scholastic center that was established by the Nyingma visionary Khenpo Jigme Phuntsok (*mkhan po 'jigs med phun tshogs*, 1933–2004) in 1980. It was populated at times by over 10,000 monastics. Larung Gar has been forcefully demolished by the Chinese authorities since 2016.
17. E.g., Havnevik (1989) in an exile community in Himachal Pradesh; Grimshaw (1994) in Ladakh; Gutschow (1997, 2000, 2004) in Zangskar; Tsomo (1987, 1988, 1999a) in the Himalayas in general; LaMacchia (2001) in Kinnaur, Himachal Pradesh.
18. E.g., von Fürer-Haimendorf (1964); Ortner (1978, 1996); van Ede (1999, 2000).

in exile have been doubly exiled: First, they are exiled from their native home Tibet and from a center of its patriarchal social systems; second, they live in exile from the center of Tibetan monastic institution and religious life. However, Tobler claims that the nuns are in the process of creating "an autonomous home, or sacred space" in Tibetan Buddhist monastic life by claiming religious education formerly offered only for monks (Tobler 2006, 59–60).

In addition to the Tibetan refugee nuns, there are Tibetan Buddhist nuns in the ethnically Tibetan regions of the Indian Himalayas (Grimshaw 1994; Gutschow 1997, 2000, 2004; LaMacchia 2001, 2016). A more extensive ethnographic work on the Zangskar and Ladakh regions is offered by Kim Gutschow (1997, 2000, 2004, 2001). Gutschow claims that women's experience and agency in previous studies of Buddhist monasticism have been neglected, which is why the history and practice of monasticism have to be rewritten to include both monks and nuns and their relationship with each other and the laity (Gutschow 2004, 12). Gutschow's primary interest thus focuses on the monastic practices of merit-making, ordination, and purification, in which monks and nuns have very different roles and status. According to her, gender is "an inescapable condition" of Buddhist monasticism in Zangskar: nuns may renounce a lay life (including desire and sex), shave their heads and put on androgynous maroon robes that signal their detachment, but they cannot transcend their sexuality, escape their mundanely gendered bodies, or flee the gender roles in which they are trapped (Gutschow 2004, 123).

Gutschow is of the opinion that in Tibetan society, the inability of nuns to obtain the highest monastic ordination may be one of the most damaging factors for their status (Gutschow 2000, 108).[19] The question of the ordination of nuns in the Tibetan tradition is perhaps most strongly advanced by Karma Lekshe Tsomo (1987, 1999b, 2003; see also Heirman 2011), a scholar and an American-born fully ordained nun in the Tibetan tradition. Tsomo has also written extensively about the position of Tibetan nuns in exile and in Himalayan areas. Like Havnevik, Tsomo (1999a) is interested in the ways in which the Buddhist teachings are reflected in the lives of women in the Himalayan regions of Kinnaur, Spiti and the Zangskar valley of Ladakh. According to her, the spiritual goal of enlightenment described in the Buddhist texts seems very distant

---

19. In most Buddhist countries today, the full ordination lineage for women has died out, and thus most Buddhist nuns are only able to receive the novice (śrāmaṇerī) ordination. For a general discussion, see Tsomo (1999b). For Theravāda countries, see Falk Lindberg (2000) (Thailand); Carbonnel (2009) (Myanmar); and Barthomelousz (1994, 2000) (Sri Lanka). For Mahāyāna countries, see Arai (1999) (Japan); Eichman (2011) (Taiwan).

for ordinary Himalayan women, who are trapped in a woman's body and living an ordinary and difficult life. This tension affects nuns the most, as they are disadvantaged by gender from accomplishing their goals.

There are also some studies of Tibetan Buddhist nuns which have been conducted in Nepal, both among Tibetan Buddhist Sherpas, an ethnically Tibetan group living in northeastern Nepal bordering on Tibet (von Fürer-Haimendorf 1964; Ortner 1978, 1996) and among Tibetan refugee nuns. A broader ethnography conducted on the Sherpa nuns is the unpublished doctoral dissertation of Yolanda van Ede (1999), which focuses on the relationships between gender, knowledge and social change. Like Gutschow and Ortner, van Ede argues that becoming a nun provides women with both merit and (upward) social mobility, along with other opportunities denied to laywomen. An alternative, communal aspect of the nunnery is also emphasized by Sara Shneiderman (1999). Life in a nunnery seems to offer young women a refuge, education and solidarity that might not otherwise be available for women in Nepalese society.

A more recent study by Kathryn LaFever (2017) focuses on contemporary *Varjayāna* nuns living in Kathmandu and especially on the ways the nuns are exercising, contesting and redefining their situated empowerment within religious communities and beyond. LaFever argues that the nuns can be empowered by articulating and sharing their own narrative stories and experiences as well as by learning about Buddhist women who teach by their own example. She also notes that the "twenty-first century nuns" are increasingly self-sufficient when compared to previous generations and this has largely to do with the Western influence, including Western feminism.

Bhutan is known as the only Tibetan Buddhist state in the world. In their article, Sonam Wangmo and Juli Edo (2016) examine Bhutanese nuns' access to monastic and philosophical education. They conclude that the nuns lack access to full spectrum of monastic education and even if they receive sufficient religious training, they are still subjected to discrimination because of their gender. This is because both the local and Buddhist communities hold prejudices against women.

It can be gleaned from previous and more recent studies of Tibetan women and nuns in specific that when comparing monks and nuns in general, there still appears to be differences, for example, between their levels of monastic ordination, religious practices and education, as well as the roles acquired in society. In spite of their shared initiation as novices, their commitment to celibacy and asceticism (ideally for a lifetime), and their uniform outward appearance – maroon robes and shaved heads – monks and nuns do not enjoy equal opportunities or privileges in monastic life (Gutschow 2000, 104). Nevertheless, life as a nun offers women rights and freedoms that are not available for laywomen. Furthermore, more recent research has highlighted the changing role of the nuns, especially in the field of education.

Thus, while the obstacles faced by Tibetan women as religious practitioners have been noted, some studies have also emphasized the agency and opportunities that the religious – or otherwise autonomous – lifestyle or status is seen to afford to women, despite the restrictions (e.g. Allione 1984; Gross 1993; Martin 2005; Shaw 1994; Tobler 2006; Haas 2013; Padma'tso (Baimacuo) and Jacoby 2020). For example, the articles in the special issue of *Revue d'Etudes Tibétaines* (2015) edited by Mona Schrempf and Nicola Schneider focus on alternative perspectives on women's lives as autonomous specialists in Tibet, Himalayas and Mongolia. It can be argued, however, that while these women gain some sort of agency and opportunities as self-governing specialists, the agency still seems to be limited to the margins.

Puzzling Status of Tibetan Buddhist Women

It appears that scholars studying Tibetan women have faced the challenge of reconciling the different and often contradicting dimensions found in the social statuses of Tibetan women. Makley, for example, calls attention to a striking ambivalence in the representations of contemporary Tibetan women. According to her, depending on the viewpoint of the observer, the Tibetan woman is "in the end either extraordinarily liberated or shockingly oppressed" (Makley 1997, 6–7). She argues that in the beginning of the early 1980s, the first serious considerations of gender in Tibetan studies – then understood mainly as relating to the status of women – coincided with the efforts of some Western Buddhist women to find a place for themselves in the tradition (Makley 1999, 17). One of the most prominent of these, Rita Gross (1993), for instance, has claimed that in spite of the doctrinal equality of Tibetan Buddhism, negative views on women and femininity emerge in the everyday conversations and attitudes of Tibetans. Karma Lekshe Tsomo, in turn, has noted that Tibetan women in the Indian Himalayan societies of Kinnaur, Spiti and Zangskar live in the crossfire of conflicting images. On the one hand, femininity and masculinity are understood as energies and counterparts which are present in all sentient beings. On the other hand, feminine energies are seen negatively as something to be suppressed (Tsomo 1999a, 176–177). Gross has also claimed that women who live within the power structures and relations of Tibetan culture are not able to see their lower status (Gross 1993, 81). According to Tsomo as well, women in Himalayan

Buddhist societies do not usually perceive the striking inequality that affects their lives (Tsomo 1999a, 176).

Makley criticizes the approach of these feminist Buddhist scholars who, according to her, try to explain social inequalities by making arbitrary distinctions between an ultimately egalitarian religion and actual social realities. Quoting Ursula King (1995), she argues that religion should be seen as completely integrated into the "everyday workings of social lives." Only then does the relationship between gender and religion become intelligible. She also urges paying attention to how people construct, contest or negotiate religious truths or beliefs in larger socio-political contexts (Makley 2005, 260).

The reason why Tibetan women can be represented as either "extraordinarily liberated" or "shockingly oppressed" – or both – may be due to the different research agendas or interests of the observer, as argued by Makley. Yet, I would suggest that dimensions of oppression and opportunities also depend on the intersection of women's status. Depending on her location, the Tibetan woman can be either disadvantaged or privileged, or both at the same time. Moreover, she can gain agency within power relations which to an external observer seem simply suppressive.

– 2 –

Intersectionality

A Theory and a Method

Questioning Power and Social Inequality

Intersectionality offers a theory and a method for analyzing dimensions of power and agency in more varied ways. In feminist research, intersectionality refers to the insight according to which various dimensions of social identities – including gender, race, class and sexuality – do not operate as unitary entities but as reciprocal components that construct, produce and maintain multifaceted social inequalities (Collins 2015, 2).[1]

The legal scholar Kimberlé Crenshaw has customarily been credited with coining the concept of intersectionality. Crenshaw was, in fact, one of the first to use the term in her article "Mapping the Margins: Intersectionality, Identity Politics, and Violence against Women of Color" (1991). However, as argued by many scholars of intersectionality, the concept had been developed by women of color over a century before Crenshaw (May 2012, 155). Thus, by the time Crenshaw introduced the term, intersectionality was part of the growing interest of feminist scholarship (Davis 2014, 17).

It was especially the African-American feminist projects of the 1960s and 1970s in the United States that laid the theoretical base for intersectionality. The goal of the projects was not to develop a theory for academia but to empower African-American women. This was done through critical analyses of the way that combined constructed systems

---

1. To offer some other definitions, Leslie McCall defines intersectionality as "the relationships among multiple *dimensions* and *modalities* of social relations and subject formations" (McCall 2005, 1771, my emphasis), whereas according to Stephanie A. Shields, "a fundamental assumption in every influential theoretical formulation of intersectionality is that intersectional *identities* are defined in relation to one another" (Shields 2008, 303, my emphasis).

of oppression of race, class, gender, and sexuality framed the social inequalities faced by African-American women (Collins 2015, 7–8).

In the 1980s, the ideas of intersectionality were incorporated into the academy with the phrase "race, class, and gender," but this approach was not named until the end of the 1980s (Collins 2015, 9; Weber 1998, 14). African-American feminists working on intersectionality argued that most feminist scholarship at that time was concentrating on middle-class, educated, white women. For them, in order to gain a broader view of women's situation, it was necessary to recognize the intersections of gender with other significant social identities, mainly race (Shields 2008, 302–303).

From the beginning, an important starting point of intersectionality in feminist research has thus been the assumption that there is an unequal distribution of power. Power is understood both as privilege and domination, and it is seen as "insinuating" itself into society (for example, through ideological, political, and economic domains and their related institutions). It is assumed that by focusing on the "complex individual, relational, structural, and ideological aspects of domination and privilege," it is possible to reveal and change them (Ramsay 2014, 455, 458).

Although first introduced as a heuristic term in social movement politics, intersectionality has subsequently been deployed in various disciplines. While there is a widespread consensus about the general outlines of intersectionality, definitions of what intersectionality actually is and what counts as intersectionality are not as clear-cut. As noted by Patricia Hill Collins, intersectionality has been characterized as a perspective, a concept, and a type of analysis, as well as a "nodal point" for feminist theorizing, a paradigm, a heuristic device, a methodology, and a theory (Collins 2015, 2, 13). According to Sumi Cho, Kimberlé Crenshaw and Leslie McCall, for instance, intersectionality has from the beginning been modeled more as a "nodal point" than as a closed system, and thus it is best framed as an "analytic sensibility." What makes an analysis intersectional is not its use of the term "intersectionality," but its adoption of an intersectional way of thinking about the problem of sameness and difference and its relations to power. This definition sees categories as always being infused by other categories, which are "fluid and changing, always in the process of creating and being created by dynamics of power." The approach emphasizes what intersectionality *does*, rather than what intersectionality is (Cho et al. 2013, 795; my emphasis). For Cho et al., therefore, intersectionality is inseparably linked to the analysis of power, and consequently it is something that is less focused on categories, identities, and subjectivities and more interested in political and structural inequalities (Cho et al. 2013, 797).

Introduction

One of the influential theorists of intersectionality has been the sociologist Patricia Hill Collins. In her book *Black Feminist Thought - Knowledge, Consciousness and the Politics of Empowerment* (2000), Collins examines the "situated, subjugated standpoint of African-American women in order to understand Black feminist thought as a partial perspective on domination" (Collins 2000, 269; see also Collins 2015). According to Collins's intersectional analysis, systems of race, social class, gender, sexuality, ethnicity, nation, and age form mutually constructing features of social organization, which shape African-American women's experiences and, in turn, are shaped by African-American women. For Collins, intersectionality originally aimed at empowering African-American women through knowledge of their situation. Accordingly, intersectional paradigms made two important contributions to the understanding of the connections between knowledge and empowerment. First, they offered new insights into African-American women's experiences; second, they clarified the relationship between knowledge and empowerment by focusing on how domination was organized (Collins 2000, 2015).

For Collins, intersectionality thus constitutes "a broad-based knowledge project" in which attention focuses on power relations and social inequalities (2015, 3, 5). She provides six guiding assumptions that direct this knowledge project. According to the first assumption, different categories of analysis are best understood in relational terms rather than in isolation. Second, these mutually constructing categories underlie and shape intersecting systems of power. Third, the intersecting systems of power catalyze social constructions of complex social inequalities. Fourth, the social formations of complex social inequalities are historically conditional and culturally specific. Fifth, individuals and groups differentially placed within the intersecting systems of power have different conceptions of their own and others' experience of complex social inequalities. Sixth, the complex social inequalities nurtured by the intersecting systems of power are unjust, shaping knowledge projects, as well as political engagement, that maintain or challenge the existing state of affairs (Collins 2015, 14; see also Pelak 2007).

Collins calls the various intersections of social inequality the *matrix of domination*, which refers to the overall and historically specific organization of hierarchical power relations in any society. Any given matrix of domination has a particular arrangement of intersecting systems of oppression (for example, race, class, and gender) and a particular organization of its domains of power (Collins 2000, 21, 320). According to Collins, any particular matrix of domination is organized around four interrelated domains of power: namely, the *structural*, *disciplinary*, *hegemonic* and *interpersonal* domains. Each of these domains serves a particular purpose. The structural domain encompasses social institutions that are organized to reproduce subordination over time. It is an arrangement of organized practices (for example, in employment, government, education, law, business, and housing) that work to maintain an unequal and unjust distribution of social resources. According to Collins, in the United States, for instance, the policies and procedures of the legal system, labor markets, schools, the housing industry, banking, insurance and the news media have all functioned to disadvantage African-American women. These interlocking social institutions have relied on multiple forms of segregation, including those of race, class, and gender (Collins 2000, 295–296).

Collins also describes how the disciplinary domain of power manages to control power relations and oppression. Disciplinary domain consists of bureaucratic organizations whose duty is to supervise and organize behavior through routinization, rationalization, and surveillance (Collins 2000, 299–300, 319). To Collins, the hegemonic domain of power is a form or mode of social organization that justifies oppression. This is done by manipulating ideas, images and symbols. Collins names school curricula, religious teachings, community cultures, and family histories as important social locations for promoting ideologies that are needed to maintain oppression. By manipulating ideology and culture, the hegemonic domain acts as a link between social institutions (structural domain), their administrative practices (disciplinary domain), and the level of everyday social interaction (interpersonal domain). To preserve their power, dominant groups create and maintain a popular system of "commonsense" ideas that support their right to reign. According to Collins, in the United States, for instance, hegemonic ideologies concerning race, class, gender, sexuality and nation are often so pervasive that it is difficult to conceptualize alternatives to them (Collins 2000, 302–303).

The interpersonal domain influences everyday lived experience and the awareness that follows. The interpersonal domain functions through routinized, everyday practices. Such practices often go unnoticed because they are systematic, repeated, and familiar. Collins argues that people have a tendency to identify with an oppression, most likely the one they have experienced, and to consider all other oppressions as being of lesser importance. Collins points out that change in this domain begins with the intrapersonal, when an individual understands her own self and experience (Collins 2000, 306–307; see also Pelak 2007, 2). The possibility of opportunities is also noted by Collins, according to whom, "each individual derives varying amounts of *penalty* and *privilege* from the multiple systems of oppression which frame everyone's lives" (Collins 2000, 306, my emphasis).

Subordinate groups thus actively resist oppression in many ways every day. Because of their situation in subordinate social locations, they often lack institutional power and thus use other forms of personal power and collective action to resist unfair treatment. Consequently, scholars drawing on intersectionality also focus on less visible (politicized) activities that are taken up by subordinated groups. Acts of resistance can range from passive forms to actions such as public protests, strikes or violence. Daily acts of resistance can vary from the individual rejection of negative group images to group activities designed to produce social change (Weber 1998, 22). Collins (2000), too, recognizes two interdependent forms of African-American women's social activism: the subtle undermining of institutions through the creation of female domains of influence within the existing structures of oppression, and institutional transformation consisting of direct challenges in the form of trade unions, boycotts, sit-ins, marches and so on (Collins 2000; Pelak 2007, 3).

There is no one methodological solution to applying an intersectionality perspective (Shields 2008, 307). Cynthia Fabrizio Pelak notes that an intersectionality framework is focused on multiple levels of analysis: individual, interactional, institutional, cultural, and structural (Pelak 2007, 1-2; 4). According to Leslie McCall (2005), this means that intersectionality has introduced new methodological problems: when the subject of study broadens to include multiple dimensions of social life and categories of analysis, complexity arises (McCall 2005; see also Jones et al. 2013).

For Mari Matsuda, intersectionality as a methodology centered on "asking the other question." She explained:

> When I see something that looks racist, I ask, "Where is the patriarchy in this?" When I see something that looks sexist, I ask, "Where is the heterosexism in this?" When I see something that looks homophobic, I ask, "Where are the class interests in this?"
>
> (Davis 2014, 20)

For Davis, however, asking the other question is only the beginning of her analysis. She notes that a problem often arises with what one should do after asking the other questions. After all, according to Davis, what is important is making sense of the connections of categories of difference and interpreting them in terms of power. She proposes that scholars should start thinking intersectionally by situating themselves. This does not mean merely listing identity categories, but rather "developing a narrative" about how we are shaped and influenced by our specific location and how this affects our research. The second step is to complicate gender which means treating gender as a category which is always related to other differences and which is mutually constituted by other differences. Finally, it is important to identify the blind spots that we all have (Davis 2014, 22–23, 25).

Applying Intersectionality

The question arises as to whether to apply an intersectionality framework to a context that is fundamentally different from that of Afro-American women. Much of the early scholarship on intersectionality has focused on the United States and is therefore often criticized as having utility solely in the context of North America. In an attempt to address this critique, later scholarship has asked what happens to the concept when it is applied to contexts outside the United States (Simien & Hancock 2011, 185).

According to Pelak, the basic assumptions of intersectionality call for historically specific, local analyses. Gender and race are not understood as predetermined or transhistorical but as structures and the category of "women" is not assumed to consist of a homogeneous group of individuals who share a common experience of oppression. Instead, individual biographies are situated within different domains of power and accordingly reflect their specific interconnections and contradictions (Pelak 2007; see also Weber 1998). For Collins too, intersectionality was never meant to explain solely African-American women's experiences in the United States. According to her, the concept is applicable for analysis of other groups as well. While "race," class, gender and sexuality constitute the mutually constructing systems of oppression for Afro-American women, other groups have unique locations in other intersecting oppressions (Collins 2000, 227). Rita Kaur Dhamoon has argued that intersectionality is not only "a normative-theoretical argument but also a research paradigm." As such, it can be widely applied to the study of social groups, relations, and contexts, thus going beyond the conventional scope of non-white women (Dhamoon 2011, 230).

I have found the analysis of different domains of power particularly useful when approaching the unequal distribution of power experienced by Tibetan women and nuns in particular. By applying the intersectionality framework, it is possible to take into account the cultural and historical context of the women I have studied.

Among other scholars, Mahmood has noted that while there have been attempts to integrate issues of sexual, racial, class, and national differences among feminist theorists, certain questions regarding religious difference have remained relatively unexplored (Mahmood 2005, 1).

Ahonen and Vuola have claimed that if religion is taken into account, this is often done only after ethnicity, sexuality and class have been considered (Ahonen & Vuola 2015, 9; Vuola 2010, 170). As Castelli points out, however, religion as a category both cuts across other identity categories and complicates them (Castelli 2001, 5). Thus, while "race," class and gender have been the traditional triad of intersectional studies in feminist research, it is possible to take any dimension under investigation (see Jones et al. 2013, 1). My book concentrates on the crossroads of gender, religion and nationality, taking religion as one such all-pervading dimension.

The central aim of intersectionality theory is that of revealing the intersecting oppressions in order to change the order of things. It can be asked whether this is my goal, and, even more importantly, whether it is even possible or desirable to discuss and analyze other people's experiences of disadvantage and advantage. Should the intersectionality paradigm only be employed by those who claim to be insiders? I agree with Lynn Weber, according to whom "to comprehend the human agency, resilience, creativity, and strength of oppressed group members, one must view the actions and motivations of subordinate group members through their own lenses, not through the lenses of the controlling images of the dominant culture" (Weber 1998, 24). In fact, the feminist standpoint approach argues that researchers cannot be neutral and objective when studying relations of power. The sensitivity to power relations also extends to the research process itself. A key issue for researchers, then, is reflexivity about one's subjects and one's own interests. Understanding the research process as reflexive means seeing the researcher as part of the research process (Neitz 2011). Thus, despite the fact that, from my standpoint, I find the status and the positions of the nuns to be unequal in many ways, I am of the opinion that the need for change should be defined by the research subjects themselves.

Finally, while intersections create both oppression and opportunities (Pelak 2007, 2–3), it can be argued that theorists of intersectionality have focused especially on the oppressive side of power. This might be because from a certain standpoint oppression seems to be more visible or more common than opportunities. Whereas my book aims at describing and analyzing unequal distributions of power, I am also interested in the ways intersections create agency.

– 3 –

Doing Research in the Contested Tibetan Field

The Field of Tibet

One of the central conventions of ethnographic studies is to introduce the location, or the field, where the research was conducted. The concept of "Tibet," however, has different meanings in different contexts.

In terms of physical geography, Tibet comprises the Tibetan Plateau, which is the largest highland region in the world. The plateau covers an area of almost two million square kilometers stretching from the Himalayas in the south to the Gobi Desert in the north, and from the Karakorum in the west to the Sichuan basin in the east (Janhunen 2008, 10).

As a modern political concept, the name Tibet is employed to refer to various geographical contexts. On the contemporary political map, Tibet belongs to the People's Republic of China.[1] Thus, for the Chinese government, "Tibet," or "Xizang," stands only for the Tibet Autonomous Region (TAR), which is located at the Qinghai-Tibet Plateau in the southwestern part of China. Established by China in 1965, the TAR is a province-level administrative entity in the Chinese state. The region covers the central and western area of the Tibetan Plateau and is approximately equivalent to the territory ruled by the Lhasa government under the Dalai Lama

---

1. The People's Republic of China has 23 provinces, five autonomous regions, four centrally administered municipalities and two special administrative regions. They are all directly under the rule of the Chinese Central Government. Furthermore, there are five levels of local government: province, prefecture, county, township, and village. A province (or autonomous region) is subdivided into autonomous prefectures, counties, autonomous counties and/or cities. A county or autonomous county is subdivided into townships, ethnic townships and/or towns (see Lahtinen 2010, 49–50). Tibetan areas constitute a large part of China's western region and nearly one fourth of the land of China as a whole.

Introduction

at the time of the Chinese arrival in the 1950s (Janhunen 2008, 10–12; Young 2000, 229; Barnett 2008, xix).

By contrast, the Tibetan government in exile and supporters of Tibetan independence, as well as ordinary Tibetans living in the PRC and in diaspora, usually understand "Tibet" to include the historical Tibetan provinces of Ü-Tsang, Amdo and Kham (Tib. *chol kha gsum*). The Chinese government splits these between the TAR and the modern Chinese provinces of Sichuan, Qinghai, Yunnan and Gansu. Furthermore, the Tibetan areas of China are divided into one region, ten prefectures, and two autonomous counties. In total, Tibetans live in 147 counties in western China. According to China's 2005 census, the estimated Tibetan population is about 7.25 million. Nevertheless, only about 2.76 million of China's Tibetan population lives in the TAR. The rest lives in Qinghai, Sichuan, Gansu and Yunnan provinces. Within these, the inhabitants of Qinghai and Sichuan account for the majority of Tibetans outside the TAR. Most Tibetans live in rural areas; less than twenty percent live in urban areas (Wang 2009, 12, 14).

In 2009/2010 the Tibetan population outside of "Tibet" was more than 128,000. There were 94,203 Tibetan living in India; 13,514 in Nepal; 1,298 in Nepal and around 19,000 in the rest of the world.[2] Since the 1960s, more than sixty Tibetan refugee settlements have been created in South Asia.[3] More than two thirds of the refugees are from Central Tibet (Ü-Tsang), about a quarter from Kham, and only a small minority from Amdo (e.g., Dawa Norbu 2003; Härkönen 2008; Powers 1995, 176–177; Samuel 1993; von Fürer-Haimendorf 1989).

Especially Dharamsala in Himachal Pradesh in northern India has become both a Tibetan administrative center and the focus of Tibetan religion, culture, and nationalist sentiment, as well as a place of pilgrimage. Dharamsala is also the main place of residence for the Dalai Lama and the location of his personal monastery. Although Dharamsala has become the focal point of the refugee community, most early refugees settled in the mountain towns and villages of northern India and Nepal, as well as in the large agricultural areas of southern India. For example, the Indian state of Karnataka, where the Indian government offered land to refugees, is now home to a considerable refugee population (e.g., Dawa Norbu 2003).

Due to its complex history and present political status, Tibet has multiple meanings and contexts, even in contemporary scholarship. Melvyn Goldstein refers to the Dalai Lama's regime as Tibet, thus suggesting that

---

2. See https://tibet.net/about-cta/tibet-in-exile (accessed 12.2.2021).
3. Thirty-five in India, ten in Nepal, and seven in Bhutan.

most of Kham and Amdo were not part of Tibet. For this wider region, Goldstein uses the term "ethnic Tibet" (Goldstein 1989, 9). Geoffrey Samuel, however, has argued that this kind of separation implies that the Tibetan regions of Kham and Amdo should legitimately be regarded as part of China (Samuel 1993, 586). A number of other foreign scholars use the term "Tibet" in a wider sense to describe all the areas now within China that were traditionally inhabited by Tibetans, including Amdo and Kham. This entity was called by Hugh Richardson "the ethnographic Tibet"[4] (Barnett 2008, xix).

In addition to the ethnically Tibetan regions in China and the Tibetan diaspora (especially in India), there are geographical regions that are Tibetan in cultural and religious terms. These areas include the former Himalayan kingdoms of Ladakh, Zangskar, Mustang, Sikkim, and Bhutan, as well as neighboring parts of India, Pakistan, and Nepal. Of all these, only Bhutan is today an independent political state (Janhunen 2008, 10–12; Samuel 1993, 100).

Despite the heterogeneity of Tibetan social and political life, the existence of Tibetan culture and its considerable uniformity cannot be denied. Robert Ekvall, an early missionary anthropologist working in Tibet in the first half of the twentieth century, noted that the Tibetan self-image did not include a concept of nationhood. Ekvall identified five criteria by which Tibetans distinguished themselves from non-Tibetans: religion, customs such as eating habits, language, race and land (Butler 2003, 48). According to Matthew Kapstein, practices such as long-distance trade[5] and pilgrimage, a sense of shared history, a common literary language, genealogy, myth and religion, as well as folkloric notions like Tibetans being eaters of roasted barley (Tib. *tsampa, rtsam pa*), gave a relative coherence to Tibetan cultural identity (Kapstein 1998, 115–119, 140; Yeh 2007; Lopez 1998, 198).

According to Toni Huber, for instance, the area referred to as Amdo by Tibetans today includes parts of the northeastern Tibetan Plateau where people consider themselves ethnically *Tibetan* because they share some form of common language, history, origin narratives, lifestyles, cultural system and identity (Huber 2002, xiii, my emphasis). Wang Shiyong (2009, 15) argues that while Tibetan areas should not be seen as monolithic,

---

4. In this work, I use the phrase "Tibetan regions/areas" when I refer to any culturally Tibetan area in any modern state. By "Tibetan regions/areas under/in/of China," I refer to the entity of three traditional Tibetan provinces. My informants, however, did not differentiate between different regions but simply talked about "Tibet" (Tib. *bod*).

5. In Tibet, trade routes were of vital importance to the economy and the social structure.

Introduction

Tibetans today share many things (e.g., similar living conditions, pride in their Buddhist culture, and a common written language).

Andreas Gruschke proposes an ethnic, not geographic, way of defining Tibet. Thus, Tibet would mean those regions whose inhabitants call themselves Böpa (*bod pa*), speak Bökhe (*bod khas*) – that is to say, all Tibetan dialects related to the one spoken in Lhasa – use the Tibetan script, and follow either tantric Buddhism or the Bön, an old Tibetan religious tradition that traces its history back to pre-Buddhist practices associated with the cult of the early Tibetan kings. He notes that while the term *Böpa* in fact refers only to the people in the former realm of the Dalai Lamas, the definition should be extended to include the complementary term of Böchenpa (*bod chen pa*), which means "man of Greater Tibet." This could be applied to the people of the Central Tibetan provinces of Ü-Tsang and Lhokha (*lho kha*), as well as Ngari and Ladakh in western Tibet, but also the ethnic Tibetan populations in various regions in the Himalayas and in Amdo and Kham (Gruschke 2001, 7).

Akhil Gupta and James Ferguson (1997) have criticized the Western tendency to see the world as a space naturally fragmented into nation-states. According to Nira Yuval-Davis and Floya Anthias, the tendency to identify state with "the nation" has to do with the historical fact that nationalism has been important in the development of the nation-state in the West (Yuval-Davis & Anthias 1989, 3). The ideas that equate a culture with a state and an ethnic group – in other words, assuming that an ethnic group living within the borders of a nation-state shares the same culture – needs some reevaluation in the Tibetan context. The nation-state as one "nationality" under a strong centralized government is a recent development in Asia.[6] According to Samuel, Central Tibet was moving in this direction in the 1920s under the 13th Dalai Lama's administration, but rule in Tibet differed greatly from what modern nation states would consider a national territory (Samuel 1993, 143). Consequently, national identity in traditional Tibet was not necessarily based on, or restricted to, the "correct" (i.e., Western) definitions of membership in a community.

---

6. Roughly speaking, a state is "a self-consciously organized institution by means of which a society is regulated and preserved." The nation-state, with its clearly defined sovereign territory, is in fact a relatively recent phenomenon. (Graham 1988, 4.) According to Benedict Anderson, the nation is an imagined political community. He wrote: "The convergence of capitalism and print technology on the fatal diversity of human language created the possibility of a new form of imagined community, which in its basic morphology set the stage for the modern nation. [...] In a pre-print age, the reality of the imagined religious community depended profoundly on countless, ceaseless travels" (Anderson 1991, 6, 46, 54).

Greg Urban suggests that instead of presupposing the existence of an ethnic culture, scholars should study cultural discourses (1996, 124). Many studies have shown that Tibetans have a shared discursive idea of an "us" belonging to a certain community. However, the discursive nature of identity should also be emphasized. As is the case with all "identities," "Tibetan identity" should not be considered as a timeless and fixed entity, but as something that is socially and politically constructed across different discourses, practices and positions (Anand 2000, 273). I thus find Urban's notion of the discursive nature of culture also applicable in the Tibetan context.

"Tibet" as a geographical and political entity is not unambiguous. However, to argue or to imply that "Tibet" is merely "imagined" would deny the fact that for Tibetans it exists and is real, and to claim otherwise would sweep away the basis of their identity. It would also call into question their ethnic struggle.

The Construction of My Research Field

My research on Tibetan nuns is based on research material I collected during three field research trips to the traditionally Tibetan regions of Amdo (*a mdo*) and Kham (*khams*) in the People's Republic of China (PRC) in 2007, 2009, and 2011, and one trip to a Tibetan exile community in Himachal Pradesh in India in 2008.[7]

My approach toward data collection can be called *multi-sited ethnography*[8]. In multi-sited approach the ethnographer moves through a spatially dispersed field and gathers research material in more than one site. What is understood as a "field" is not assumed to exist by itself but is thought to be constructed in the ethnographic process (e.g., Marcus 1995; Falzon 2012, 1–2).

Even if the approach of multi-sited ethnography was not unknown before, it was George E. Marcus who most comprehensively articulated the method in his famous paper "Ethnography in/of the World System: The Emergence of Multi-Sited Ethnography" (1995). Here Marcus discusses the growing methodological trend in anthropological research

---

7. In 2004, I also stayed three months in an exile nunnery in Himachal Pradesh for my master's thesis (Härkönen 2005), and in the spring of 2007 I studied Tibetan and volunteered at the Tibetan Women's Association in Dharamsala for two months. During my stay, I lived in a nunnery guesthouse and regularly visited the nunnery I had studied in 2004.
8. Multi-sited ethnography is also called multi-site ethnography, the multi-sited approach or multi-sited method.

Introduction

for ethnography to move from its conventional single-site location to multiple sites of observation and participation. According to Marcus, in its more obvious applications, multi-sited ethnography examines "the circulation of cultural meanings, objects, and identities" across and within the multiple sites of activity (Marcus 1995, 95–96). In addition to these applications, multi-sited ethnography is interested in phenomena where there is very little actual contact or exchange between the sites and where the functioning of one of the sites depends on *imagining* what is happening elsewhere. The object of the study is thus the complex relationship between these separate sites (Marcus 1999, 6–7, my emphasis).

Mark-Anthony Falzon identifies three main reasons for the formation of the multi-sited approach in the late twentieth century (2012, 3). First was the notion that space is socially produced (see also Marcus 1995, 104). As a consequence, a rethinking of the concepts of space and place in ethnographic research led to the realization that ethnographic space – like any other space – is produced (Falzon 2012, 3–4). Second, multi-sited ethnography arose as a response to empirical change in the world (Marcus 1995, 104). For Marcus, the need for multi-sited ethnography grew from the fact that his students of anthropology found themselves in the middle of distributed knowledge systems.[9] The most significant interpretative framework in the twentieth century was globalization, which has posed a challenge to the ethnographic methods of inquiry and the units of analysis (Falzon 2012, 4–6; see Marcus 1995, 97; 1999, 6). The third reason behind the growth of the multi-sited approach has to do with the fact that due to other academic requirements, it has become increasingly difficult for ethnographers to stay in the field for long periods of time (Falzon 2012, 6). Marcus also adds the fact that some typical examples of multi-sited ethnography have emerged from interdisciplinary arenas such as media studies, feminist studies, science and technology studies, and various strands of cultural studies (Marcus 1995, 97).

Multi-sited ethnography challenges many of the premises of traditional ethnography and Marcus anticipated criticism, noting that three sets of methodological concerns might arise among anthropologists: (1) concern about testing the limits of ethnography, (2) worry about weakening the power of fieldwork, and (3) fear about the loss of the "subaltern" (Marcus 1995, 99; see more about criticism in Coleman and von Hellermann 2011, 6). The Malinowskian way of doing focused and long-term ethnography in communities that are distinctively different from ours is thus thought to be endangered (Marcus 2005, 4). The

---

9. This refers to the fact that especially in the globalizing world, "knowledge" can no longer be found in one location, as was often assumed in traditional ethnography.

unavoidable connotation of multi-sitedness as a term is that it refers to something that is "profligate, impatient and unfocused," emphasizing surface rather than depth, and requiring effort beyond the capacity of the single fieldworker (Marcus 1999, 9). The biggest problem of the multi-sited approach is, in fact, thought to be its lack of depth (Falzon 2012, 7). Multi-sited ethnography has also been criticized for being nothing but a natural and logical extension of the study of the same peoples, only now in motion (see Ferguson 2011).

The advocates of the multi-sited research have objected to this criticism. According to Ulf Hannerz, it is important to realize how one site, as it is understood in a multi-site study today, differs from the single site of the mid-twentieth-century anthropologists. While the aim of traditional ethnography was to study the entire culture and social life of the people (Hannerz 2003, 202, 208), the goal of the multi-sited approach is not a holistic representation or "an ethnographic portrayal of the world system as a totality" (Marcus 1995, 99). Thus, the ethnographer does not claim to have an ethnographic grasp of the fields in their entirety, but sites are almost always selected among many which could be included (Hannerz 2003, 207). Furthermore, not all sites are treated with a uniform set of fieldwork practices, and the depth of focus varies due to the nature of the field and its accessibility (Nadai & Maeder 2005, 9; Marcus 1999, 8).

Nadai and Maeder note that classical ethnography itself has been criticized. The debate, particularly in terms of the crisis of representation, has shown that there are various problems related to the production of ethnographic data. They wish to demonstrate that multi-sited ethnography in what they call "fuzzy fields"[10] can represent an important contribution to qualitative sociological research in general. According to them, sociological ethnography in and of complex societies hardly ever studies a clearly bounded group in a single place and its research objects are derived from theoretical knowledge and questions (Nadai & Maeder 2005, 1, 8, 10). According to Nadai and Maeder (2005, 4):

> The field of sociological ethnography cannot be founded somewhere out there, but is constructed by the researcher. Moreover, a field for sociological ethnography is most likely not restricted to one observational site. Its contours emerge only during the research process as the ethnographer traces informants across multiple sites that turn out to become relevant in the light of the research question.

---

10. "Fuzzy fields," that is, fields without clear boundaries with regard to many dimensions.

Hannerz has also criticized some anthropologists for having a rather romantic view of their fieldwork sites and their relationships with the people there. According to him, anthropologists tend to find it difficult to describe their informants because they would rather see them as friends, or they may be proud to announce that they have been "adopted into families and kin groups." They do this not only because it suggests something about their skills as fieldworkers, but also because it carries a moral value (Hannerz 2003, 208–209).

The multi-sited approach has been applied to different kinds of research designs (see Coleman & von Hellermann 2011; Falzon 2012). Simon Coleman and Pauline von Hellermann (2011) note that the physical practice of following spatially disjunctive sites has dominated much of the discussion of multi-sitedness. Yet, they suggest that there is more potential in the term. According to them, Marcus wanted to make a point that the "world system" was not to be understood merely as a contextual framework where the local happened, but as already embedded within the object of study and thus as an integral part of "local" situations (Coleman & von Hellermann 2011). Kaushik Sunder Rajan, a close colleague of Marcus, argues that it cannot be known in advance what constitutes a multi-sited project, and successful multi-sited projects cannot be done simply by following the instructions given by Marcus or anyone else. For him, multi-sited ethnography "is not literalist methodology as much as a conceptual topology, whose construction depends on ethnographic modes of production" (Rajan 2011, 175). While multi-sited ethnography cuts across the geography of area studies, it does not deny the importance of particular cultural histories. The starting point of ethnography is to learn which questions are actually understandable in a given culture.

Falzon has noted that the multi-sited approach has produced its own little "road to Damascus storyline." By this he means that very often the original plan of the researcher is to conduct more conventional single-sited fieldwork, which he or she then realizes to be inadequate (Falzon 2012, 12).

It was also my initial intention to conduct more traditional, single-sited fieldwork. Unfortunately, the limitations of access maintained by the Chinese authorities after 1950 have made fieldwork in Tibet nearly impossible, and after 2008 the situation has gotten even worse. Robert Barnett (2008, xiii) writes:

> The procurement of permits for research remains today an arduous, complex and protracted struggle, particularly within the TAR. Even if permits are obtained, the results are often fraught with the limitations

that researchers have to impose upon themselves to avoid placing their respondents at risk of repercussions from the state.

Nevertheless, in order to do research in Tibetan regions, I began the research project in 2007 by making a three-month field trip to the Tibetan regions in China. The aim of this preliminary trip was to find a nunnery that I could study in more detail the following year. During the first field trip, I traveled mostly in the Amdo regions in Qinghai and Gansu, but I also made a trip to Lhasa in the TAR and to the Kham regions of southern Qinghai and Sichuan. During my stay, I visited various monasteries and nunneries. I also visited Yachen Gar which was at that time said to be a home for about 6,000 nuns and 4,000 monks, along with lay practitioners of Buddhism. I also conducted twenty-seven semi-structured, focused interviews: nine with Tibetan laywomen, seven with laymen, six with monks and five with nuns. The purpose of the interviews was to gain a general idea of the significance of the monastic institution in the Tibetan communities in Amdo and Kham and to achieve an initial understanding of the reasons for living as a monastic in present-day Tibet. In addition, I visited an English class of Tibetan college students in Xining and asked them to write about their ideas of Tibetan monasticism. I got a short answer from thirteen students (see Appendix).

During my first field trip, I also stayed a few days in a nunnery in the Yushu Tibetan Autonomous Prefecture in southern Qinghai Province.[11] The head lama of the nunnery granted me permission to stay with one of the nuns, and I was welcomed to come back the following year to do more extensive research in the nunnery. The support of the spiritual and administrative head of the nunnery was very important, because in Tibetan monastic institutions the main gatekeepers are usually lamas and the head monks.

Thus, my plan was to return to the nunnery in Yushu to conduct more fieldwork in 2008. However, due to the political turmoil brought by the Olympic Games and the fact that China refused to grant me a Chinese visa, it was impossible to travel to the Tibetan regions of China that year.[12] From that year on, ethnographic fieldwork in the Tibetan regions of China became even more difficult for non-Chinese researchers. Because I was not able to travel to the Tibetan areas, I decided to

---

11. Yushu TAP comprises the counties of Chumarleb (*chu dmar leb rdzong*), Dritö (*'bri stod rdzong*), Dzato (*rdza stod rdzong*), Thrindu (*khri 'du rdzong*), Yushu City (*yul shul grong khyer*), and Nangchen (*nang chen rdzong*).
12. In 2008, China tightened its control over Tibetans and Tibetan regions. Many foreigners staying in Tibetan regions as teachers or NGO workers were forced to leave the country. This also meant tighter visa procedures.

return to the Tibetan community in India where I had previously studied Tibetan nuns for my master's thesis. I stayed in Himachal Pradesh for about one month. In addition to living in a nunnery, I interviewed five exiled Tibetan nuns who had taken their vows in Tibet and had later escaped to India. All of them had been detained at some point before or during their escape, and two older nuns had been political prisoners in China.

In 2009, I was again granted a Chinese visa for one month and was thus able to return to the nunnery in Yushu Prefecture. However, due to the sensitive political situation in the Tibetan regions, I found it unwise to stay in a nunnery overnight. At that time, foreigners were permitted to stay only in certain hotels in the Tibetan areas. Long stays in any monastic compound would have attracted too much attention from the state authorities. I continued doing the life story interviews that I had started in India, and I interviewed eighteen nuns at two different nunneries. The first was an old nunnery that belonged to the Kagyu school of Tibetan Buddhism, which was re-opened in 2005. There were more than 300 resident nuns at the nunnery at the time of my research. The other one was a nunnery that belonged to the Sakya school of Tibetan Buddhism. The nunnery was established in 2000 and had about 100 resident nuns. Unfortunately, I was forced to leave Yushu prematurely due to an outbreak of pneumonic plague reported in July 2009 in Qinghai Province (Hu Wang et al. 2011).

In the spring of 2010, I received devastating news of a major earthquake in Yushu Prefecture that had destroyed 85–90 percent of the township of Gyegu. The nuns' houses at the nunnery where I had stayed in 2007 and 2009 had mostly collapsed and a newly built temple of the nunnery was damaged. Luckily, no lives were lost at the nunnery during the earthquake. Due to the unforeseen events that took place at my field site, I decided to broaden my focus from the Khamba nuns in the Yushu area to nuns living in the Amdo regions of Qinghai.

In 2011, I made my final field trip to the Tibetan areas in Qinghai. During my five-week stay, I traveled around Qinghai, looking for nuns and nuns' communities to study. I interviewed nineteen nuns in five different locations in Qinghai: eight in Xining, two in Kumbum (*sku 'bum*, Ch. Ta'ersi),[13] three in a nunnery in Chentsa (*gcan tsha*, Ch. Jainca) in Huangnan and six nuns in two sites in Rebgong (*reb gong*, Ch. Tongren). To supplement my data, I also did twenty-one interviews with lay Tibetans, mostly in Xining. The lists of the interviews are presented in Appendix.

---

13. Kumbum monastery (*Kumbum Jampa Ling, sku 'bum byams pa gling*) is located in Huangzhong at about 25 km southwest of Xining.

Hannerz has noted that while the actual combination of sites included in a study may be based on a research design, site selections are to some extent made gradually and cumulatively, "as new insights develop, as opportunities come into sight – and to some extent by chance" (Hannerz 2003, 207). This is what happened during my research. Because of the changing political situations in my field site, as well as the natural disaster that was impossible to anticipate beforehand, I had to change my preliminary plan of a single-sited ethnography into a multi-sited one.

Applying a multi-sited approach to the study of Tibetan Buddhist nuns proved to be very illuminating. As was shown in the previous chapters and as will be demonstrated in the following, belief in Tibetan Buddhism and the Tibetan Buddhist monastic tradition are almost ubiquitously shared by the dispersed Tibetans. The Tibetan nuns I studied at different sites in China and in India shared the notion of a common Tibetan culture and identity, of which monastic status was one of the most important articulations. Interestingly, when talking about Buddhism and monasticism, the nuns and other Tibetans I interviewed emphasized their common "Tibetanness" instead of regional differences between Amdo, Kham, Central Tibet or Tibetan refugee communities. This was probably at least partly due to the political situation under which they lived at the time of the research. Had I conducted one long, single-sited research, I would not have realized the widely shared notion of this common feeling of Tibetanness and thus would have been unable to witness some dramatic changes that took place in the Tibetan regions.

In my research, the "field" is thus constructed out of various geographical and spatial locations. What connects these different locations is the notion of shared Tibetanness defined principally by Buddhism, Tibetan monasticism, Tibetan culture and, at least to some extent, by a sense of Tibetan nationalism.

Methods and Data

According to Barbara Aziz, one of the most useful sources of "women's experience" is life history, comprised of either autobiographical or third-person accounts (1987, 84). I chose to conduct life story interviews in order to increase my understanding of individual nuns. I believed that knowing the life history of a nun could shed light on, for example, her decisions, motives, experiences and present status. However, as put by Ann Marie Leshkowich, "life histories are not direct mirrors of experience but mediated, intersubjective commentaries that require tellers to offer ad hoc interpretations that in turn shape how they subsequently view and lead their lives" (2006, 279). A personal narrative is thus not an exact or value-free account of a person's life, and it should not be evaluated in terms of its reliability or validity. Sometimes stories are invented or strategic. The interviewer and the interviewee always compose and construct the life story together: the interviewee is the narrator and the interviewer is the guide (Atkinson 1998, 7–9, 20, 59–60).

Despite the narrative nature of life stories, a lot of information can be gained from them. Life stories can provide the researcher with information about a social reality existing outside the story, as well as about the story itself as a social construct. A life story can help the researcher delineate an individual's place in the social order and the process used to reach that place. It can help explain an individual's understanding about social events and political causes and how they see, experience, or interpret those events (Atkinson 1998, 13–15).

I give a short biography of each of the nuns interviewed in the Appendix. The biographies are based on the age, status and situation of the nuns at the time of the interview. The names of the nuns are pseudonyms, such as "Ani Karma." Here "ani" means "nun." Usually Tibetan names have two parts and there is no distinction between first names and family names. In fact, only some Tibetans have a family name or use it. The nuns also have two names in addition to "ani," such as "Ani Karma Rinchen" or "Ani Tenzin Palmo." It is also very common for at least one of their names to be the same as others who were interviewed. For simplicity, I refer to the nuns by one name only.

In addition to the life story interviews, I conducted 49 focused and semi-structured interviews. The 38 interviewees were lay Tibetans of different gender, age and social backgrounds. Six of the interviewees were monks and five were nuns. Focused interviews were conducted in order to gain a general idea of the significance of the monastic institution in the Tibetan communities of the region, and to achieve a preliminary understanding of the reasons for living as a monastic in present-day Tibet. I also wanted to know about the importance of nuns in the society and about the general attitudes of the laity toward female monastics. The interviews with laypeople offered a background and additional information that contextualized the life stories. According to Anna Davidsson Bremborg, there are two different modes of handling interviews and interviewees. One emphasizes the interviewees as individuals; in the other, more stress is put on theory, categories or research questions (Davidsson Bremborg 2011, 318). The purpose of interviewing lay Tibetans was thus not only to grasp their subjective conceptions, but also to achieve a more general picture about the existing ideas of female monasticism in contemporary Tibetan regions. In order to make at least some suggestive generalizations, I also asked the informants to judge if their ideas were common or representative, or how they thought people generally viewed the matter (see Hammersley & Atkinson 2007, 106).

All of the life story interviews and most of the semi-structured, focused interviews were tape-recorded and translated from Tibetan into English. Three of the interviews were conducted in English. Most of the interviews were carried out in one of the Tibetan dialects with the help of a translator. The reason for using translators was that despite my previous studies of (mainly) Central Tibetan dialect, I had not mastered Kham and Amdo dialects, not to mention various other local dialects based on these, spoken by the interviewees.[14] Thus, for example, the interviews with people speaking Kham dialects were translated by Khamba translators, while the interviews with people speaking Amdo dialects were translated by Amdo-speaking translators.

Obviously, an ethnographic study cannot be based merely on interviews, which are always part of a larger context. The research material needs to be contextualized, for example, with regard to what the interviewees do, what other informants say and do, and what the researcher says, does and observes, as well as in relation to official documents, etc. (see Huttunen 2010, 40, 42–43). During my field trips to the Tibetan regions in China, I visited dozens of nunneries and monasteries (including the five great monasteries of the Geluk school of Tibetan Buddhism)[15] in the TAR, Qinghai, Gansu and Sichuan, in order to gain at least a superficial understanding of monastic life in present-day Tibet. I visited public events such as religious teachings and monastic celebrations, as well as important Buddhist sites (*mani* walls,[16] relic monuments, or *stūpa*s, and other religious monuments). By taking part in the religious events and visiting religious sites, it was possible to observe religious practices and behavior, as well as social interaction between the monastics and the laity and between the monks and the nuns. I spent time with my Tibetan lay and monastic friends, discussing my research issues but also many other topics that helped me to gain a deeper understanding of Tibetan culture and the everyday concerns of Tibetans.

Nevertheless, because of the sensitive political situation in Tibetan regions under China, I found it too risky to stay in any monastic community for an extensive period of time. For example, during my stay in Yushu in

---

14. There are many dozens of dialects in the Tibetan language and many of them are not mutually comprehensible (see Denwood 1999; Samuels 2014).
15. Sera (*se ra dgon pa*), Drepung (*'bras spungs dgon pa*) and Ganden (*dga' ldan*) in the TAR, Kumbum (*sku 'bum byams pa gling*) in Qinghai, and Labrang (*bla brang bkra shis 'khyil*) in Gansu.
16. Mani walls are walls made of stones that are inscribed with mantras.

2009, with the permission of the head lama, I used to come to one of the nunneries every morning and leave the place in the evening. Spending time in the nunnery offered the possibility to observe and participate in the day-to-day there, but it hardly provided an all-encompassing impression of the nuns' life. In the Amdo regions of Qinghai, the nunneries and nuns' communities were mainly located in remote areas and it was difficult and time-consuming to reach them. Thus, in 2011, I spent most of my trip traveling across Qinghai and looking for communities of nuns mentioned by other informants. Finding a nun in Amdo was often hit-and-miss.

In addition to observations and notes based on periods of participant observation, interviews and informal discussions, I tried to gather information, for example, about the history and statistics of monasticism from official sources (from Tibetan and Chinese authorities and printed material) as much as possible. However, gathering administrative information in China can be very difficult. Anja Lahtinen, whose research focuses on questions of governance in Qinghai, writes how during meetings with some officials, she asked for data and documents relating to the issue in question, but soon discovered that the information was not available. Sometimes, however, she was later and unexpectedly given all of the information that she had asked for (Lahtinen 2010, 41). Not surprisingly, officials were not willing to provide me with information about monasticism, such as the number of monasteries and nunneries, or the number of monks and nuns in Tibetan regions.

In ethnography, analysis of the research material begins already in the field and finishes only when ethnographic writing ends (Hammersley & Atkinson 2007, 158). Thus, fieldwork itself alternates between collecting and analyzing data. In my research, the research material was collected during four fieldtrips. This made it possible to view and analyze the research material while not in the field and to fill in any gaps during successive fieldtrips. Unlike in statistical sampling, in qualitative interview research it is not possible to know in advance how many people need to be interviewed. Usually when nothing new or significant emerges from the interviews, it is thought that saturation has been reached and the collection of data may be ended (see Davidsson Bremborg 2011, 313–314; Tuomi & Sarajärvi 2009, 87–90). It was this notion of the saturation of the interview material that led to my decision to finish interviewing. In other words, I could notice that the interviews were becoming repetitive and nothing significantly new was emerging.

Both types of interviews and the field notes were analyzed thematically. Thematic analysis involves searching through data in order to identify any recurrent patterns. A theme is a group of linked categories which carry similar meanings. The analysis begins by reading the interview material through several times and looking for any patterns. The next step of the analysis is to identify all data that relate to the already classified patterns. In other words, everything that fits under a specific pattern is identified and placed accordingly. After that, related patterns are combined into sub-themes in order to do a more detailed analysis of the data. After the data is organized by means of categories, it is possible to start analyzing those aspects that seem to be central to one's study. The process of systematic sifting and comparison leads to seeing the mutual relationship and internal structures of categories. The categories that emerge in the analysis are very often used to simply produce a description and/or explanation of the case or cases investigated (Braun & Clarke 2006; Aronson 1994; Hammersley & Atkinson 2007, 162–166; see also Tuomi & Sarajärvi 2009).

In practice, I started the analysis by reading the notes and transliterations and listening several times to the tapes that had been transcribed. After that, by using the comment function of MS Word, I noted key sentences or comments, organizing them under a specific topic or theme. For example, in a life story, when an interviewee related how she became a nun, various subthemes and phases emerged: how she first came up with the idea of becoming a nun, how her family reacted, how her wish was finally realized, who ordained her, and so forth. The focused interviews were treated similarly. For example, I looked for the ways in which people talked about nuns or what kind of interactions they had had with nuns.

While it is less common for ethnographic analysis to start with a well-defined theory, the process of analysis always relies on the existing ideas of the ethnographer and those she has acquired from research literature. What is important is that these do not take the form of prejudgments, forcing interpretation of the data into their mold. According to Hammersley and Atkinson, theorizing ought to involve a repetitive process in which ideas are used to make sense of data and data are used to change our ideas (Hammersley & Atkinson 2007, 158–159). In my research, intersectionality theory was chosen as a tool for more theoretical analysis only after the thematic analysis.

Some Remarks on Positionality and Research Ethics

The researcher can never become identical with the people she studies. Even if the interviewer and the respondent are both women, they do not necessarily share the same standpoint (Warren 2001, 95). Different standpoints and unbalanced power structures between me and my research subjects had various consequences for the research material and ethics. Charlene Makley (1999) noted that most Tibetans she interviewed, regardless of status, were wary of her tape recorder and refused to work with it. Makley first assumed that they refused due to fear of recrimination from authorities (e.g., if criticism of the state reached the wrong ears). However, she later realized that tape recorders were also associated with recording the words of people with religious authority. Thus, for an illiterate layman or woman to record his/her opinions about religion and ritual was potentially very embarrassing (Makley 1999, 44). While none of my interviewees rejected the use of the tape recorder and it did not seem to have an effect on the topics they chose to talk about, some of the younger nuns in particular were brief when telling about their life. Most of the informants were inexperienced as research interviewees and many did not regard themselves as having the knowledge or authority to talk even about their own lives.

Anna Rastas (2010) writes about how certain unequal positions can also lead to some expectations toward the researcher on the part of the research subjects. Most of the expectations toward me were financial, but sometimes also political. A few times it also happened that the interviewee had her own visible "agenda," according to which she constructed her story and, in fact, the whole interview. Once, for example, during the whole interview a young nun listed different illnesses that she and her family suffered from in order to receive a donation. Another time in India, a refugee nun asked me why the UN was not doing anything for the Tibetans and wondered if I could tell the "UN office" about the situation in her country. I found these requests justified, but I also had to convey that all I could probably do to help was to write their stories and let their voices be heard.

In spite of the different standpoints and the apparent power hierarchy between me and the nuns, the hierarchical positions were not fixed or absolute. Many of the nuns saw themselves as my teacher: I was a novice who was learning about Buddhism, Tibetan culture and Tibetan language. I was someone who was asking them silly questions, but who could also from time to time surprise them with her knowledge and understanding of their religion and culture. While I shared a certain position with the Tibetan laywomen I interviewed, I also shared a certain independence with the nuns. I also shared with many of them an interest in studying and understanding Buddhism. Despite our different standpoints, it should also be noted that my inquiry is by no means value-free. First of all, I am sympathetic toward the plight that many Tibetans face under the Chinese rule. Second, I appreciate Tibetan Buddhism as an important and valuable worldview. And third, I am not indifferent toward oppression – be it based on gender, nationality or any other aspect – or the oppressed themselves.

Methodological – as well as many epistemological – aspects are closely related to research ethics in general. For example, the constructed nature of the research process and data, the question of understanding, and the problem of the power balance between research participants have also to do with research ethics.

In ethnographic research, a certain level of intimacy or familiarity between the scholar and the research respondents is seen as necessary for building mutual trust and openness. However, mutual trust, openness and closeness raise many ethical questions. Despite that fact, there is not necessarily any one correct answer to the many ethical dilemmas that we face as researchers. I agree with Anne Ryen (2011), according to whom "many of the problems that we encounter in ethnographic research are emergent and contextual and call for situational responses." There are limitations, therefore, in universally applying Western research ethics (Ryen 2011, 432; also Palmer et al. 2014; Miller 2013).

Nevertheless, this does not mean that there are no general ethical guidelines. For example, the Finnish Advisory Board on Research Integrity, which is an expert body appointed by the Ministry of Education, Science and Culture, has drawn up guidelines for good scientific practice and procedures. According to the Advisory Board's guidelines (2012), ethical principles of research in the humanities and social and behavioral sciences include three areas: respect for the autonomy of the research subjects, avoidance of harm, and privacy and data protection.

Autonomy of the research subjects entails that participation in research should be voluntary and based on informed consent. Research subjects need to be told what the research is about and what their participation in the research means. Research subjects also have the right to withdraw from a study whenever they want (Finnish Advisory Board on Research Integrity 2012, 6–7; see also Ryen 2011).

Harm resulting from research can potentially stem from the collection of data, the storage of data and consequences following publication. In short, research subjects should be treated with respect and ensured that no mental or physical harm is caused to them during the data collection, in the course of storage of data, and when findings are reported in research publications. Finally, in order to protect the privacy of the research subjects, it is necessary to remove identifiers from the data that is stored and published (Finnish Advisory Board on Research Integrity 2012, 8–9, 13; Ryen 2011).

Introduction

Frederick Bird and Laurie Lamoureux Scholes (2011) also name three general and fundamental ethical principles that guide how research on religion ought to be done: first, researchers should respect the dignity and integrity of the subjects; second, they ought to communicate honestly and objectively to the subjects and audiences; and third, researchers should use good judgment when gathering, analyzing and evaluating the data and reporting on their research (Bird & Scholes 2011, 84).

There are various ethical questions to be considered when studying Tibetans. To start with, when negotiating access to the field, there is a question of whose permission ought to be sought (see Hammersley & Atkinson 2007, 42): that of the Tibetans involved in the study or that of the Chinese authorities? In fact, this type of question most obviously arises in relation to those who occupy subordinate positions in the setting under investigation. For my study, in addition to applying for a Chinese visa, I asked for permission to conduct research from the heads of the monastic institutions, as well as from the individual nuns and laypeople (and monks) I interviewed.

Because my study is mainly based on interviews, it was easier to ensure that all of the participants were fully informed about the research. I agree with Davidsson Bremborg who argues that ethical agreement is best achieved through the structured form of an interview. In fact, the main ethical issue arises before the interview even starts: the interviewee must be made aware that the situation is a research interview and not a common conversation (Davidsson Bremborg 2011, 310–311, 319; see also Ruusuvuori & Tiittula 2005). Therefore, I openly disclosed the purpose of my study and that it would be published. I told participants that they could quit the interview whenever they felt like it, and I also told them that their anonymity would be preserved in the final report, as well as when the data was stored. However, at the same time I asked them not to talk about anything that they felt was too sensitive in any way, either at that moment or afterwards.

Researchers do not operate in situations of complete freedom. Hammersley and Atkinson (2007, 220) write about ethnographers and their research subjects this way:

> Those they study not only may have different needs and interests that should be taken into account, but also will have differential power to protect themselves and to pursue their interests in relation to researchers and others.

It has been my priority to prevent any possible negative consequences for my research subjects. This has been done by safeguarding the anonymity of my informants and by making sure that their backgrounds and the specific research sites cannot be identified. In order to protect my informants, I also decided not to gather information that might be harmful to them in the future.

In the following Part II, I present the life stories of the nuns as told by them. I start by describing the not-so-straightforward process of becoming a nun in the present-day Tibetan areas. Based on the life stories of nuns, but also on interviews with my lay informants, I first depict how the decision to become a nun matured, what motivated it, how it was rationalized, and what kinds of obstacles nuns met with in the course of this process. After that, I describe the process of actually becoming a nun. This includes taking monastic ordination and finding a place to lead life as a monastic. After that, I illustrate the everyday life of the nuns and the challenges they were faced with when it came, for example, to livelihood and religious practices. Finally, I quote passages from the interviews that describe how some of the nuns decided to flee Tibet to India. In Sections III and IV, I analyze the life stories and other data from the perspective of intersectionality.

Part II

FROM LAITY TO MONASTIC LIFE

– 4 –

The Idea of Nunhood Matures

Various Motives

When I was young, I knew that my parents were impermanent. Of course they are impermanent; even I will die someday, right? So I always wanted to become a nun. After that, there would be nothing that would make me feel sad. When I could barely speak, I used to say I wanted to become a monk. Then, as I grew up, I thought that monks are very happy and I was happy when they visited my home. And I never envied wealthy people. At the age of 10 or 11, I really wanted to become a nun. In fact, I was the girl who hated to wash and comb hair. I thought it would be so pleasant if I had no hair. And I also hated to wear a chuba,[1] the typical Tibetan chuba with fur.

Poor parents! They used to ask that if I got married and led my own life, wouldn't that be good. Poor them! Then, they also used to ask that if I became a nun, would that be good then. Am I really able to be a nun forever? They were thinking of my reputation. Before I became a nun, I had hair, right? After I cut it, it would be hard to return to be a layperson, isn't that right?

Ani Tashi

The above quotation from the interview with 38-year-old Ani Tashi brings up many of the central themes of becoming a nun in the present-day Tibetan regions. First, she talked about the central Buddhist doctrine, according to which nothing is permanent. Impermanence means that she and her parents, like everyone else, will die someday. Impermanence and the suffering caused by impermanence are abstract philosophical teachings, but they are also very concrete realities of everyone's everyday life.

Second, according to Ani Tashi, monastic life is a solution to the problems of impermanence and suffering. Nuns and monks will die, too, but unlike laypeople, they attempt to step out of cyclic existence and its

---

1. A traditional Tibetan dress made typically of sheepskin and wool.

continual cycle of death and rebirth. Thus, monasticism presented for her an ideal way of life that is free from worldly sorrows and worries.

Third, Ani Tashi was inspired by other monastics, in this case monks, whom she considered happy people.

Fourth, her comment about wealthy people was probably meant to imply that it is better to become a monastic than a rich person, because merit gained in monastic life is more durable than the worldly riches accumulated by wealthy people. Fifth, the passage reveals that Ani Tashi got the idea of nunhood when she was still very young. Elsewhere she explained this in terms of karma: because of her previous positive deeds, she was naturally inclined toward religious life. Sixth, by viewing herself as a girl who never cared about her appearance, she implied that her "faith" was not to be pretty in order to get married, but to become a nun. Finally, she mentioned her worried and reluctant parents, who did not support the idea of nunhood without reservation, but instead expressed their concerns regarding their daughter's reputation. In the following, I will examine each of these themes in more detail by looking at other nuns' stories as well.

"I Was Destined to Become a Nun"

Like Ani Tashi above, some of the nuns I interviewed emphasized that the idea of nunhood first came to them when they were very young. Some told that even before they could walk or talk properly, they had expressed their wish to become a nun. They had admired monks who had visited their homes and some had engaged in roleplaying in which they assumed the role of a monastic. The 44-year-old Ani Dikey from Amdo was one of the nuns who thought it was her *karma* to become a monastic. This is how she recollected her childhood:

> As a child, when I was around 12 or 13 years old, we played lots of impersonating games. I always took the role of a nun, whereas some kids took the role of a wife and a husband. But, I preferred to be a nun. I used to get a red cloth to wear and take the role of a nun in the game. So, there was a natural impulse in me to become a nun.
>
> I was very fascinated by and attached to the idea of reciting prayers and studying religious texts. As a kid, I thought that would be the happiest thing in life. The same way as there are some other girls who get fascinated by the idea of milking cows and doing house chores, my interest was different. I had the idea that family life can never provide genuine happiness. When I told my idea of becoming a nun to others and they reacted mockingly by laughing and other stuff, it really hurt me and I used

to cry. There were some girls of my age from my place, and together we nurtured the idea of becoming nuns, but eventually I was the only one who became one.

When I was young, there was no freedom to practice religion. We hardly saw monks and nuns around in those days. There was one nun named Shongmo in my locality and she was revered by all our people. My father told me that he was going to meet her. Then later on, as the situation improved, a few monks, those who had not broken their vows during the suppression, started resuming their religious practice. There was a monk named Tabba here – he is still alive – and he is a highly respected monk. I was so happy to see him in his monk's robe at that time. I got thrilled by imagining myself in that robe. My natural attraction to that kind of life, I believe, must be due to my karma. I was destined to become a nun.

She continued by describing how she finally became a nun:

I used to be very romantic about the nun's life. The idea of living in a small house without anyone with me thrilled me. But until I turned 15 years old, my parents never let me become a nun, saying that the nun's life is very difficult.

Those days, some among my family agreed with my decision to become a nun, but some didn't. Then, I was struck by a serious disease and it really drove me almost to death. But I was still very adamant about cutting my hair. In bed, I used to appeal to my father to cut my hair. My father thought that I would never get cured, so he wanted to make my only wish come true. Then he went to seek a prophecy from a Dolma[2] statue and got a message that my original name should be replaced with a new name, and then [he should] cut my hair. After performing this, the illness would disappear like a cloud in the sky. So, after all this was done, I miraculously recovered to normal.

In Ani Dikey's account, many incidents suggested that she believed it was her "destiny" to become a nun. When other children played house, she played a nun and dreamed of chanting prayers and leading a solitary religious life. There were not many chances to meet monks, and particularly nuns, during her childhood because religious life was suppressed. Meeting with religious figures was thus especially fascinating for Ani Dikey, and she thought that her enthusiasm was due not only to her innate tendencies but also to dictation of karma. Finally, there was a serious illness that brought her close to the brink of death. However, she miraculously recovered as soon as she received the monastic ordination she had so persistently asked for.

---

2. Dolma or Drolma (Skt. Tārā; Tib. *sgrol ma*) is a popular female bodhisattva in Tibetan Buddhism.

Religious life was suppressed or only beginning to revive during the period of childhood of my older nun interviewees. For this reason, there were not many nuns they could meet. In many Tibetan regions, it is still much rarer to come across nuns than monks, as I discovered myself and I was told by many of my lay informants. Despite this fact, some of my interviewees claimed that although they had never actually seen a nun before, they still got the idea of becoming one. As 36-year-old Ani Yonten from Amdo put it:

> It is hard to recollect all that happened in my mind and what drew me to become a nun. As a kid of nine or ten years of age, though I had never seen a nun before, the impulse in me to become a nun was very strong. Those days, I didn't know that the life of a nun is so happy. But the desire to become a nun was so strong. From the Buddhist philosophical point of view, all those things can be attributed to karma. [...] I heard about nuns but I never saw any. My intention to become a nun came to me even before seeing a nun. I heard from others that once you become a nun, you are supposed to wear a robe.

Like Ani Dikey, Ani Yonten believed that the reason for her becoming a nun was her karma. She emphasized that she had a strong desire to become a nun from an early age and that she had this impulse in spite of the fact that she had never seen a nun. Ani Dikey's and Ani Yonten's determination to don the robes arose when they were still young. The story of 23-year-old Ani Lhamo from Amdo also includes the fact that she was inclined and very determined to become a nun when she was still young:

> When I was a child, the nuns and monks, and especially their clothes, fascinated me a lot. One time, I was in the town and met a nun. I approached her and learned that she was from a village not far from mine. I told her that I wanted to become a nun and she replied to me that becoming a nun is not that easy. But I said I surely will become a nun one day.

On the contrary, 35-year-old Ani Rinchen from Kham told me that she wished to become either a doctor or a nun when she was a child. It turned out later that she actually became both. First, however, she became a nun. As in the case of the nuns above, Ani Rinchen's account strongly emphasized karmic consequences. She recalled:

> When I was getting older and was around 21 years old, my relatives thought that I should get married. However, since I was very young, I hadn't given thought to that. If I got married, I would be able to help only my family, especially being a daughter-in-law. One night, I had a good dream and the next day I went to visit a lama who lived nearby our town, and I decided to become a nun. [...] I told him that I wanted to be a nun and he said he had

been waiting for me. Ha ha. He gave me a khata,³ which he had prepared for me earlier, and brought me to his bedroom where he shaved my hair. He told me that I should change into a robe on that same day. I did as I was told and became a nun that day. I didn't ask for my father's permission.

Ani Rinchen did not say more about the good dream she had had, but she clearly interpreted the dream as a sign that encouraged her to make the decision to become a nun. Furthermore, the dream led her to a lama who, according to Ani Rinchen, had been waiting for her arrival. This suggests the idea of a karmic connection between the lama and Ani Rinchen. Ani Phuntsok, a 31-year-old nun from Kham, told how she became a nun after she had practiced religion and felt the "blessing of the dharma." She recollected:'

> I used to practice the dharma and as I studied dharma books I felt like I wanted to be a nun. I think it must be a blessing of the dharma. You know, lamas say that the dharma always blesses us. Every time I practiced dharma I felt delighted, it is the same now. So I wanted to become a nun. [...] My uncle who is a monk used to tell me a lot. He used to tell me how the earth was formed and about suffering in a worldly life. So I believed him. I believed him and I believed in the cycle of existence. Then I practiced the dharma and I could feel the blessing of the dharma. And I wished that this would bless all others and they could feel the same.

It is not evident what Ani Phuntsok meant when she talked about the "blessing of the dharma." From a Buddhist point of view, the blessing of the dharma can simply mean that practicing religion generates positive merit, which in Ani Phuntsok's case matured into the wish to become a nun. She may also refer to the Buddhist doctrine that the teachers of unbroken lineages pass on the blessing of dharma, that goes back to the Buddha. She might have also been referring to the prevailing idea that certain objects and people, such as religious texts and amulets or highly accomplished religious practitioners, can retain and generate sacred power. Nevertheless, it seems that Ani Phuntsok also referred to karmic consequences rather than a rational choice when she told about her path of becoming a nun.

Thus, these nuns believed that becoming a nun was a result of their karma. They believed that their good deeds and religious practice – in this life and even more in past lives – had generated positive merit, which had led them to donning the robes and receiving ordination. Hence, instead of choosing to become nuns, they had been chosen for the nun's life, to use the description of Gutschow (2004, 134).

---

3. *kha btags*, a ceremonial silk scarf used in the Tibetan tradition.

"Wonderful Changes in Her Inspired Me"

Many of the nuns I interviewed told that they had not seen other nuns before they got the idea of becoming nuns themselves. However, some, like Ani Tashi above, stated that they were deeply impressed by other monastics, either nuns or monks, and that this is what inspired them to become a nun themselves. In the case of 22-year-old Ani Palden, who was born in the TAR but lived in Yushu during the interview, encountering monks who could not only recite but also read and write inspired her to become a nun. She told me:

> There weren't any other nuns in the village, but there were monks. So, we respected them and invited them to our home and asked them to chant for us. I thought that if I was like them, I could read and write. How happy I would be! So, I wanted to become a nun.

Although few in number, there were also some nuns who had motivated my nun interviewees. There also seemed to be some learned nuns, and their lifestyle inspired Ani Wangchuk, a 35-year-old nun from Amdo, who recollected that she had a strong desire to become like these nuns. While the idea of learning to read and write fascinated Ani Palden and Ani Wangchuk, especially inspiring were those few accomplished nuns who acted as teachers to younger nuns. Ani Wangchuk told me:

> There was a blind nun who most of the time stayed confined in a particular place. When she went somewhere, someone needed to clutch her hand and give guidance. She taught Buddhist texts to young nuns like me. There were many people who attended her teachings.

37-year-old Ani Dolma from the TAR had not only heard about nuns, but had also heard about their good deeds. She thinks that this "planted special seeds of happiness" in her heart, and brought her close to the nuns and their activities.

Most of the nuns I interviewed did not have any other monastics among their close family members. Nevertheless, it is probable that many of the informants did have monks among their more distant relatives. I assume this because, as in traditional Tibet, becoming a monk is still highly respected and relatively common in contemporary Tibetan culture. Consequently, it would not be an exaggeration to claim that every Tibetan living in the traditionally Tibetan regions knows a monastic person. Fifteen of the nuns interviewed had at least one monastic in the family, most often a brother. The nuns had brothers, uncles and male cousins that were monastics more often than nun sisters, nun aunts and nun cousins. Nevertheless, those who had a female monastic in the family told that their example was important in their own decision to become a nun. For 29-year-old Ani Dechen from the TAR, her sister's example was crucial:

> One of my elder sisters is a nun. Soon after becoming a nun, there was such a visible change in her lifestyle. She became so gentle and kind, and there was always a certain degree of calmness within her. Later, these wonderful changes in her eventually inspired me to become a nun and pursue spirituality.

Ani Dolkar, a 40-year-old nun from the TAR, and Ani Pasang, a 32-year-old nun from Amdo, were inspired by their aunts, who were nuns. Ani Dolkar remembered:

> I was ordained as a nun at the age of 15. We had two nuns, my father's sisters, at home. I was, as far as I can remember, very much attracted to nuns from a pretty young age. I think all these events were fuel for my inspiration to be a nun. Besides, these two nuns used to narrate all these wonderful things about being a nun, a hassle-free life, and they instructed me how to recite and read some rudiments of Buddhist mantras.

Ani Dolkar's aunts acted as an example, but they also convinced Ani Dolkar about the positive aspects in a nun's life. Ani Pasang's aunts, who lived with her family, were relieved of at least some of the household chores, such as herding. Ani Pasang, who did not like herding, confessed that she was envious of their way of life:

> I didn't like to herd. At that time, there were already two nuns [in the family] and I really envied their lives. So, I wanted to become a nun. There was a discussion going on regarding one of my younger sisters becoming a nun, so I insisted that I also wanted to become a nun.

Unlike the excerpts in the previous chapter that emphasized the karmic causes of becoming a nun, these fragments stress the example of other monastics. The inspiring example of other monastics was also noted by Charlene Makley, some of whose informants in Labrang had seen monastics coming to their village and noted that their lifestyle and commitment to Buddhist practice had fueled their own decision to become a nun (Makley 1999, 190). It also seems to be relatively common that when a woman leaves her village to become a nun, other girls in the same village are inspired by her example and follow her into monastic life. In the nunneries, I met many nuns from the same village. This is explained also by the fact that many people in a certain village follow the same school of Tibetan Buddhism and end up in a nunnery or monastery of that school.

Tibetan history includes stories of highly accomplished female practitioners in Tibetan Buddhism, who are said to have inspired both men and women (e.g., Allione 1984; Gross 1993; Martin 2005). My nun interviewees did not mention these stories as examples that they themselves followed. The inspiring figures for the nuns I interviewed were learned or otherwise noteworthy male and female monastics they knew, in particular close monastic relatives (see also LaFever 2017).

"I Was Tired of the Enduring Sufferings that Fate had Brought upon Me"

One of the motivations for becoming a nun most often repeated by my informants was the suffering experienced in lay life. In Buddhism, the lay life, or "worldly life," is considered to be problematic in many ways. It is a source of the five poisons (Skt. *kleśa*, Tib. *nyon mongs*), which are the mental states of ignorance, attachment, aversion, pride and envy. The *kleśas* are seen as leading to suffering,[4] which was the most common reason for ordination – and doctrinally one of the most important ones – given by my nun informants. The greatest source of suffering that the nuns said they had experienced was the death of their family members. A 40-year-old nun from Amdo, Ani Tsomo, explained how losing her parents inspired her to become a nun:

> I lost my parents in an accident when I was at a tender age. I had been working on the farm and helping my family with other things. Since there were no parents, I didn't want to stay there anymore. [...] After I lost my parents, I faced many problems. Then, I realized that there is no point in living a layperson's life. So, I thought that if I became a nun, I could do something good for my dead parents by saying prayers and performing rituals.

53-year-old Ani Changchub from Amdo was another of the two nuns I interviewed who had been married before becoming a nun. She had decided to become a nun after losing her husband, brother and parents. She recalled:

---

4. The Tibetan tradition distinguishes between three types of suffering: (1) the suffering of misery; (2) the suffering of change; and (3) compositional suffering. The first type of suffering refers to physical and mental affliction, while the second type includes enjoyments that ordinary beings mistakenly think of as being pleasurable. The third type of suffering, the fundamentally unsatisfactory nature of cyclic existence, is the basis for the first two (Powers 2006, 119).

> I had a brother. [...] He was a blacksmith by profession. My brother and his wife died in an accident. When I was 29 years old, I lost my dad. And then at the age of 40, I lost my mother, who was 77. At the age of 43, I lost my husband. So, my life is very terrifying. [...] Because of being an ill-fated woman, I had been facing all these terrible problems. After [I was] left alone, I thought that by becoming a nun there would be some change in my life. [...] In fact, I was tired of the enduring sufferings that fate had brought upon me. I was really tired of living a layperson's life. So, I thought that it would do me good if I became a nun and said some prayers.

The death of their beloved ones meant that Ani Tsomo and Ani Changchub found it difficult to find meaning in a lay life. They also believed that as nuns they would be able to better benefit their deceased relatives (for example, through prayers). Losing her mother and a fear of death also motivated Ani Phuntsok to don the robes:

> Around three years later, my mother passed away. My father used to tell me to practice the dharma, but I didn't really realize [what he meant] until my mother died. Of course, I had been chanting and praying, but not really understanding it. [...] Only at that time did I realize how scary death was. Then I realized that I could not lead a worldly life. So, I dreamed of being a nun.

In the case of most of the nuns I interviewed, both of their parents were alive. Those who had suffered had lost a mother slightly more often than a father. In the interviews, the nuns also mentioned much more commonly that their mothers had serious health problems than their fathers.

Sickness or different kinds of ailments were another common source of suffering experienced by the nuns I interviewed. One of the nuns, 22-year-old Ani Gyurmey from Kham, suffered from various sicknesses, as did her whole family. Unfortunately, the family was poor and unable to afford proper medical treatment. Despite her sickness, or because of it, Ani Gyurmey wished to become a nun when she was young:

> When I was about two years old, I was paralyzed. Everyone said that I might die or go crazy and I would not be able to talk. If I was put together with other people, I could only be treated as a dog. I didn't understand anything. I was like that until seven years old. My family is quite poor. We didn't have money to see doctors. So it was like that and I was not able to see the doctors. Then a lama performed some rituals for me and I got better. I mean I changed back into a human being. But I still have some mental problems. I don't have money to see the doctors. It is said that my illness can be treated. But I don't have the money. Sometimes when I get worse I can't distinguish people. When my sickness got a little better – I was eight at that time – I started saying that I wanted to be a nun. In my

family, there is a monk. I was told that I wore his robes and said that I would like to be a nun.

Then, when I turned twelve, I started to get a little better and began to recognize things. I thought if I didn't become a nun and if I led a worldly life like that, I couldn't take it. I thought that if I kept faith in the Buddha, even if I died I would die at once and suffer no more. If I led a worldly life, how much suffering would I have to endure? Such as giving birth. When looking at my parents, I know how difficult it is to lead such a life. If I think about my parents, I would also cause them more suffering if I led a worldly life.

I had been saying that I wanted to be a nun since that time. But my parents did not let me become a nun. They said that I couldn't live alone with my illness. They said that if I got worse I couldn't even boil a cup of tea for myself and there would be no one to take care of me. So they asked me to stay home until I was nineteen years old.

In Ani Gyurmey's life, sickness and poverty caused tremendous suffering for the whole family. She thought that monastic life would offer some relief for herself, but also for her parents.

Death and illness are probably the most dramatic manifestations of impermanence and suffering. These motivated already the historical Buddha to renounce the world. Fear of death and experiences of sickness also motivated some of the nuns I interviewed to leave lay life and become a nun. For them, monastic life was an antidote for the suffering experienced in mundane life.

"If You Don't Work until You Cry, You Don't Get the Food to Make You Laugh"

Most of the nuns studied came from rural, fairly isolated areas of traditional Kham and Amdo.[5] Ten of the nuns I studied were from families that practiced agriculture and ten were from pastoralist families. Almost as many came from families leading a semi-nomadic lifestyle and from families whose livelihood was something else, such as small-scale business, collecting caterpillar fungus, working as a state cadre, or doing

---

5. The majority, altogether twenty-two nuns, were from Kham, and most of them came from Yushu Prefecture in the southern part of Qinghai. Only two of the Khamba nuns were from the Kham region of the TAR. Twelve of the nuns came from Amdo. The majority were from Amdo/Qinghai, while one was from Amdo/Gansu and two were from Amdo/Sichuan. Five of the nuns came originally from Central Tibet or Ü-Tsang (TAR). Four of the nuns lived in India at the time of the interview.

occasional menial work. Most of the nuns from the Amdo regions of Qinghai and Gansu came from families practicing agriculture whereas the nuns from the Kham region of Qinghai were from families whose sources of livelihood was most often "something else." Animal husbandry and agriculture are the dominant modes of subsistence in the Tibetan regions, despite the fact that due to changes implemented by China, there are nowadays many Tibetans who have given up traditional livelihood, either voluntarily or under compulsion.

Whereas childhood for most of the nuns meant freedom from worldly worries and hard work, this seemed to change by the time they reached adolescence. All the nuns I studied started to take part in domestic work and in the family's livelihood as soon as they were considered able to do so.

Thus, besides death and sickness, the lay life was seen as a root for many other causes of suffering. My nun interviewees saw the two primary modes of Tibetan livelihood, agriculture and pastoralism, as particularly busy and exhausting ways of life.[6] This is what Ani Tashi, a 38-year-old nun from a nomadic family from Kham had to say about nomadic life:

> I am a nomad. I am familiar with the hard work that nomads have to do. Herding is so hard; doing other nomadic work is also very hard. But if I was a laywoman, I would starve if I didn't herd the yaks, isn't that right? And I would have a lot of children. I would have to find food not only for myself, but also for my children. So, I thought that monks and nuns are happier. I always thought that monks are very happy. I thought it would be happy to be a nun.

She continued:

> But once the person is stuck in the worldly life, no matter if he is a Han Chinese or a Tibetan, a nomad or a farmer, he has to work for survival, right? There is a saying "If you don't work until you cry, you don't get the food to make you laugh." If I had to work, I really couldn't. It is too tiresome. So, even if it seems that it is happy to get married, you still have to work and earn the living, isn't that so? Some nomads are very rich, but then they have the suffering of being wealthy. They have to work a lot. There is a saying that if you are rich, you are the servant of wealth and if you are poor, you are the servant of other people. You have to work in rain and mud, isn't that right?

---

6. The majority of Tibetans are farmers, but many also keep yaks, sheep and goats. In fact, herders are found throughout the Tibetan regions and animal husbandry is important in Tibet's economy. Agriculture involves a variety of grains and vegetables, of which barley is the most widespread and important (e.g., Wang 2009, 14).

> If you have many yaks, you have to get up at three in the morning and start working. There are families with 100 yaks to milk. So, even if you wanted to sleep, you would not have time, isn't that so? They have to take care of the livestock. If the weather is good, if there was only summer and no winter with wind and rain, then it would be better. In the winter, there is a lot of snow. In the summer, when you have to get up around three in the morning and it is raining, then you'll get totally soaked. So, it is like that, and I thought nuns are happy.
>
> I just feel so happy that I don't have to go in the mud to herd the livestock, that I don't have to commit any bad deeds. It is maybe too much to say that I am not afraid even if I died.

The hardships of nomadic life were obviously an important motivation for Ani Tashi to become a nun. Nomadic life represented to her endless work and continuous worries related to providing for herself, the family and especially children. Due to the natural conditions in the Tibetan areas, agriculture and animal husbandry are often a risky business. The altitude is high, winters extreme and summers short. The weather can change rapidly, and hailstorms and blizzards may wipe out the livestock or destroy the harvest. The lay life with its hard work and uncertain future also motivated the 21-year-old Ani Yongtsen to become a nun. She spoke about her choice this way:

> I wanted to become a nun, and my family was also saying that I would be happy if I became a nun. I was watching the tiresome life that they were leading. My parents' life was quite difficult. My uncle and aunt were nomads and I saw them taking care of the yaks and sheep. They always had to work, so I learned that life was really difficult. When I saw this, I realized it was so difficult to lead a worldly life. If I led a worldly life, I couldn't do well at all. If I had to lead a worldly life and if I couldn't pass the exams, then I wouldn't have any job, isn't that right? I would become a person without a job; life would be hard if I had to work as a laborer. My family's condition is also poor. If I still chose to get married, I would have to think that life would be very hard for me.
>
> For instance, in my family, there are only four of us, and still my parents have to worry about our livelihood. If they have something for today, they have to worry what tomorrow's food will be. If I became a nun, I wouldn't have to worry about these things, isn't that right? So, I thought that being a nun would be very happy.

Ani Yongtsen's parents did not have any permanent job, which led to impoverished living conditions in the family when she was a child. According to Ani Yongtsen, the life of her relatives, who worked as nomads, was not any better. She had thus witnessed the hardships of a traditional livelihood, but she also experienced the difficulties her family faced in the changing society with poor opportunities for employment.

In the busy life of agriculturalism and nomadism, most of my informants were not able to attend school. In fact, the main reason for not going to school was the fact that their input of labor was needed by the family. 38-year-old Ani Tashi, quoted above, had never had a chance to go to school. She explained:

> I didn't go to school. I helped my parents at home and did household chores. My mother used to get sick all the time. [...] My mother got paralyzed and she stayed in bed for seven years. I had to serve her. So I did not go to school. I thought of being a nun when I was young. But since we were nomads, I didn't have time to go to school and study. [...] I didn't have any teachers [at home]. At that time, the nomadic children were not sent to school. The children were sent after the yaks and sheep. Both the parents and the government think now that children should be sent to school. But at that time, we were not [sent]. I knew that as a nun, I should have learned to read and write, but I didn't have a teacher. So I just chanted whatever I could and stayed at home.

Those nuns who had gone to school for some years told that they had attended school in theory but not in practice. Ani Gyaltsen, a 44-year-old nun from Kham recollected:

> When I was young, I had to work for the community. We didn't have much chance to study. I went to a communal school for a month or two. I started school when I was eight, but we didn't have much time to study. Instead, we always worked. I stayed in school until I was fifteen years old.

Ani Wangchuk, a 35-year-old nun from Amdo also told that she never attended school regularly because of the work she had to do at home:

> I went to school for a while after looking after the goats, from the age of 11 until I reached 13 years old. But I never attended school on a regular basis; I always had to take breaks and look after the goats and do house chores.

According to Ani Dikey, a 44-year-old nun from Amdo, it was not common in her childhood to attend school, but the situation has changed now. She said:

> The family condition was not that good. There was no permanent job for any of my brothers and sisters. Most of them are involved in temporary jobs that bring them some money. During our childhood, none of our siblings attended school. We were only running after the animals. Now we send kids to school and expect that they will get education and find nice jobs.

22-year-old Ani Palden, who was born in the TAR but lived in Yushu during the interview was the oldest of her siblings and was able to go to school only after her sister's children needed someone to accompany them there. She recollected:

> I stayed at home taking care of the livestock and only later went to school. Nobody sent me to school so I stayed at home. There wasn't anyone at home to take care of the livestock. All the other siblings in my family are younger than me and they couldn't take care of the animals. My younger sister got married and she sent her children to school in the village. After they finished primary school, they had to go to town to continue their studies. We were afraid that they might be hit by a car, so I went to school with them in the town. [...] I went to school for three years: the middle school grades one, two and three. I was probably 19 years old at that time.

When asked about the reason for not attending school, Ani Lhatso, a 37-year-old nun from Kham also thought that she was not to sent to school because she was among the oldest in the family and someone was needed to help at home. For those who had been to school, one of the reasons for not continuing schooling was the fact that the family could not afford to pay the school fees. Ani Kalsang, a 37-year-old nun from Kham told that she was able to go to school for two years but after that her family was not able to support her. 22-year-old Ani Gyurmey from Kham said:

> At first there were four siblings in our family who went to school. Then, after my brother reached the sixth grade of primary school, they said that we had to pay tuition. So, we could not afford the tuition and withdrew him from school. My older sister went to school until the fourth grade. I also attended until the fourth grade and was then withdrawn from school. Then the one who is younger than me went to school until the sixth grade. Although she is the youngest in the family, we still weren't able to pay for her tuition.

There was also a problem of the remoteness of schools. Ani Dolkar, a 40-year-old nun from the TAR had to quit going to school because the road there was too dangerous. She said:

> I attended school for three months when I was ten years old. I dropped out after three months due to its inaccessibility and treacherous mountain tracks and streams. I didn't have the heart to cross those scary paths every day.

I also asked the nuns about the education of their siblings. Based on my interviews, it seems that the sons in the family were more likely to be educated than the daughters. According to Ani Lhatso, two of her brothers went to school while she stayed home and cooked for them. Among my informants' families, it also seemed to be more common to withdraw a girl than a boy from school. According to Ani Phuntsok, a 31-year-old nun from Kham:

> When my elder sister got married, I was taken out of school. There was no one to work at home so I was withdrawn from school. Then, after I got back home, I had to work. My younger brothers were doing the Association Degree, one in Sichuan and one in Xining. So the younger ones could not help me much.

Two of the nuns among my informants were more educated than an average Tibetan. One of them – 35-year-old Ani Rinchen from Kham, who as a six-year-old had lost her mother – said:

> When I was nine years old and my younger brother was five, we moved to a village and my father sent the three of us to school. I finished primary school in six years and spent another three years in middle school. However, I didn't pass the exam for further studies, for higher education. Then I went to work at a factory. I worked there for around two years and then I got sick. Since I was eight or nine years old, I had had a dream of being a nun or a doctor and I prayed that I would become either one someday. Afterwards, I went back to my hometown and did business probably for one year. During that time, I sometimes gained money and sometimes lost, but either way I didn't feel happy.
>
> When I was working at the factory, I was told that one of the Tibetan students would be sent to self-study for one and a half years. Fortunately, I was chosen. I studied philosophy and public relations and economic management in the Qinghai Normal University. [...] Then my Chinese friend said that since my father had brought me up so far, it was time to pay back in the way of learning something. Hence, she suggested I should study medicine at a foundation in Gyegu. I studied there for three years, as she suggested. [I studied] both Chinese and Tibetan medicine. I studied there for three years and worked one more year as an intern, in total four years.

Apart from the traditional lifestyle of nomadism and agriculture, many young Tibetan women appear to face new pressures belonging to the modernizing society. Ani Yongtsen mentioned that not being able to pass entrance exams for further studies would mean a life of work and no education. Thus, even if a girl was lucky enough to go to school, the future seemed to be full of uncertainties. This is evident in the case of Ani Choedron, a 32-year-old nun from Kham. Ani Choedron was one of the most educated nuns among my informants. She had gone to school for thirteen years, but her worry about not being able to find a job led her to monastic life. She explained:

> I didn't pass the entrance exam, but I still had a chance to go to Xining to continue with my studies. However, I thought it would be very difficult to get a job. So I told my parents that I wanted to become a nun. They let me. Then I became a nun. I thought that the nun's life is happy. Aside from my parents, I don't have to be concerned for or be afraid of anyone else, right? I am not sure, but I am just afraid of leading a worldly life. I don't know. I just don't like the idea of getting married. […] You know, being a nun means that you are all on your own. If you are full, it is only you and if you are starving, it is only you, right? Besides, as a nun I cause only a little burden for my parents, isn't that correct?

When the type of work done by the nuns before entering monastic life is considered, the most common seems to be various domestic chores. The domestic work done by them included work done inside, as well as outside a house or a tent. In addition to housework, such as cooking, making butter, cleaning and taking care of the younger siblings or grandparents (or parents), the most common work for young girls was herding animals, most typically sheep and goats. A few nuns had had a chance to go to school, and they mentioned studying as their main duty before nunhood. Most of them, however, probably had to participate in domestic work, not being in school.

Besides being heavy and burdensome, life as a layperson was seen as offering few choices. When talking about the standard of living of the childhood family the nuns described it as poor or moderate. None of them considered the living conditions of the childhood family high.

Most of the nuns I interviewed had had no opportunity to attend school. One of the most important reasons was labor being needed by the family. Endless work and the fact that many of them were not able to go to school seemed to be among the main reasons for the growing feeling of dissatisfaction with lay life.

"But as a Girl, I Don't Like the Idea of Getting Married and Leading a Lay Life"

A lay life is not only closely related to hard work, but also, and perhaps especially, to family life, as the quotations above suggested. Anna Grimshaw (1994) noted how the Ladakhi nuns she studied often referred to the hardships of laywomen when contrasting lay responsibilities with their own lives as religious practitioners. In particular, they talked about the burdens associated with marriage and motherhood, which are the two primary roles of village women (Grimshaw 1994, 102).

Marriage and motherhood were also among the most common reasons for donning the robes mentioned by my informants. Many of them told me that they had found the idea of marriage repugnant. 23-year-old Ani Lhamo from Amdo recollected: "My parents used to tell me that they will find a boy for me and let me take care of the family. But as a girl, I didn't like the idea of getting married and leading a lay life."

Ani Lhatso, a 37-year-old nun from Kham, also told me that she did not find any meaning in married life. She said:

> At that time I was a young girl, right? I saw other women getting married and leading their own life as they reached the age of 23 or 24. I saw them building their own houses and establishing their own homes. I felt like it wouldn't be happy to follow this kind of style of life. So you know, in my mind, I used to think that being a nun would be better than leading a life like they were leading. I wanted to be a nun and I told my parents that I wanted to be a nun. They agreed and I became a nun.

This is what Ani Jamyang, a 44-year-old woman from Kham, told me about her path to nunhood:

> A lama came to our hometown and held a religious ceremony. During that time, all my relatives and neighbors suggested I should get married, but I couldn't find meaning in a marriage life. Since my father had already passed away, I wanted to be with my mother for the rest of her life. Also, I thought I could benefit from being a nun not only in this life but also in the next life. I had such a thought. I discussed my thoughts with my mother and she said she was happy with my decision. Then we became nuns. We went to the lama together and got a *genyen* ordination from him. Then we went to the mountain. Since my father had passed away, my mother decided to get a *genyen* ordination and become a religious woman.

The undesirability of marriage was also brought up by a 44-year-old Khamba nun, Ani Samdup:

> I thought I could not really endure all the worldly work. And I thought if I got married I would also have to have my own dowry, otherwise no one would just take me, right? My family is not rich and I knew that my family couldn't afford that.
>
> You know, every girl gets married. And then some of them lead a difficult life. And some, when they get married, can't live with their parents any longer, right? Even when I was ten, I thought of becoming a nun. And then I actually became a nun when I was around thirteen years old. Watching the kids who got married, I find I am happier even if they seem to be happy. And some of them got married with a bad husband. These husbands beat them and scold them. I wish that they would have become nuns like me.

Ani Samdup mentioned many of the disadvantages that marriage is thought to bring, in particular to a woman. She talked about needing a dowry and the fear that because her family was not rich, no one was likely to marry her. She also spoke about the fact that because of the prevailing patrilocal residence system, it is the bride who usually leaves her natal family and moves to live with the groom's family. Finally, she mentioned abusive husbands that could make the wife's life miserable. In fact, not all Tibetan men were considered to be ideal husbands. 21-year-old Ani Yongtsen from Kham said:

> In some families, there are husbands who drink and do all those bad things. So, these people lose everything that the family has. There are also good ones who help the family and take care of the family members.

68-year-old Ani Pema became a nun after she divorced her husband, who had suffered from a drinking problem. She recollected:

> As a kid, my parents gave me to my grandparents. So, I was looking after my grandparents. As I grew up, my grandparents decided to get me married and so I was married to a man. Later, due to some family problems, my husband and I had to move to another place and we left our kids with the grandparents. My husband got a good job after passing an entrance test for a post, but he started drinking a lot and ignoring me. That was one of the most hurtful and difficult periods of my life. So, finally we divorced. Eventually, I decided to come here to the monastery and make prayers and prostrations to the Buddha. I am a person who has faced many sufferings, but I don't want to tell about all those things. My husband was a drunkard and we had some serious problems between us.

A related source of suffering my interviewees mentioned was motherhood. Like many of my other informants, Ani Tashi considered marriage, and especially motherhood, as causing pain for Tibetan women. She stated:

> People say that for a monk to study for three years is the most difficult thing. The reason for this is that monks have to study hard for these three years. But no matter how hard they study, I think it is not even comparable with the difficulties of a woman in three years of worldly life. I think like that, even though I have not studied for three years. If you get married, you will be happy for three days. You will have a party for three days, then after that you will be in hell. You have to work all the time. You will get pregnant and you have to carry a child in you for nine months. How difficult is that! I think that being pregnant is the worst. I saw people who are pregnant. I have sisters and I have my parents, right? I think it is very hard to do nomadic work, such as to collect yak dung, while you are pregnant. I can cry for no reason when I see someone giving birth. As nomads,

we don't have time just to sit, right? So you have to work even when you are pregnant and sometimes it is so hard to reach the teat of the yak. You know their bellies are too big, isn't that so?

She continued:

> The happiest ones in this world are the nuns and monks. They don't have to raise children. And they don't need to fight with their spouses. If I am dead, I am alone, and if I am alive, I am also alone. If I can't chant on my own, then surely I can chant in a shrine room with all the other nuns. If I was stuck in a worldly life and I had a lot of wealth, I would become a servant of the wealth; I would have to worry about losing it. Or, I might be happy when I am alive but then, when I am dead, I would not have accumulated any merit. Then, if I had a lot of children, I couldn't even get good food for myself; I would always have to think of the children. Although I did not experience these things personally, I know because I saw. I have sisters and brothers and uncles and aunts, right? Even if I wanted to go to a festival, I would have to carry some children on my back and take others with me. If I had one mouthful of food, I would have to feed the children, and then there would be nothing left for me. So, I realized that to be a monk or a nun is the best choice. In my family, one child died. I think my parents must have suffered a lot. They had to worry about the food, the clothes. If you have children, you are not even able to sleep well at night. So everyone is the same if they fall into this samsaric life.[7]

Ani Tashi's account brought up many problems faced in motherhood and family life. In addition to hard work and marriage, which she thought offered only contemporary happiness, Ani Tashi talked about the disadvantages of expecting, delivering and raising children. There is no maternity leave for a pastoralist woman, which means that she has to work even if she is near her due date. Due to poor facilities, giving birth can be extremely painful, but also risky. Once the children are born, there is a constant worry about feeding them. According to Ani Tashi, children are also an important reason for women's limited possibilities to take part in religious teachings and festivals. She also mentioned that losing a baby caused extreme suffering for her parents. According to 31-year-old Ani Norzom from Amdo, too, the death of a child is among the most painful

---

7. Falling into *saṃsāra* refers to becoming a married laywoman. According to Sarah Jacoby, becoming a lay householder (*korwa zungwa, 'khor ba bzung ba*) literally means "taking hold of cyclic existence (*saṃsāra*)." It means wasting one's life enmeshed in menial tasks that accumulate further negative karma instead of dedicating oneself to religious pursuits that lead to liberation. The primary mark of "entering *saṃsāra*" or becoming a householder" is marriage because of the family responsibilities and economic imperatives that follow in fulfilling them (Jacoby 2015, 87).

things for a mother, and as a nun a woman is free from all family and motherly problems.

The motives mentioned by my interviewees echoed those mentioned by Sarah Jacoby (2015) in her paper on Khandro Rinpoche, a distinguished religious specialist from Golok (Ch. Guoluo). As a pastoralist woman, wife and mother of five children, Khandro Rinpoche continuously had to balance between her lay life duties and religious calling. In the interview, Khandro Rinpoche said:

> [Lay]women do not have the power to practise the dharma. They are controlled by others. They only work. Even if they want to do a dharma practice, they are powerless to go [see Jacoby 2015, 87].

She continued:

> It is difficult to have a family and practice dharma. Even if you think you want to go [on a retreat], your husband won't send you. If you have many children, you won't be able to go. If you go, [your husband] won't give you food and so forth and then you fight [see Jacoby 2015, 92–93].

It was also a very common idea among the laypeople I interviewed that women became nuns because they wished to avoid marriage and family life. For example, a 73-year-old laywoman from the Kham region of Qinghai assumed that marriage, and mainly an unhappy marriage, were among the most important reasons for becoming a nun. Some of them thus brought up abusing husbands but the patrilocal residence system and problems in one's love life were also given as important reasons for becoming a nun. It was also thought that women had no other choice than to become a nun after a divorce or after the death of a husband. My impression was that there were many more nunneries in Kham areas than in Amdo areas. I was eager to know whether that was true and whether there was any reason for that. Comparing the different regions, a 35-year-old male teacher from Amdo/Qinghai said: "I don't know [the reason for fewer nunneries in Amdo]. Maybe there should be more widows here" (IN2011/9). Even though the man was laughing when he said this, his statement strongly indicated that mainly widows were thought to become nuns.

"Only by Becoming a Nun Could I Genuinely Devote Myself to Religion"

While there seem to be powerful factors in Tibetan society that lead to the impulse for a woman to leave lay life, there are also attractive factors in monastic life. I asked my nun informants what they thought was the best thing about being a nun. Although the motives given above were also mentioned, purely religious reasons were now offered more often. Ani Kalsang, a 37-year-old nun from Kham, said:

> It is happier here. I had to suffer a lot in a worldly life there, right? You have to care about one thing or another. Here I don't have anything else to think about except the dharma. Then, I have accomplished what I thought. So, I feel happier here.

She continued:

> I can practice the dharma. When I see someone pass away, I can chant for him. If I was leading a worldly life, I wouldn't have this chance. But now, if I want to practice the dharma, of course I have the chance. I also have free time. If I was leading a worldly life, even if I wanted to I would not have time, isn't that correct? Even if you wanted to practice the dharma, you would still have to take care of your livelihood, and it is not practicing the dharma. So, when I saw this, I realized how happy it is to become a nun.

32-year-old Ani Palkyi from Kham also emphasized the possibility to devote oneself to religious practice:

> I think the happiest thing in my life is that I became a nun and I have this chance to practice the dharma. And now that I am away from the worldly life, I did not fall into that. There are women my age and they got married and they gave birth to children. Some got better and some got worse. So, compared to them, I think I am much better off and I feel happy about that. In terms of the meaning of the dharma, I can find more happiness in it. I don't know how I can tell you. Now I only understand a very slight portion of the happiness in the practice of the dharma. And it is very superficial. I can slowly go very deep into the search for happiness.
>
> I think as a nun, now that I understand a little about the dharma, I wonder why they get married. I feel like they are playing kids' games. There is suffering in the cycle of life, not only for myself but also for children. So life is wasted like that. [...] You don't need to take other examples; you can just look at my sister. When I asked her to become a nun, she didn't want to. She thought that getting married is a happy thing. Then, from a dharma book I learned how difficult it is to lead a family life and this worldly life. When I read those words, I wondered why they get married. You know, when you get married you have to get married to a person you don't know, right? And you can only have this one body, right? And since you came into this world you have not accumulated any merit and you have done a lot of bad deeds, right? So it is like you have just wasted your precious life. So, I think like that. In the nunnery, there are teachers, and when they taught I learned the dharma. Only then did I realize the importance of knowledge. The dharma is such precious knowledge, how sad it is that I did not know it earlier.

This is how Ani Lhatso, 37-year-old nun from Kham, reflected on her previous life:

> At home I didn't think much about religion. I used to just waste my time by talking to people, staring at people. Here it is different. After staying at home for some time, I feel like returning here quickly. If I stayed at home for too long, I would get bored and anxious about being there. [...] I feel very happy that I became a nun. When I see others of my age... Some of them are fine, but some of them are quite poor, since they don't have a permanent job, right? So, I thought it would be very hard if I was like them. I would have to suffer a lot. [...] The suffering of worldly life means all sorts of suffering, the suffering concerning food, living, drinking, and so on. Doesn't it include all sorts of suffering that we suffer in this worldly life? Think about this worldly life – everything is suffering. [...] At home, even if you wanted to practice religion you would not have time, right? So, when thinking about it from all the perspectives, I think it is better to be a nun.

For these women, in addition to freedom from worldly suffering, life as a nun offered a chance to devote themselves to religious life. The excerpts show that there are various reasons for becoming a nun in the present-day Tibetan regions. For some, it was their karma that made them nuns. Some were inspired by the example of other monastics, either nuns or monks. Furthermore, an important motivation was suffering in lay life. Suffering was caused particularly by death and sickness, but family life and work were also seen as causes of unhappiness. While I have categorized the different motives brought up by the nuns individually, it should be emphasized that these were often intertwined. Ani Palkyi, for example, said:

> The parents had told us that we should practice the dharma, right? And, there were monasteries and monks even at that time, but there weren't any nunneries. I thought nuns are as happy as monks. I used to think like that, but I didn't know much about the deep meaning of being a nun. If I had gotten married, I would have to work a lot at home, isn't that right? So, at that time I thought that the worldly life is a bit meaningless. Then, I told you that my eldest brother passed away, you remember? Then, there was a teacher in the community who taught Tibetan and we were sent there. At that time, I was thinking of becoming a nun. The other reason is that if you are a laywoman, then of course a laywoman and a man get married, right? Then, of course I would have to look after making a living, like my parents do, and I couldn't just leave it and then go wherever I want, isn't that correct? So, at that time I had the idea of being a nun.

Various reasons inspired Ani Palkyi to think about nunhood: her parents' piety, the belief that monastic life was happy, and the restrictions she thought laywomen faced, as well as the death of her older brother. For Ani Yonten, too, the most important reason to be a nun was to help others. She stated:

> The best part of being a nun is, of course, the freedom we have because we are not bound by family life. The intention to become a nun and the process of living the nun's life are for others. We always have this intention of living for others. Whether we can contribute to the welfare of others or not [is not the point]. Merely the very presence of such a comprehensive intention is worth becoming a nun. [...] The only expectation for a nun is to study religious texts and help those who are in need. The religion is something to be practiced and observed; only by doing that can you benefit others. [...] I don't have any special thing to say. As a nun, my wish is to devote myself to religion and others as much as I can.

According to Ani Dawa from Amdo, the altruistic attitude is easier for nuns because they are not bound to family:

> The most important thing in life for a laywoman is her family. As nuns, we always think about the well-being of others. Having said that, it doesn't mean that there are no laywomen who also think that way. There are some among the laywomen who think in a very comprehensive way.

In fact, Ani Gyurmey, who suffered from various health problems, claimed that merely practicing selfishly for her own benefit would not help her but could lead to her taking birth in a lower realm.[8] She said:

> The dharma is not only for one person. It is for all beings, and we should think of helping all and praying for all. If I only thought of myself and prayed for myself, I would surely go to hell instead of the peace-realm. So, I always pray for all beings. I am doing this also because I hope that my sickness would get better.

Previous literature on Tibetan nuns has argued that while men are generally regarded as having purely religious motives for becoming a monk, the motives of women are often called into question. For example, it is often assumed by Tibetans that only unsuccessful women become nuns, such as those who are too ugly to find a husband or those who are physically or mentally handicapped (e.g., Havnevik 1989). According to Gutschow, for women, the decision to renounce lay life in the Zangskar area was seen as "selfish," "unnatural," or "unreasonable" (Gutschow 2004, 126–127). I was interested in knowing if the nuns' ideas and experiences were equivalent to those of laypeople. Interestingly, like the nuns,

---

8. Sentient beings are believed to take birth in different realms of existence. In Tibetan Buddhism, the lower realms are the animal realm, the *preta* or hungry ghost realm, and the hell realms.

the laypeople I interviewed often distinguished between two different sets of motives for becoming a monastic: those considered more religious and those thought to be more mundane. This is what a 20-year-old layman from Amdo said when he was asked about women's motives for becoming nuns:

> I think there are two kinds of reasons that are pervasive among women who become nuns. One type is those who out of sincere devotion and realization of the greatness of spiritual life become nuns. Then, the other type is those who become nuns due to personal problems. Out of long-established tradition, girls are expected to get married outside the family and their appearance counts for the kind of life they are likely to have. So, those who are not attractive prefer to become nuns. Whatever I shared shouldn't be taken as a truth, it is purely my personal observation. For girls, appearance matters when it comes to finding a good and suitable husband.
>
> (IN2011/1)

It seems reasonable to argue that there were both more religious and more mundane – even if closely intertwined – reasons behind the choices of the nuns I interviewed. The hardships faced in lay life seemed to motivate some of them to look for a solution to suffering in monastic life. It also seems that the motives changed somewhat over the time spent in the nunnery. It thus appeared that more "mundane" reasons were stressed when the girl first got the idea of becoming a nun, while more religious motives were mentioned after she had led a monastic life for some time.

–5–

Donning the Robes

"My Parents Initially Didn't Support My Decision"

Even though nunhood has always been one of the accepted careers for Tibetan women, the interviews among monastic and lay Tibetans suggest that, in practice, women are often not encouraged to join monastic life. Many of the laypeople I interviewed also highlight this. Thus, most parents do not expect their daughters to become nuns and some are very much against the idea. Many of the nuns I interviewed stated that their family did not at first support their idea of becoming a nun.

In the previous chapter, the interviews showed that many of the nuns thought of becoming a nun when they were very young. Most, however, became nuns only much later. There seemed to be various reasons for postponing nunhood. The most common reason mentioned by the nuns was the reluctance of the parents to lose a working pair of hands. Ani Dechen's parents were not happy about her idea of becoming a nun because they needed her help with work. Ani Dechen said:

> There were no other children in our family who could lift the increasing burden which was lying on the aged shoulders of our parents. Therefore, my parents initially didn't support my decision and showed reluctance toward me going to a nunnery.

Ani Palkyi also wished to become a nun, but had to postpone it. Among the reasons was the death of her brother, who had taken care of the family matters. She recollected:

> But then my brother passed away. I thought that even when my brother was at home I wasn't able go to a nunnery, because I thought I had to help my parents take care of the family. But now that my brother had passed away there was no one to take care of the family. You know, at that time my younger brother was very small. So, I thought I could not leave home. And I stayed at home.

> Of course, my parents said that we could go anywhere we wanted and there was no need to worry about them. But I can work and I can do any work. My elder sister should have taken the responsibility for the family, but she did not. She is very kind and gentle and people really like her very much. I, on the other hand, am very bad-tempered and no one else would take it, except my parents. So, I felt very sorry for my parents because they had been very sad due to the death of my brother. That was the saddest time I have ever experienced in my life. If my younger brother hadn't taken care of the family, I would surely still be with my parents. Even my parents said that I should go, I just couldn't. I felt bad for them.

Ani Dechen and Ani Palkyi clearly felt that they were morally responsible for taking care of their parents and home. The feeling of responsibility toward her childhood family also made Ani Samdup postpone her wish to become a nun. She recalled:

> My father was a beggar before and there were lots of children at home. Moreover, one of my mother's sisters passed away and she left two orphans. We adopted them. So, I thought it would be better for the parents and the family if I stayed at home and took care of the children and home. Then later, after my siblings moved to town, I also got some tailor work in Gyegu and earned some money from that. I gave the money to my parents and let them use the money to buy clothes for the children. You know, I am the oldest and try to help the family. [...] My other siblings used to tell me not to go the nunnery and to stay with the parents. And they said I could open a tailor shop and earn a lot of money. But I like staying in the nunnery. There was a little boy with my parents, so I thought it would be okay [to leave].

Some of the nuns interviewed were sent to help their aging grandparents. Ani Phuntsok was one of them. She said:

> At that time, I had a grandmother. So, I thought of serving her first and then becoming a nun. Two or three years later, my grandmother passed away and I really wished to be a nun. [...] At that time, I did not tell anyone that I wanted to be a nun. My grandmother was very old, you see? So, I was just practicing the dharma but I didn't tell anyone. I thought that if I told that I wanted to be a nun and left home, she might be sad.

In addition to the obligations these nuns felt toward their families, there were some parents who rejected the idea of nunhood because they hoped that their daughter would continue with her studies. In particular, some fathers seemed to wish that their daughter would get a good education and a good job that would guarantee a happy future. Ani Choedron recollected:

> After I finished the third grade in middle school, I wanted to become a nun and I asked my parents. My mother kind of agreed, but my father did not agree. Then, after I graduated from high school, I asked if I could be a nun and they agreed. [...] They said no at first and that I should go to Xining, because I got a chance to go to Xining [to study]. So, they said I should go and continue with my studies. But I said that I didn't want to go. There were also my classmates who weren't able to get a job. So I said I wanted to be a nun and I didn't go. Maybe he [the father] thought I would get a good job. I am not sure.

Ani Dawa, a 41-year-old nun from Amdo, also thought that the reason why her father did not support her idea of nunhood was that he hoped she would finish school and get a job. She said:

> My mother was not that disturbed by my decision, in fact, she agreed with it. But, my father didn't support my idea, which is the reason why they forced me to continue schooling until I was 17 years old. Finally, due to my insistence and persuasion, they sent me to a nunnery. [...] I am not exactly sure, but he [the father] must have been thinking that by completing education and getting a job I would be assured of a happy and comfortable life.

The third reason mentioned by my informants was the parents' worry about the reputation of their daughters. Some parents were concerned that a daughter might decide to return to lay life later. As shown above, many of the nuns I interviewed said that they wanted to become nuns when they were still children. It is possible that the parents thought that they were still too young to make such a far-reaching decision. Ani Wangchuk's parents did not let her become a nun because they thought that she might change her mind later. She recollected:

> Once the conviction to become a nun had solidified, I informed my parents. For a while they didn't comply with my wish because of the suspicion that I may not stay a nun forever. But I didn't listen to them and finally they let me [become a nun].

Tibetans believe that parents can gain merit by sending a son or a daughter to monastic life. It is widely thought, however, that there are negative karmic consequences for those who give up their monastic vows. Parents may prevent their daughters from going into monastic life out of fear that the decision is being made in haste. As noted by Gutschow, as Buddhists "they know the terrible burden ex-nuns or monks bear in their future rebirths." According to a common belief, a nun or monk who breaks the four root vows – to abstain from killing, lying, stealing, or having sex – cannot be reborn as a human or in any of the upper realms (Gutschow 2004, 134). On the other hand, it is also thought that life as a monastic accumulates a person's merit, even if he or she decides to disrobe. Furthermore, it is likely that the parents are also worried about their daughter facing problems in this life if she decides to renounce her monastic vows. She might have difficulties with her livelihood and finding a spouse. Attitudes toward ex-monastics seem to vary in Tibetan society. It appears, however, that a woman's reputation is more damaged than that of a man.

Related to the concern of breaking the vows is the fear that someone would make the daughter to act against her vows, voluntarily or involuntarily.[1] This is why some parents were also reluctant to keep their nun daughters at home. Ani Samdup told about her parents' worries in this way:

> In my hometown, there were men chasing girls. I thought that if something like that happened to me, I would never change the idea of being a nun. But of course since everyone knew that I was a nun, nothing like that happened to me.

Like many of the other nuns I interviewed, Ani Tashi lived at home as a nun for years before she was able to enter a nunnery. Some people were worried about her reputation, but she was determined. She explained:

> Some people said that it was not good that I was staying at home, because someone might make me go back to being a laywoman. I said it won't happen. There were people saying that "the abstinence of a monk is in his hand but the abstinence of a nun is in other people's hands." Therefore, they told me not to stay at home. But I thought I would not return to lay life even if I had to die. I am a stubborn person.

The quotations above indicate that nuns need to look after their chastity and reputation much more carefully than monks. It is considered a risk for a nun to remain at home because it is thought that there is a chance she might break her monastic vows or, even worse, that someone forces her to break her vows by sexually assaulting her.

Finally, there seemed to be a practical reason for not sending a daughter into monastic life: the lack of nunneries. In fact, it is possible that some parents would have let their daughters don the robes had there been more nunneries for them to join. However, because of the small number of nunneries, especially in the Amdo region, some might think that it is better to deny a girl nunhood altogether.

Ani Tenzin's parents seemed to accept her nunhood only after she went to live in a nunnery. She said:

---

1. There are many cases of Tibetan nuns in exile being raped in India, but I am not aware of the situation in the Tibetan regions of China.

> During that time, my parents were not happy about my decision, knowing the apparent lack of nunneries in our village and places nearby. They were also worried about my life as a nun. Knowing that I have joined a nunnery, they are now very happy about my decision.

The scarcity of nunneries was also pointed out by the male scholar from Amdo:

> To be frank, for most of the boys monkhood is arranged by their parents when they are young, maybe around eight or nine years old, whereas most of the nuns run away from their families. The intention to become a nun is purely their own. Generally, due to the scarcity of nunneries, most of the families have to take the risk of sending their girls far away from them, which they don't prefer. So, girls have to run away from the family. But on the contrary, in places near Namdzong nunnery,[2] parents are willing to send their daughters to become a nun. Suppose, if a girl from Machu[3] wants to become a nun, she has to come to Labrang. Most of the time, looking after the livelihood of a nun is done by the respective family. In that case, for a family, having a nun far away is a great problem when it comes to attending to all her needs.
>
> (IN2011/10)

Many parents decided to let their daughters become nuns only after lengthy consideration. Confirmation for their decision was sometimes sought from high religious authorities. Ani Lhamo's family went to a lama for a prophecy in order to decide whether she should become a nun. Ani Lhamo stated:

> It is really difficult to speak about that, but when I first decided to become a nun my parents told me that becoming a nun is not as easy as I thought. They said that wearing the robe is not that difficult, but the things that you need to observe after that are difficult. So, we went to seek a prophecy from a lama who is our relative. He also asked me about my reason for becoming a nun, but I didn't have anything to say. I just liked the idea of becoming a nun and I felt it was good. He said it was going to be good. After three months, I became a nun.

In some cases, while the parents might not be so much against the idea of nunhood in general, they may think that their daughter is not suitable for monastic life. Ani Palkyi's parents wanted to send her elder sister to a nunnery, but she refused. Because Ani Palkyi was determined to become a nun, the family sought a prediction from a lama. Ani Palkyi recollected:

---

2. Namdzong Samten Phelgye Ling (*gnam rdzong bsam gran 'phel rgyas gling*) or Namdzong Jomo Gön (*gnam rdzong jomo'i dgon*) is the largest nunnery in central Amdo, in Achung Namdzong (Jainca, Qinghai).
3. The name *rma tshu* refers to Machu County in Gansu.

> My parents used to say that they would let us do whatever we want. If we want to be nuns, we can be nuns and if we want to be monks, we can be monks. They allowed us to follow our own way of life. [...] There were three girls at that time and I was the middle one. I was told that I used to say that I wanted to be a nun. [...] My elder sister is a kind and gentle woman. She also looks nice with a round face. My parents asked her to be a nun but she refused. Of course, it is her decision, right? Even at that time, I used to say that I wanted to be a nun. Then my mother had three pieces of amber. You know, in old times, it was a very expensive item, isn't that right? My mom said that she would give one of the three ambers to each of the daughters, but I refused. I didn't like them at all. Then, since that time I never let my hair grow. [...] My mother used to say that she believed that I would be a nun if I still was so determined when I was 20 years old. Otherwise she wouldn't. She said that if I really became a nun, I would be a good nun.
>
> When I was 18, she took me to a lama in our area. She said to the lama: "She is saying that she wants to be a nun. So, will she be able to be a nun? If she won't be able to be a nun [forever], you know, that is a bad thing, isn't that right? Then, it would be very bad if she is not able [to continue] to be a nun; it would be bad for her. So, can she really be a nun?" she asked the lama. Then the lama asked her how old I was. At that time, I was 18. The lama said: "She has been at home and serving her parents for 18 years and she is still a nun, so that means she can be a nun. If she didn't want to be a nun she could have become a layperson when she was 15 or 16. There are lots of cases like that. My sister was like that." Then my mother said: "She has been saying that she wants to be a nun for so long and now I believe her. So I will let her get ordained in front of you." Then the lama agreed and I became a nun.

Even though Ani Palkyi was not technically a nun when she went to meet the lama, she was unmarried, had no hair and was probably wearing a red Tibetan dress (chuba). For these reasons, the lama seemed to consider her a nun. I will come to the question of monastic vows and the definition of a "nun" in the next chapter. What is interesting here is the fact that both Ani Lhamo and Ani Palkyi needed a lama's support for their wish before their parents let them become nuns. In some cases, certain supernatural episodes convinced reluctant parents that their daughter had the karmic preconditions to be a nun. Above I quoted Ani Dikey, who recovered miraculously from a disease as soon as she had received the monastic ordination.

It thus seems that women are not expected to become nuns. According to a 41-year-old male university teacher from Amdo, the reason for fewer nunneries is that people think that becoming a monk is easy while becoming a nun is more difficult. This idea is shared by many of my lay informants. In light of the quotations above, it can be concluded that girls in the contemporary Tibetan areas are not encouraged to become nuns. It is difficult to estimate how many girls or women wishing to enter monastic life have to give up this dream. I met many laywomen who told me that they actually wished to become a nun, but for one reason or another were not able to do so. Despite the obstacles, my nun informants finally ended up becoming nuns. In general, there are two stages in the process: the act of leaving home in the process of renunciation and the act of receiving ordination.

"I Ran Away from School and Became a Nun by Myself"

Some of the nuns I interviewed became nuns with the support of their family and some just shaved their hair and never grew it back. Often a family member or a close relative accompanied the nun-to-be to a lama in order to receive an ordination. Despite this fact, surprisingly many interviewees had run away from home to become a nun. In the beginning of this book, Ani Sherab from Ü-Tsang told how she had run away to become a nun. This is how Ani Sangmo, a 23-year-old nun from Amdo, became a nun:

> The decision to become a nun was purely mine. First, my family didn't like the idea, so I ran away three times to become a nun. Finally, I managed to fulfill my wish. [...] I ran away to a monastery in Rebgong and went to the second highest lama there. I told a monk about my intention of becoming a nun and he helped me to get this information to the lama. After the lama accepted my request, I went to the marketplace to cut my hair. Then I went back to the lama and he gave me ordination. [...] My family had been rejecting my idea of becoming a nun for quite a long time. They even beat me. But after becoming a nun, when I visited my family, they didn't say anything.

Ani Yonten's account reveals that she ran away to become a nun just before the final exam at school. In this way, she made sure that she was not able to continue her studies, as her parents hoped:

> I ran away from school and became a nun by myself. It was just before an exam when I ran away. I was not that bad at the studies, but my intention of running away before the exam was that if I passed the tests, then my parents would think that I am capable of studying and they wouldn't comply with my decision. So, I intentionally skipped the exam. [...] Then I went to Labrang. We have a nunnery there called Namdzong, but they didn't let individual girls become nuns without the accompaniment of the

From Laity to Monastic Life

> family members. So, I went to Labrang. [...] After coming to Labrang, I was staying for a while with a monk who is my close relative. Then I thought that if I didn't become a nun as soon as possible and if my family found me, they would take me back home. So, with the help of the monk relative I joined the nunnery.

Ani Palden, a 22-year-old nun from the Kham region of the TAR, took a long journey in order to join a newly opened nunnery in Yushu. She recalled:

> After everyone went to sleep, I got up at midnight and came here. The next morning, when my family found that I was not there, I assume that they already guessed that I had gone to become a nun. After I arrived here I also phoned home. I phoned home and told them that I had arrived here.

Ani Dolma and her friend also ran away in order to become nuns. However, their attempt succeeded only later. She described their journey this way:

> I just ran away from school with one of my classmates to Shugsep nunnery.[4] We had heard many times about Shugsep nunnery, but neither of us knew its location. Anyhow, we managed to find the nunnery by asking people on the way. [...] It's just three or four days from our village. We had only 4 RMB for our trip. This was to cover the cost of transportation and food during the trip. At last, after crossing tall hills for more than three days, we reached our destination. [...] We were told that in order to join the nunnery we needed to have letters of approval from our village head and other high-ranking Chinese officials. But we were lucky enough to be allowed to stay in the nunnery for two days with the help of nuns from our village. They were studying in this nunnery. Later, our family members came to the nunnery to pick us up. We told them that we were willing to lead a life as nuns, but the senior nuns assured us that we were always welcome here after getting those letters from our village head. After that, we went back home. After six months, our dream came true. We became nuns.

Ani Dechen ran away to become a nun, too. As happened with the other nuns, her family who was opposing nunhood in the beginning was happy about her decision in the end:

> When I noticed that there was such a tiny chance for me to fulfill this enduring wish under my parents' roof, I ran away from home. I was accompanied by my sister, who is a nun and who by being a nun realized my dream in the end. [...] I enthusiastically learned from my sister how to write and read. Time flew and my hard work begun to bear fruit. Later, my

---

4. Shugsep (*shug gseb*) nunnery is located about thirty miles from Lhasa. It is also established in exile in India.

parents came to know that I was studying brilliantly at the nunnery and were amazed by my decision. And they were very happy.

Running away to become a nun can be seen as a traditional act in Tibetan culture. There is rich folklore in Tibet of stories and legends about highly accomplished nuns and religious female figures who ran away in order to avoid lay life and the conventional expectations faced by women (see Allione 1984; Gross 1993). Even though these stories were not mentioned by my informants, they seem to continue this historical tradition. What is noteworthy is the determination to become nuns among those I studied. Many of them went through considerable trouble in order to make their dream of nunhood come true.

"I Gave My Hair to Him and Then He Dressed Me in a Nun's Robe"

Renunciation of the householder's life is the first step on the path to nunhood. The second is taking monastic vows. What technically makes a person a Buddhist monk or nun is thus monastic ordination.[5] After the decision to become a nun is made, the next step is to go to a lama or rinpoche[6] for ordination. At least in theory, three levels or stages of ordination exist for Buddhist nuns: novice (Skt. śrāmaṇerī, Tib. getsülma, dge thsul ma), probationary (Skt. śikṣamāṇā, Tib. gelobma, dge slob ma)[7] and full ordination (Skt. bhikṣuṇī, Tib. gelongma, dge slong ma).

In practice, in the Tibetan tradition, ordination to become a nun starts with a haircut. The person who gets the haircut is usually called rabchung (Tib. rab 'byung; Skt. anagārika, "one who has gone forth fully"). The rabchung is often considered as equivalent to lay vows or the genyen (dge bsnyen) ordination when it is taken as the first stage of a monastic career.[8] According to Gutschow, the haircut nevertheless signals a

---

5. Since laity are not allowed to participate in ordination rites in Tibetan Buddhism, there are apparently no firsthand accounts of these rites (Gutschow 2004, 180). I have heard that during the "vow" ceremony, one is among other things asked if the parents permit one to become ordained. The ordinand is supposed to answer either "yes" or "no."
6. The title rin po che, which literally means "precious one," is an honorific term used in Tibetan to refer to high-ranking lamas.
7. This is an intermediary level of training during which candidates for bhikṣuṇī ordination train for two years by holding precepts similar to those of śrāmaṇerikā while meanwhile practicing the bhikṣuṇī precepts.
8. The more conventional practice is to take genyen vows first, followed by the rabchung and finally getsül ordination.

lifelong intention to reject the call of sexual desire. After the haircut, the novitiate remains in a liminal realm between household and monastic life and may stay at home with her parents before a more formal ordination (Gutschow 2004, 177–178; Gutschow 2001). At least in theory, if not always in practice, the next and final step for Tibetan women is that of novice ordination. Thus ideally, the nuns adopt the *getsül* precepts of the *Bhikṣuṇī Prātimokṣa Sūtra* (Tib. *dge slong ma'i so sor that pa'i mdo*) (Tsomo 1996, 7, 75). The vows taken during the haircutting become permanent by means of this ordination. Novice nuns observe ten precepts, which are divided into 36 precepts.

Ordained women practitioners in the Tibetan tradition can thus only undertake the equivalent of the first two of the three monastic grades, the *genyen* or *rabchung* and *getsül* (Samuel 1993, 286–287). The *vinaya* texts require a complete assembly of nuns (*bhikṣuṇī saṅgha*) to be present in order to administer the full ordination. In the Mūlasarvāstivādin tradition followed by Tibetan Buddhists, this consists of twelve nuns: a precept master, an instructress, and ten more nuns, all of whom must be *bhikṣuṇīs*. The ordination must be conducted by the *bhikṣuṇī saṅgha* first, then confirmed the same day by a *bhikṣu saṅgha* comprised of at least ten fully ordained monks (Tsomo 1987, 120–121).

For me, one of the most confusing questions during my research was the ordination status of my nun informants. For most of them, ordination seemed to mean merely a haircut conducted by a lama or in some cases by a distinguished monk. Ani Karma, a 60-year-old nun from Kham, recollected with her sister how she ended up becoming a nun:

Ani Karma:	At about six, seven years old, I had already become a nun. I became a nun when I was young.
Ani Karma's sister:	It was a remarkable lama who suggested to her that she should become a nun, so she cut her hair and did so.
Ani Karma:	My parents also suggested that I should become a nun. After I cut my hair, the lama gave me a lump of sugar as a tribute. I only remember that. I didn't know anything about what it meant to become a nun. We were just listening to the lama. I didn't quite understand how to practice religious things, but I knew how to chant the Triple Gem [the Buddha, Dharma and Saṅgha] and understood to respect lamas. At that time, I was six years old. After the [Cultural] Revolution it was restricted and Buddhist religion was forbidden.

Ani Karma was very young when she became a nun and, as she said, she did not understand what the ordination actually meant. Most of the nuns I studied, however, were older when they received their ordination. Ani Changchub had taken monastic vows in her forties. When asked about her ordination, she explained it in this way: "I bought a robe myself and went to meet a lama at Rebgong. He cut my hair and made me take the promise. I did all this and then I became a nun."

When I asked her if she could tell me more about the precepts she took, she said that she suffered from heart disease and because of the strong medication was not able to remember much about them. For Ani Yongtsen as well, ordination meant giving a portion of her hair to a lama, or in this case to a monk:

> I told my family that I wanted to be a nun. In our area, we had a relative called Uncle Juga. He was an old monk, but everyone respected him as a lama. So I got ordained there. I gave my hair to him and then he dressed me in a nun's robe.

The literature on Tibetan female monastics often mentions older women who shave their heads, wear simple dress and live as nuns without receiving the formal ordination of śrāmaṇerī. In fact, there are a large number of these kinds of women in the contemporary Tibetan regions. Women who become ordained later in life, after having raised families, are referred to as "senior practitioners" or *genchö* (Tib. *rgan chos*) (Tsomo 1987, 121). Ani Kalsang told that she knew these kinds of women who cut their hair by themselves when she was young. Ani Phuntsok also told about these women in this way:

> The nuns, they were not like us, wearing the cassock, since there weren't many nunneries, right? So, people said that they were nuns. My grandmother was also a nun. She cut her hair and wore a red dress.

It is not clear, however, how the status of Ani Phuntsok and many others differed from the status of these older women. In fact, many of my informants seemed to be nuns who were not technically ordained, but despite that fact were still considered nuns. One of them was Ani Ngawang, a 39-year-old nun from Kham, who never let her hair grow and who was considered a nun by other people because of that.

It may be recalled that above, the lama who called Ani Palkyi a nun when she went with her mother to ask for his opinion about the ordination probably based his impression on her bald head. It seems that Ani Palkyi also perceived herself as a nun long before she took any ordination. This is what she said when I asked her about when she became a nun:

> Since I was born I have shaved my hair and never let it grow. The reason is that at that time there were lots of children at home. My parents had to work in a communal group and they did not have time for us. There were not many good clothes for us. My father was a herdsman of the communal group and my mother had to work in the community. So, all the children were shaved. So, I was bald since then.

Ani Palkyi was bald not because she chose to be, but because her parents were poor and busy. In spite of that, she thought that her bald head meant that she had been a nun since she was born. For Ani Samdup also, her bald head signified monastic status:

> I only started to wear the cassock when I joined this nunnery here. Before that, I wore a red Tibetan robe and a yellow belt and my head was bald. I became a nun when I was young. I was bald so people knew I was a nun.

It seems that for these nuns, becoming a nun was not marked by a formal ordination procedure, but rather by cutting their hair and starting to wear a red dress. It is possible that they also took some lay or rabchung vows, but they did not mention that. Charlene Makley also found that for Tibetans in Labrang, the crucial defining feature of a monastic was the public renunciation of family life and (heterosexual) sex evidenced by the *rabchung* (Makley uses the spelling *rab tu byung ba*). This was marked by shaving the head, donning the monastic costume and leaving home (Makley 1999, 204–205). While my nun informants renounced sex, they did not necessarily, and at least not immediately, renounce family life, as will be discussed in the next chapter.

It is usually thought that of the Tibetan Buddhist schools, the Gelukpas accord particular importance to monastic life. Perhaps because of this, it was primarily the nun informants who belonged to the Geluk school who gave me a more detailed explanation about their ordination. This is how Ani Pema, a divorced woman who became a nun when she was 64 years old, told about her monastic status:

> I became a nun at Rebgong Monastery, but I got my getsülma ordination at Labrang from a geshe[9] monk. At that time, there were around 12 nuns from different regions to receive the ordination. The monk suggested to us that we wear the robe wherever we go and that if we don't do that, it is equivalent to breaking the vows that we take.

Existing literature on Tibetan nuns would probably refer to Ani Pema as a "senior practitioner" (Tib. *rgan chos*) because of her previous marriage

---

9. *Geshe* (*dge bshes*) is a Tibetan Buddhist academic degree for monks, and nowadays also for nuns, especially in the Geluk school.

and older age.[10] However, she was very clear about her ordination status and said that she had a novice, or *getsülma*, ordination – which even many of my younger informants appeared to lack. Ani Pasang, another Geluk nun from Amdo, provided me with the most comprehensive explanation of the ordination status of Tibetan nuns in her area:

> The first is *genyen*, the second is rabchung, the third *getsül* and the fourth is *gelong*. *Gelongma* is equivalent to gelong, but no one has attained gelongma so far. But His Holiness the Dalai Lama has been trying to find a way for the nuns to achieve this supreme spiritual degree. Nothing has been finalized so far. When it comes to us, we can attain the second ordination. Whatever ordinations there are after the second are meant for monks. Most of the nuns don't go beyond the second ordination, and we don't know any nuns who have gone beyond that. But we heard that at a place called Trikha (thri ka), there are some nuns practicing both *getsül* and *gelong*. It is at Trikha in Hainan. People say that the leader of that group of nuns is a *khandroma*[11] from Yushu. Those nuns under her have the *getsül* and the gelong, but we really don't know how they have achieved that.

I heard about the *khandroma* Ani Pasang mentioned above from my other (lay) informants. In fact, I traveled to Hainan to meet this exceptional woman.[12] I was told that she lived in a monastery close to Qinghai Lake. When I arrived at the monastery, however, I was told that Ani Khandroma had passed away the previous year at the age of 70. A monk I talked with told that Ani Khandroma, whose full name was Lobsang Tsingtsab Dolma, was originally from Rebgong but had come to Hainan and taught monks, nuns and laypeople for years there. The monk told that Ani Khandroma had had many nun students around Qinghai, but he could not locate any of them in more detail. He also told me that there was a plan to look for Ani Khandroma's incarnation after five years.

Ani Rinchen, belonging to the Kagyu school of Tibetan Buddhism, told how she attended a *getsül* ordination. The discussion with Ani Rinchen continued with the question of *gelongma* ordination. The full ordination of *gelongma*, or *bhikṣuṇī*, is not available for Tibetan women, as discussed previously.

---

10. Gutschow has noted that in the scholarly literature, nuns are confused with elderly renunciants, because both are called by the same name, *jomo*, in the local idiom. A jomo can also refer to a woman who has not taken formal monastic vows, but lives a celibate life, shaves her head and wears red clothes (but not robes) (Gutschow 2004, 174–175).
11. *Mkha' 'gro ma* (Skt. *ḍākinī*) refers here to an accomplished female teacher.
12. There is also said to be another incarnation of Ani Khandroma living in Labrang called Khangri Dolma.

From Laity to Monastic Life

Ani Rinchen: No, there aren't *gelongmas* in Tibetan areas so far... Let me think... What did the old lama tell us about where that country is? [to another nun] [...] Might be in some foreign country.

M.H.: I heard that hundreds of years ago there was a *gelongma* ordination in Tibet.

Ani Rinchen: Yes, I also heard of it but now it isn't here. It's probably Malaysia. Anyway, it's a small country outside Tibet. I have a hope of getting a *gelongma* and the lama suggested that I visit a small country where I can receive it. I can't remember the exact name of the country.

M.H.: Taiwan?

Ani Rinchen: Is it Taiwan?

Another nun: Yes.

I discussed the *gelongma* ordination with many of the people I interviewed, both monastic and lay. How Tibetans understand the question of *gelongma* was interesting, as it seemed to contradict somewhat the technical definition of this ordination. A monk living at Kumbum Monastery stopped by to chat with us while I was interviewing Ani Pema:

Monk: Attaining gelongma nowadays is very difficult. Suppose there are 100 nuns. There is a possibility for only one nun to get the *gelongma* degree. But out of 100 monks, three have the possibility of getting the *gelong* degree.

M.H.: But for a nun who aspires to attain *gelongma*, the ordination has to be done by a *gelongma* nun, and if in Tibet there is no *gelongma* ordination, what can one who wants to become a *gelongma* do, since the lineage is broken?

Monk: It is difficult, but if one really studies and tries to find a way, there must be some possibilities. So, a nun must put her heart and soul into finding that way for attaining *gelongma*.

This monk thus understood the *gelongma* ordination to be more of a question of individual capacity or aspiration than a problem of broken lineage. Making the question of ordination even more difficult to grasp, I ran into a nun who considered herself a nun (ani) but in many ways with her long hair and earrings she reminded me of a tantric religious practitioner. She told me that she had the "highest" ordination available and that it included all the possible levels of ordination.

For most of the nuns I studied, becoming a nun seemed to culminate in the act of leaving home and/or cutting their hair. It is possible that I was not able to ask them the right or meaningful questions when it came to their monastic ordination and vows taken. However, it is also probable that many nuns did not give the technical monastic ordination as much emphasis as it is given in the scholarly literature on Buddhist nuns.

– 6 –

Finding a Place to Stay

Monastic Life

Ideally, monks and nuns live in a monastic community set apart from lay society. What is exactly meant by a "monastery" in the Tibetan setting, however, is not entirely agreed on among scholars of Tibetan Buddhism. Geoffrey Samuel (1993), for instance, argues that the Tibetan word for a monastery, *gompa* (*dgon pa*), refers to a heterogeneous category of different kinds of religious institutions and can mean hermitages of *yogīs* and *yoginīs* and small local communities of monks and nuns, as well as large town-like central monasteries, which function as scholastic centers for smaller and local *gompas* (Samuel 1993, 309–312, 322–323).

However, Dreyfus (2003) is of the opinion that the Tibetan word *tratsang* (*grwa tshang*) is the term more properly translated as "monastery," and that it is of two types: local monasteries, with perhaps only the four monks needed to form a *saṅgha*, and central monasteries, which function as training centers for monks from other monasteries and may accommodate thousands of monks. According to Dreyfus, hermitages should be distinguished from monasteries because they do not meet the important characteristics of Tibetan monasticism. In other words, they are not corporate entities, but are owned by a person or a limited group; they are devoted to a particular purpose beyond providing a residence; and rituals are rarely performed in them (Dreyfus 2003, 47, 346).

Nunneries were found all over historical Tibet: In Central Tibet, in the areas of Ü-Tsang, Hortso and Barkham (*'bar khams*), there were 160 nunneries belonging to the Geluk school, with a total of 6,831 nuns. In addition, there were 290 nunneries of the Nyingma school, comprising 7,141 nuns; 227 Kagyu nunneries with 3,697 nuns; and 40 Sakya nunneries with 1,159 nuns. In Kham, there were 52 Geluk nunneries with 4,468 nuns; 29 Nyingma nunneries with 2,467 nuns; 10 Kagyu nunneries with a total of 1,017 nuns; and a Sakya nunnery with 80 nuns. In Amdo, there were eight Geluk nunneries with 290 nuns and one Nyingma nunnery with 30 nuns

(Havnevik 1989, 37–38). It is, however, very unlikely that these statistics are correct. There were presumably more Nyingma nuns in Amdo, for instance. It is likely that there were also more Kagyu nuns and nunneries in the Kham regions.

In terms of administration, a nunnery was often a sub-branch of a monastery. Monks usually occupied the office of abbot in the nunnery. There were a few cases of abbesses (Tib. *a ni mkhan po*), but they were rare. Nuns were appointed to some positions within the nunnery, such as that of a disciplinarian or chanting master (Havnevik 1989, 40–41, 47; Willis 1987, 104). There were thus very few recognized formal positions for nuns. Most of the larger monasteries were and still are centered around one or more series of reincarnated lamas or tulkus (*sprul sku*) (Samuel 1993, 271, 279–280, 473). It seems that an institutional structure for recognizing and maintaining lines of female incarnations never developed.

The nuns in my research lived either in a nunnery (*ani gompa*), with a group of few other nuns, stayed at their birthplace, or moved from place to place. The nunneries they stayed at resembled Tibetan monasteries with monastic administration and a daily schedule. All of the nunneries I visited were officially founded by a male lama, but this does not mean that nuns were not active in establishing them. Each of the nuns had her own little house built with the help of her family. In addition to the nuns' houses, the monastic compounds included a main temple where the nuns gathered for common religious activities and for studying. Many of the nunneries I visited were still under construction.[1]

The groups of nuns – or what I call nuns' communities – were smaller entities. They seemed to have come into being when some individual nuns had gotten together and started to practice together. More nuns joined, while some left the community. One of the communities I visited consisted of one small house where four nuns lived together. The other was a cluster of small houses, or quarters, where each of the six nuns or so lived on their own. Those nuns who were not affiliated with any nunnery or nuns' community either had their own house or lived with their family. In practice, however, they did not stay in one place much but wandered often from place to place (for instance, to monasteries), in order to receive religious teachings and empowerments.

---

1. In many cases, there were, for example, no proper lavatory facilities.

"There Were No Nunneries so I Stayed at Home"

After donning the robes, my informants likewise needed to decide where to carry out their calling as a nun. The decision was not always easy, because there are far fewer nunneries than monasteries in the Tibetan regions. In fact, in almost every life story, the lack of nunneries is brought up. Because there were no nunneries to enter or since the existing ones were too far away, many of the nuns had stayed at home for years before entering a nunnery. One of them was Ani Samdup who became a nun when she was eleven or twelve years old but since there were no nunneries she stayed home.

Ani Tashi had to continue with the household chores despite her monastic ordination. She recollected:

> I became a nun when I was twenty years old. At that time, there were no nunneries so I stayed at home. After my father passed away, I served my mother, who was paralyzed. I didn't gain much merit through chanting, but I stayed at home and served my mother. I also took care of the children of my younger sisters. I felt compassion toward those children, so I looked after them.
>
> So, I became a nun and I stayed at home for many years. There was a nunnery in Jari.² My relatives told me to go there, but I could not because of my mother. After my mother passed away, I was still not able to go, because I had to help the younger siblings who got married. They had children and I felt sorry for them. We didn't have parents, so I helped them to take care of the children.

For many, the opportunities to perform religious activities at home were limited. Some were luckier and despite staying at home were able to engage in some religious practices. Ani Kalsang from Kham recollected:

> I stayed at home but participated in all the empowerments and prayer festivals that were held. Wherever there was a chance for a dharma practice, I attended it and other times I stayed at home. There wasn't a nunnery, right? So I stayed at home.

Ani Choedron, who was educated for years before becoming a nun, was not only able to attend religious events but was active in teaching other nuns as well. She and some other nuns also built a house for practicing. As she explained:

> I stayed at home for seven, eight years [after becoming a nun]. Only after this nunnery was built did I move here. [...] My uncle is a monk. He asked

---

2. I have been unable to locate this nunnery.

me to do *ngöndro*.³ After that, he sent me to all kinds of religious rituals and to do some circumambulations. And at other times, I just stayed at home and read and wrote. And he also let me teach others. There were several nuns at that time; they are in Serta now. I taught them to read. We did *ngöndro* together. We built a small house there. So, we stayed there and I taught them. There were a few nomadic nuns.

The scarcity of nunneries meant that some nuns were sent to nunneries which were very far from their native places. There are some remarkable Buddhist centers in the Tibetan regions. Especially two of them, Yachen Gar and Serta in Sichuan, house thousands of monks, nuns and lay practitioners. When I visited Yachen Gar in 2007, there were said to be 6,000 nuns and 4,000 monks residing there. Ani Yongtsen told me:

> At that time, we still didn't have this nunnery here. My parents asked me if I wanted to go to the Yachen nunnery or to the Jari nunnery. I had heard about the Jari nunnery before. So, I told them that I wanted to go the Jari nunnery and they sent me there.

The lack of nunneries was mainly felt in the Amdo regions of Qinghai where there are only a few nunneries. In these regions, nuns seemed to find their place more often in the nuns' communities. It is very difficult to estimate the prevalence of the nuns' communities or the number of nuns staying in these communities in the present-day Tibetan regions, but it is probable that at least in Amdo/Qinghai, many of the nuns stay in communities like this. Ani Changchub and Ani Tsomo stayed in a community of six nuns in Rebgong. This is how they described the founding of the community:

> Before I came here, there used to be a monk and a nun staying here. The nun did not wear a robe, but she was a nun. In those days, the facilities were not as good as today. Then, my brother's daughter came here. It was she who built the walls here. For that, she went around the whole of Rebgong to collect donations and eventually managed to build this.
>
> (Ani Changchub)

> When I first came here, there were two nuns. One of them passed away. Then the one who stayed and I started staying together. Both of us built these walls together. Then, later on, young nuns started coming and the houses were built with the help of their respective families.
>
> (Ani Tsomo)

---

3. As a set of preliminary practices in Tibetan Buddhism, *sngon 'gro* consists of taking of refuge in the Buddha, Dharma and Saṅgha in conjunction with the performance of 100,000 prostrations, 100,000 recitations of Vajrasattva's hundred-syllable mantra, 100,000 maṇḍala offerings and 100,000 guru yoga practices.

A wandering lifestyle was one of the options for the nuns in premodern Tibet. There are still many nuns who lead this kind of life. This type of lifestyle often involves intense meditation practices. Ani Jamyang was one of these nuns before she entered a nunnery. She recollected:

> After I became a nun and shaved my hair, I meditated around 20 years on a mountain. Our lama meditated near here, but once he came to my native place where there is a cave for meditating. Most families there visited him, and I became a nun on that day; I shaved my hair. From that day on, I have been a follower of my guiding lama, and I meditated in a cave for around 20, 21 years. Before, I used to follow my lama, who traveled around in order to meditate. Now I am in the lama's newly built nunnery.

Thus, when compared to monks, there have always been far fewer nuns and nunneries in Tibetan regions. In the Amdo region, for example, many of the people I interviewed or talked to did not know nuns personally, and some said they had hardly ever seen a nun. I asked my informants what they thought the reasons were for the fewer number of nunneries and nuns in Tibetan regions. Many said that they were unable to think of any reason for fewer female monastics. According to a 26-year-old male university student from Amdo/Qinghai, historically nunneries were less supported by the Tibetan government and this is also the reason for fewer nunneries today. Among the reasons for fewer nunneries thus seems to be the fact that nearly all the distinguished religious figures in the history were male who founded monasteries but not nunneries. As said by the 35-year-old male teacher from Amdo/Qinghai the support of the lamas is crucial for nunneries. He brought up the importance of male lamas when it comes to founding nunneries. Because of the Geluk dominance in the Amdo regions, the nunneries are fewer in number. In the Kham region, where there are also many Kagyu and Sakya monasteries, the male lamas are more willing to build nunneries. One of the informants, a 28-year-old male student from Amdo, thought that the reason for fewer nunneries was the fact that there were fewer women wanting to become nuns. The male student thus seemed to think that becoming a nun was up to the girl. If she was willing to become a nun she could find her way. A 22-year-old female student from Amdo/ Qinghai thought that because nuns are less respected by the laity, they are fewer in number. She also thought that the fewer number of nunneries and the difficulties faced with finding them prevented women from joining. Interestingly, the female student also thought that because women today have more choices, they do not need to become nuns. This statement points to the prevailing assumption that women become nuns because the society forces them to, not because of religious motives.

Because it seemed that the number of nuns and nunneries, at least in some Kham regions, has been increasing in recent years, I asked my informants to estimate if they felt this kind of change. While almost all of my informants from the Kham regions of Qinghai agreed that there were more nuns and nunneries now than before, my informants in the Amdo regions had not noticed that kind of change in their area. The answers to my question about the fewer number of nunneries thus reveal many different ideas about nuns in general. Women are not expected to become nuns and some think that they do not even want to, because life as a nun is generally thought to be full of hindrances. The primary reason for these obstacles seems to be based on gender.

"We Requested Him to Rebuild the Nunnery"

According to Charlene Makley, the number of nuns in Amdo/Sichuan has been increasing: since the reopening of the famous Labrang monastery in the early 1980s, exceptional numbers of young women have found their way to Labrang in order to join the three nunneries being rebuilt there. Makley states that about two hundred nuns were affiliated with the Labrang nun communities in 1995 and this was over twice the number of nuns reportedly living in Labrang just prior to the Communist takeover in 1949 (Makley 2005, 260, 265). When I visited Labrang in the autumn of 2007, two of the nunneries I visited already housed more than two hundred nuns.

As mentioned above, there thus seemed to be an increasing number of nuns, especially in the Kham regions of Qinghai. As I traveled in the Yushu region and interviewed people, I got the impression that many new nunneries had been opened there in recent years. When I requested data about the demography of Yushu, a regional authority I met was willing to give me other information about the region, but refused to say anything about the number of monasteries, nunneries and monastics there. I tried to get information about the number of nunneries in Qinghai from the authorities in Xining as well, but they also refused to give me or my Tibetan assistants any information that related to monastics.

Consequently, my hypothesis about the increasing number of nunneries in Yushu is based on my own observations and interviews with the nuns and lay Tibetans. A head monk of one of the nunneries in Yushu, for example, told me in 2009 that the nunnery was first founded in 1840 but was destroyed during the Cultural Revolution (1966–1976) and reopened in 2005. When I first visited the nunnery in 2007, there were 250 nuns residing there. In 2009, when I visited the nunnery for the second time, there were already more than 300 nuns there. I heard that after the earthquake in 2010, the nunnery was divided into two parts, but I do not have information about the present situation.[4] The same phenomenon might apply in other places, too. For example, a Geluk nunnery I visited in Garze, Sichuan in 2007 had opened six years before. By the time of my visit, it was already the residence of 120 nuns.

According to my informants, there were hardly any nunneries in many parts of Yushu, but this seemed to have changed in recent years. 60-year-old Ani Karma from Gyegu in Yushu, for example, told that when she was young there were not any nunneries in the region and after the Revolution it took almost twenty, thirty years to (re)build them. Together with her sister, she described how the situation in Yushu had changed:

M.H.: Are there many nuns in Yushu just staying at home, practicing religious things? Those who have never been to a nunnery?
Ani Karma: There were a few in the old days, but no longer today.
Sister: The younger nuns are usually in the nunnery.
M.H.: Do you think there are more nuns now than before?
Sister: Yes, yes.
Ani Karma: The number of nuns has been increasing recently. In the old days, there was only one monastery around this place.
Sister: At that time, there was only one monastery around the corner, but recently we got Jiegu Monastery,[5] Domkar Monastery,[6] Thrangu Monastery[7] and so on. Nowadays there are many nunneries as well.[8]
Ani Karma: Serta Monastery and Yachen Monastery have a great number of nuns.
M.H.: Do you know why the number is increasing?
Sister: Nowadays the Buddhist religion is flourishing and it's good to get rid of the suffering of life. You can enjoy benefits in this life and after you are dead.
M.H.: Is the number of monks increasing or decreasing?
Ani Karma: How can I say, generally the number of nuns is increasing. I think so.
Sister: When comparing, at Jiegu monastery there are more monks than nuns.

---

4. I refer here to a major earthquake that took place in Yushu in 2010. Many monastics also died during the earthquake. The monastic community was also reported to have been extremely important in the aftermath of the disaster.
5. Jyegu Döndrub Ling (*skye rgu'i don 'grub gling*) in Gyegu.
6. Domkar Lhündrub Dechen Sadön Chökhor Ling (*'dom dkar lhun drub bde chen sa don chos 'khor gling*) is in close proximity to Gyegu.
7. Thrangu Gompa (*khra 'gu dgon pa*) is south from Gyegu.
8. All these monasteries today have a nunnery.

From Laity to Monastic Life

> Ani Karma: There are more nuns than monks at Domkar, and at Thrangu Monastery a number of monks passed away during the earthquake. I don't know what happened at the other monasteries.

Why does there seem to be more nunneries than before? The building and rebuilding of nunneries is, of course, a part of the revitalization process taking place in the Tibetan regions under China. Interestingly, it is also associated with the changing status of women. A nun I interviewed in Yushu in 2007 told me that previously no one cared about nuns, but now that lamas understand that women have lots of problems they build nunneries.

In fact, it is not only lamas who are involved in building nunneries. Nuns have also had a central role in establishing them. They have taken part in collecting donations for building nunneries and have been active in the construction work. In many places, I saw nuns building a nunnery along with their families or Chinese construction workers. Ani Dolkar from Ü-Tsang recollected how she and her aunt requested their teacher to rebuild the nunnery and how they finally built it:

> Since our present nunnery in Tibet wasn't rebuilt after the complete destruction it suffered under the Chinese invasion, I stayed with my aunt, a teacher. I was helping her and learning how to read and write religious texts. She was living in a small retreat house in a nunnery near Lhasa. After she completed her nine-month retreat, we left the nunnery and went back to our rinpoche, who was living in a nomadic tent and requested him to rebuild the nunnery. Rinpoche instructed us to go to the cave near his tent to spend a few days there and we stayed in that cave for two days. My aunt didn't sleep at all during the whole two days and nights. She kept herself busy by doing her daily prayers and rituals while I collected firewood and prepared food for her.
>
> Meanwhile, I came across another nunnery on the other side of our cave and we left the cave to see the nunnery. Seeing this nunnery which was completely destroyed by the Red Army – although there were some aged occupants still alive – a cloud of sadness engulfed my aunt and she sat at a corner, gazing at the crumbled nunnery, while I went around the nunnery three times. I was thinking that given the way they had built their quarters, those resident nuns must have been very religious and devoted.
>
> The foundations of all the living quarters were well laid and I visualized that one day I might get living quarters like this. We went to see the rinpoche again and spent one night at the rinpoche's house. My aunt told me to recite all the religious texts I had memorized while I was with her and the rinpoche was quite impressed by my ability to memorize. Finally, after much persuasion and repeated requests, he undertook the rebuilding of the nunnery in 1987. Five elderly nuns and three younger nuns like me helped to build the nunnery. All of the villagers from the nearby villages

joined us daily in the building process. We, the nuns, kept memorizing texts while fetching the water and stones. Our day normally started at three in the morning. We used to go to the forest to cut trees for pillars. As soon as the nunnery was completed, I was sent to a chapel near the Potala palace[9] to do daily prayers and take care of the altars.

Ani Dolkar and her aunt were clearly very active in promoting the nuns' monastic life in the TAR. Ani Rinchen described a more recent episode, the founding of a nunnery in Nangchen in Kham. She said:

> A place such as a monastery is necessary for practice. Our lama didn't have his own monastery since he was doing meditation and moved from one mountain to another and was followed by some students. Afterwards, we, his followers and servants, suggested to him to build a nunnery for us. He realized our wish.

The early nuns who left Tibet did not usually have a nunnery to join. Ani Dolma told how she and other nuns were active in refounding the famous Shugsep nunnery in exile in India:

> Not so long after reaching Delhi, I went to the teaching of His Holiness the Dalai Lama in Varanasi. At that time, I met a lot of nuns who were from our nunnery in Tibet. We made a big group of twenty nuns and decided to build the Shugsep nunnery in India. We made our journey to Dharamsala right after the teaching. We met a generous Indian lady who accepted to offer us land for rebuilding our nunnery in India near Nālandā University. Later, we were able to go there after receiving financial and moral support from the Department of Religion at the Center of Tibetan Administration in Dharamsala. We were luckily accepted by His Holiness the Dalai Lama to have all of our traveling expenses sponsored by his office, and he assured us that we could always count on him whenever we needed help in the future. After receiving lots of support from associations and individuals, we arrived there. But unluckily we were not able to rebuild our nunnery there, due to numerous problems. So, we came back to Dharamsala again.

Despite the obstacles met by the project, the nunnery was later built in Dharamsala and is now a home for around a hundred nuns. While nunneries and monasteries have been reopened in recent years, the fact remains that, at least in theory, building a monastery or a nunnery requires a permit from the state authorities. Ani Dechen was highly critical of the state's support of the rebuilding of monasteries. She claimed:

> The primary objective of renovating the monasteries and nunneries in Tibet is only [to have] a showcase to the world. In reality, they don't even provide a proper education for us to learn about Buddhism and our

---

9. The *pho brang po ta la* was the main residence of the Dalai Lamas in Lhasa.

identity. Buddhism doesn't only mean worship. Even if there is a dedicated master in our nunnery, they directly put him in prison with a baseless compiled accusation of [him being] a "separatist" of the nation.

The accounts above reveal that many nuns have been highly active in creating a monastic life for themselves. This is either done by establishing new nunneries or rebuilding old ones or by founding nuns' communities. My observations correspond observations of Cho (2015) who claims that the nuns in Yachen Gar have been extremely important in establishing the monastic community there.

"I Couldn't Believe that I Was Finally Able to Join this Nunnery"

Many of the nuns told how they first heard the news about the opening of a nunnery and how this changed their life. Ani Kalsang told how people in the village started talking about the establishing of a nunnery and how her relatives made sure that the news was reliable. Ani Palkyi, who in 2007 had lived in a nunnery for about three years, recollected:

> Later this nunnery was established and I joined. I couldn't believe that I was finally able to join this nunnery. I used to say that I would get too old if I waited until this nunnery was completed.

According to Ani Lhatso, when the nunnery was being planned to open, a list of women who wanted to join was collected. As mentioned above, especially in some areas of Kham, the number of nunneries had increased and it was sometimes possible to choose between them. It turned out that there were different kinds of motives for choosing a certain nunnery. One of the most important factors in choosing a nunnery seemed to be its vicinity. Ani Ngawang from Kham, Qinghai told that the nunnery where she was staying was the only practical option:

> I thought of going to Yachen [Gar], but then it was too far and my parents did not let me go there. They thought this one is near and sent me here. At that time, there was not a nunnery here and there is a nunnery in Yachen, right? So, since I was a nun already I thought of going to a nunnery. I thought of escaping there, but my parents would not have allowed it. I wasn't able to go to any other nunnery except this one.

Ani Yongtsen first stayed in a nunnery that was far away, but moved to a closer one as soon as it opened. She said:

> I stayed in Jari for one year. After this nunnery was established, my family asked me to stay here. Besides, Jari Nunnery was quite far. It was rather difficult to send food there. You have to go there just to bring food, otherwise you wouldn't go there. Then at home, our family didn't have many people, and my mother was always sick and father had to go to work, so there was no one free to bring me food. Thus, it would have been a burden for the family if I had stayed there. I came here and became a nun here.

Nor was it uncommon for some of the nuns to have moved from one nunnery to another. Seven of the nuns I interviewed had stayed in another nunnery before the present one. Among other things, the location of the nunnery was also important for Ani Gyurmey's family. She said:

> The lama is good here. In addition, my family condition is not good, right? My parents and my whole family are sick. If I went to Yachen, then they would have to travel for three or four days to get there and it would be very hard for them, isn't that right? But, if I stay here and take a retreat, even if it is just one bowl of tsampa, they will surely bring it to me. So, I can take a retreat here and they can send me food here. I don't have to tell them to send me food; they bring it here. It is very close to the vehicle road.

In addition to practical reasons, there are also other reasons for choosing a nunnery. Supposedly, some families favor the nunneries of their own school of Tibetan Buddhism as in Ani Sangye's and Ani Sonam's case. Ani Sangye explained: "I heard that there will be a nunnery here and then I said that I want to go. I belong to the Sakya school and this is also a Sakya nunnery. So I came here."

Sometimes, as in Ani Tsering's case, a lama proposed a nunnery belonging to his own school of Tibetan Buddhism. While the right school is important, it did not always determine the choice of the nunnery. The head lama of the nunnery was often valued very highly when choosing a nunnery. Ani Phuntsok joined a Kagyu nunnery, even though her family belonged to Sakya school of Tibetan Buddhism. This is what she said:

> Later it was said that there is a nunnery in Gyegu. And our family holds great faith in the rinpoche who rebuilt the nunnery. So I joined the nunnery here. There are nunneries in Gyegu and Yachen and in other places. We belong to Sakya, but our family does not really care much about the sects. Basically, as a Sakyapa, I should go to the Sakya nunnery, right? But it is so far and our family doesn't care much, so I came here. [...] Some people said that I should go to the Sakya nunnery, but we have this great rinpoche here, so because of that I came here. Of course, besides rinpoche my family also had to take the distance into account. For me, the most important reason is rinpoche. Otherwise, I have relatives in the Sakya nunnery and it is also the same school.

Ani Samdup also chose the nunnery from another school of Tibetan Buddhism. Important reasons for her choice were her respect for the rinpoche and the fact that the Kagyu nunnery was established before the Sakya nunnery, where she was supposed to go.

> There were some people who heard that this nunnery will be built. There were people in our area who brought the news. So, I thought of coming here since then. As soon as this nunnery was built I came here. Then I asked if they [my family] could build a house [for me]; it would be good. If they couldn't, that would be fine, too. I told them that all I want is to go to a nunnery. I would be happier in the nunnery. Then my parents said that I could do whatever I want. So, I came here. My family belongs to the Sakya school. This one was established earlier. Otherwise, I should have gone to the Sakya nunnery. I have a monk brother in India and he was scolding me, saying that I should have gone to the Sakya nunnery since we belong to the Sakya school. I did not know that the Sakya nunnery was to be built and I came here, since this one was established much earlier. I came here because of the rinpoche.

Most Tibetans highly respect religious specialists, who are often consulted about problems and big decisions. One way is to ask for a divination, as Ani Tashi did. She explained:

> Before my mother passed away, she said that she would send me to India. But she was still sick then, and I was not able to go. At that time, there were not many nunneries. There were monasteries, but none of them had a nunnery. Now there are lots, aren't there? At that time, there was only Jari Nunnery. However, I was not able to go there. Then, when I heard about this nunnery, I came here. Before I came here, I made a divination and it was good. We do that, don't we? At that time, they said that Lab Monastery[10] and a Sershül Monastery[11] were also going to establish nunneries. So I made a divination, including Yachen and Serta. The divination said it is good here. So I came here.

Ani Rinchen also went to ask for a prophecy, which finally brought her to meet her lama. As she said:

> My friend and I went to visit the Gesar Epic singer Dawa Draba[12] in Gyegu and asked him to predict our futures. As a nun, I didn't know actually what to ask. However, I asked him how my future would be and what difficulties I would face in the coming years, and in what way I could help living

---

10. Lab Gompa, or Lab Gön Ganden Dongag Shedrub Phelgye Ling (*lab dgon dga 'ldan mdo sngags bshad sgrub 'phel rgyas gling*), is in Thrindu county.
11. Sershül (*ser shul*) is a county in the northwestern part of Sichuan.
12. The life of Dawa Draba is depicted in a documentary called *A Gesar Bard's Tale* produced in 2013 (China/Finland) by Donagh Coleman and Lharigtso.

creatures. He said that I would meet difficulties while practicing religion and suggested that I look for a lama, in order to be guided. Probably I asked him who had been my guiding lama in my previous life. He told me there would be some difficulties in my future and that my previous lama was Wesal Dorje, and that I was from a certain place in my previous life.

Since he said I would face some difficulties in terms of practicing religion, I went to look for Lama Wesal Dorje. That's the first time I saw the lama, because I am from Chumarleb and he was in Nangchen. After I had decided to look for Lama Wesal Dorje, I told my father that I was leaving for three years and asked him to not look for me, not to worry about me. He asked, what if he died during that time. I answered that even if I stayed with him, when destiny was to come, he would still die. If I left this time, I couldn't help him in this life, but in the next life [I would be able to help him]. I went through Gyegu to Nangchen. In Nangchen, there are some of my father's friends. In Gyegu, I bought all the necessary things and went to Nangchen by taxi.

After I arrived there, I heard the lama was at another monastery and I went directly to the monastery. I got there and unloaded all my things in the yard and paid money to the driver. I went to visit the lama and told him I was from Chumarleb and I came because I wanted to become his follower. At that time, the lama was already 84 or 85 years old. He was very old, so he said he didn't need any students. I didn't give up. I unpacked all my things and started prostrating in his yard. I saw a dog lying there and I thought that if this dog could find a place here, I could certainly find a place, too.

The lama's consort, named Tashi Tsomo, offered me tea and a place. The next day, I was asked to come to his place. The lama sometimes drinks alcohol. In the daytime or late in the evening, he becomes a little bit muddy. But in the morning he appears very peaceful and calm, treating us nicely. One morning, he called me and said I should stay there with him. One evening, after some cups of drink, the lama told Tashi Tsomo that I had been his follower in the previous life and we were together as a family. What the lama said matched what the foreseer had said. Afterwards, I again did the ordinations there. I read scriptures and practiced ngöndro again. Then the monastery invited a *khenpo* from Serta and I took the ordination and practiced with both the lama and the khenpo. Sometimes I came here; traveling back and forth I spent three or four years there. After four or five years, we figured out that the lama had his own treasures and suggested to him to build a nunnery as a stable place for practicing, and then the nunnery was built. It's been four years now.

Ani Rinchen's lama was a tertön (gter ston), or a discoverer of ancient texts or terma (gter ma, "hidden treasure"). For this reason, his disciples thought that it was necessary to build a place where to keep the texts and establish the tradition.

It is also common that girls or young women choose a nunnery in which they already have friends or relatives. Women from the same village tend to join the same nunnery. Ani Gyaltsen, a 44-year-old nun from Kham, for example, lived in a nunnery that was housing around sixty nuns in 2009 when I interviewed her. According to Ani Gyaltsen, there were thirteen nuns from her village at the nunnery. She had heard about the nunnery from the nuns who were residing there, and eventually she joined them.

While the opportunity to live in a nunnery was highly appreciated by the nuns I interviewed, there were certain individuals that did not want to live in a nunnery. Ani Dikey, who lived in a nuns' community in 2011, was one of them. She recollected:

> I went to Namdzong nunnery and stayed there for a while, but I didn't have a good time there. Then I came back home and started wearing a robe. After that, I went to Namdzong for ordination under a lama and joined a group of nuns who were staying at one place. I was tutored by a nun named Shongmo. [...] I stayed there for a few years. Later, Ani Shongmo came back to Khangra in Chentsa and we followed her. Then, after her demise, we settled here.

Some of the nuns, however, found it so important to live in a nunnery that they left Tibet in order to fulfill their dream. For Ani Tenzin from the Kham region of the TAR, an important reason to leave Tibet was to escape the restrictions that made it impossible for her to find a nunnery to stay in. She explained:

> I was ordained by one rinpoche in our village. [...] I left our village to find a nunnery in Lhasa and I stayed with my uncle for two years, hoping that one of the nunneries would accept my admission. [...] Since there weren't any nunneries in our village, I tried to find a nunnery in Lhasa. I was hoping that one of nunneries in Lhasa would accept my application, but to no avail. My main intention was to join a nunnery close to Sera monastery, but I was told that they had no space for new recruits. [...] Finally, I decided to go to India after a string of failed attempts to get admission. [...] The main reason why I didn't get a seat in Lhasa was the new rules imposed by Chinese authorities. Only a limited number were allowed to enroll. I have no idea how it worked in other parts of Tibet, but in Lhasa this was the case.

There are different procedures when one wishes to enter a nunnery. Some nuns, such as Ani Sonam who lived in Kham/Qinghai, told that she needed written permission to join a nunnery. She thought that it was relatively easy to get the permission, but she was not sure because her brother had taken care of the matter. The restrictions of the Chinese government also meant that Ani Palkyi from Kham/Qinghai was forced to postpone her enrollment in a nunnery. She recollected:

> My mother is the type of person who does things immediately if she wants to do something. When I was at home, I used do a lot of work. But then she said it was fine if I left home and became a nun. "If she really can be a nun and a good nun, I will let her stay here in your nunnery." "So, I will leave her here and she can be a nun here." "We don't have permission now." At that time there was no permissions. It was said that at that time there was permission only for seventy or eighty nuns. There was only permission for that amount of nuns from the government. Later, it was three hundred or four hundred. Then my mum said: "When should I send her here? If she stays at home there might be some accidents." Of course, the lama knows, right? Then he said, "It is okay, one day she will find a place where she likes to go." So, then my mum also believed that and I stayed at home until now.

At least in some exile nunneries, there are now entrance examinations for those willing to join. This is how Ani Sherab told about the process of enrolling in a nunnery in India:

> One day I came here [the nunnery where she was staying at the time of the interview] with my friend and asked who the manager was and if we could get admission. But the manager said it is not easy to get admission. "We have to see your discipline because we don't know what kind of people you are. You have to take an exam. If you pass the exam and have a good discipline then everything is checked. Therefore, in the daytime you can study here and at night you have to go to your own room. You can do like this." After I left school I rented a small hut and we stayed there and in the daytime we studied. For one year, my friend and I studied very hard. And later we passed the exam. And when the exam was passed, I didn't need to pay any money to stay here.

It seems that entrance examinations are also becoming more common in some Tibetan regions. I have heard about entrance examinations, for example, at some nunneries in Sichuan. Ani Palzon, a 33-year-old nun from the Amdo region in Sichuan, told that her nunnery also had an entrance examination:

> When we become nuns, we first need to go to a lama for a haircut. Then we go to the monastery to take an exam after listening to an abbot and his teaching. After passing the exam we can join the nunnery. After cutting my hair, I went to the temple and took an examination. You could not have enrolled if you hadn't passed the exam. You needed to wait for the next year.

Despite the revitalization of monastic life in the Tibetan regions, there are far fewer nunneries than monasteries in most Tibetan areas. The interviews showed, however, that nuns have been highly active in rebuilding the destroyed nunneries and founding new ones. Today it is sometimes even possible to choose between existing nunneries. Whereas the school of Tibetan Buddhism was still important, a lot of weight was put on the vicinity of the nunnery and the head lama or *rinpoche* of the nunnery. In those areas where there were still only a few nunneries during my research, nuns had been active in founding and maintaining smaller nuns' communities.

Many of the nuns I interviewed had taken considerable measures to become a nun. Some had escaped home or Tibet in order to be a nun and many had struggled to search for a place they could dedicate their lives to religious pursuits. Whereas many of my interviewees stressed the happiness they found in monastic life, there still were various difficulties that they encountered in monasticism.

– 7 –

Life as a Nun

"First She Has to Learn How to Read"

When a person joins a Tibetan monastic community, the ability to read is considered a necessary skill. Despite Chinese efforts to get rid of high illiteracy rates in the Tibetan areas, illiteracy is still very common, as I will discuss later. Consequently, when a girl or a woman enters a nunnery, she often has to first learn how to read. She is usually taken care of by an older nun, who is appointed as her teacher. After learning how to read, the novitiate still has to get accustomed to reading and chanting religious scriptures. Later, the interpretation of the texts is done mainly by the lamas or *khenpos*. As explained above, it was rare for nuns in traditional Tibet to receive a monastic education. According to Havnevik, the formal status of nuns gave limited opportunities for ritual or scholastic development. In addition, most nunneries did not have the economic or organizational facilities to provide higher education. It is thus likely that Tibetan nunneries never functioned as Buddhist universities as some monasteries did. Those few nuns who studied mainly belonged to the Geluk School of Tibetan Buddhism (Havnevik 1989, 51–52, 54–55).

Nevertheless, Georges Dreyfus mentions that before the seventeenth century, Tibetan nuns had their own educational institutions that produced sophisticated scholars. He claims that there are even (mostly oral) reports of public debates taking place between nuns and monks (Dreyfus 2003, 6). Nicola Schneider (2011) also questions the assumption that Tibetan nuns in the past were mostly engaged in ritual activities. According to Schneider, there were at least two lamas from a small Geluk lineage called Dragar (*brag dkar*) after their monastery Dragar Jangchubling in Kham, who supported nuns' education in their region from the eighteenth century onwards. The writings of the 3rd Dragar Lama show that his predecessor, the 1st Dragar Lama, founded three nunneries and had hundreds of female monastic followers. Furthermore, his biography indicates that women engaged in religious study and practice.

However, in the beginning of the twentieth century some groups of Tibetan society were against the idea of women becoming so involved in religious life. The lack of support seems to be the main reason why there were so few nuns and nunneries in this area of Kham at the time.

While some nuns were offered a scholastic education in traditional Tibet, it seems fairly safe to argue that most nuns did not receive an equivalent religious education to that of the monks. Until recently, therefore, it was difficult for nuns to gain access to the same education as monks. The situation seems to have changed considerably in recent years. Thus, while some of the nuns I interviewed were still learning how to read, many were also starting to receive a formal education in Buddhism. In exile, the most significant shifts in the status of nuns have, in fact, been in the field of religious education, particularly in the introduction of philosophical studies. In some of the exile nunneries I visited, the nuns were learning debating, which was previously only performed by monks. Philosophical studies seem to have also become more common in nunneries in the Tibetan regions. Ani Phuntsok told about the education in her nunnery in Kham this way:

> We have *khenpos* who are invited here every month. They give teachings, but they don't tell us what to do or what not to do in detail. [...] Now I have done *ngöndro* and I know a lot more. So, now I have some practices that I have to do in the morning, like meditations. So I try to wake up earlier now. [...] At first, I usually read autobiographies, mainly Milarepa. Then we had teachers teaching scriptures. I have studied that. Now we are taught The Words of My Perfect Teacher.[1] So we practice and read the teachings taught by teachers.

For some of the nuns, the opportunity to receive a monastic education and knowledge was among the most precious things in monastic life. Ani Yongtsen said:

> It is very happy to be a nun in the first place. Then, every time I hear the *khenpos* teaching, I feel enormously happy. If I was a laywoman, I might listen to the teaching of *khenpos*, but I wouldn't understand as much as I do now. I might know a little of what not to do, but I wouldn't know as much as I know as a nun, isn't that right? Since I became a nun, I have had this chance to listen to the teachings of these *khenpos*. Only through their teachings have I learned the suffering of all the existing beings. I realized that every being is suffering under this cycle of *saṃsāra*. I feel sorry and pity for these beings. Thus, I am so lucky to have these great *khenpos* and to be able to listen to their teachings, and I have this great lama that I can be faithful to.

---

1. kun bzang bla ma'i zhal lung.

For older nuns, especially uneducated ones, these new academic requirements caused problems. Now that they were finally able to stay in a nunnery, they did not necessarily have the skills to make the most of it. 44-year-old Ani Samdup said:

> At that time, there were no nunneries, right? This was the biggest disadvantage for me. Now the nunneries are established and even if we wanted to learn reading and writing, it is too late. We are getting old. Now that there is an English class[2] I would like to participate, but my brain does not work properly. I can't even catch up with chanting. I can chant only few prayers that my father taught me when I was at home.

Ani Palkyi also found it difficult to meet all the requirements of contemporary monastic life:

> The most regretful thing is that I didn't have time to study. If I don't have knowledge, I can't understand the meaning of dharma books. So because of that I can't – I don't know how to – practice the dharma well. Of course, teachers teach us how to practice it, but I can't study on my own. The teachers tell us that we have to meditate and practice, but I don't know how. I feel pity and regret that I don't have the knowledge. But I feel happy because of all other things and I think there would not be any time happier than now.

In fact, I heard that after the earthquake in the Yushu region, one of the nunneries founded a Buddhist college for the nuns. The nuns are divided into three groups: a "higher learning group" of nuns who can read and write well and who can chant scriptures fluently; a "literate group," which consists of nuns who are somewhat literate but do not know many scriptures; and an "illiterate group" of new nuns, who are not able to read or write. The higher learning group receives (unspecified) dharma classes and they chant scriptures together in a main temple. The second group and the third group are gathered in a room and taught separately by two teachers, a *khenpo* and a lay teacher. Nevertheless, nuns interviewed in India criticized the educational standards of Tibetan nunneries. Ani Dolma said:

> Life looked simple. Food and all other necessary things were provided by the nunnery. And we renovated everything that had been destroyed during the Cultural Revolution. We were taught Tibetan philosophy only orally, rather than by writing on the blackboard. [...] In the evening, we revised our lessons that we had been taught in the morning. And we memorized the texts and so forth. [...] We lacked a qualified abbot and good philosophy teachers. We were specialized only in the oral practice and its

---

2.   I gave the nuns at some nunneries basic English lessons.

activities. The main difference between life in India and in Tibet is that in India we don't have to think much about other things besides studies. In Tibet, chances to get an opportunity to study are slim because there are other obligations to be fulfilled.

This is how Ani Sherab who lived in India in 2008 compared the education in the nunneries in Tibet and in exile:

> We had all the facilities in our nunnery except a debate class and the teaching system of Tibetan philosophy. Our nunnery was mainly for ritual studies and meditation. And we had to memorize lots of texts. We had to bring food from our home, as the nunnery couldn't afford it. [...] Nuns in Tibet can practice what they have learned; they can do prostrations and some meditations. Doing these is also good, but they don't really know why they are doing these practices. They cannot study very deep. Such as the truth, what the truth of life really is. They can do prostrations and these kinds of things are free, but really deep study is not possible. That's why I think life is better in India.

As shown above, many nunneries in the Tibetan areas in China now also offer at least some kind of scholastic education. In addition to reading, the nuns in the nunneries had to learn to chant various prayers and perform tantric liturgies or sādhanas,[3] such as that to Tārā. They also studied some elementary Buddhist doctrines, as well as calligraphy under the guidance of (male) teachers, and practiced individual religious activities, such as the preliminary Vajrayāna practices (ngöndro), meditation, fasting, circumambulation, prostrations, retreats and so on. Sometimes the nuns were occupied by preparing ritual objects, such as torma[4] and other utensils to be used in temple ceremonies. At a nunnery in Yushu where I stayed in 2007 and 2009, the nuns were also practicing *cham* dances,[5] which were previously only practiced by monks.

"We Follow the Same Routine"

According to Havnevik, nuns had three main careers in traditional Tibet. The majority of nuns staying in nunneries primarily performed rituals and did not engage in advanced religious practices. A second group of nuns concentrated on meditation and yogic practices. The third

---

3. Sādhanas (Tib. *grub thabs*) are tantric rituals.
4. Used in tantric rituals or as offerings in Tibetan Buddhism, *gtor ma* are sculptures made mostly of flour and butter.
5. The '*cham* dance is a masked and costumed ritual performance practiced within some schools of Tibetan Buddhism and Buddhist festivals.

category consisted of a large number of generally uneducated nuns, who neither stayed in nunneries nor engaged in yoga and meditation. Many of them had only taken formal ordination at an old age. Their main religious practice consisted of saying prayers, reciting mantras, turning prayer-wheels, performing circumambulations, and going on pilgrimage (Havnevik 1989, 45).

There is usually a daily schedule in monastic communities. Previous studies of Tibetan nuns, particularly those conducted by Gutschow and Grimshaw in Ladakh, have shown that nuns are not freed from household chores, even in monastic life. According to Grimshaw, the nuns she studied were "a striking expression of the historical marginality of women within monastic Buddhism." The majority of them lived in the household of their parents or brothers, where they were treated mainly as domestic servants. Occasionally these women were attached to monasteries. In these cases, nuns cooked for the monks and took responsibility for the cleaning and upkeep of the temples (Grimshaw 1994, 12). This is how Grimshaw described life in a Ladakhi nunnery:

> While Sonam [one of the nuns] was absent, I remained indoors tending the fire and reading religious texts, which neither she nor the other nuns had time to do. [...] While we toiled, the monks sat around the fire, reading religious texts and planning what chores were to be undertaken at the nunnery in the future.
>
> (Grimshaw 1994, 7, 11)

A short period of time between dusk and night was the only opportunity these Ladakhi nuns had for religious practice. I did not have a chance to participate for long periods of time in the everyday life of many nunneries in the Tibetan regions of China. Nevertheless, based on my more extensive stays at exile nunneries, as well as shorter stays and participant observation in Tibetan regions in China, it can be suggested that the daily activities of the nuns were very similar in different Tibetan regions and in most of the exile nunneries in India. This notion was also confirmed by the nuns I interviewed.

In general, the daily activities of the nuns consisted of regular temple ceremonies, religious studying and the personal spiritual practices mentioned in the previous chapter. In addition, the nuns cooked food, fetched water, cleaned their small houses and socialized with other nuns. In those nunneries where construction was still ongoing, the nuns took part in the work, shoveling dirt or carrying stones. Occasionally the nuns could leave the nunnery and go shopping, for example, in a nearby village or town. On longer holidays, they could visit their families or go on a pilgrimage.

A day in a nunnery usually started early in the morning, for most at five or six o'clock. However, some nuns might have woken up as early as at three or four in the morning in order to do their personal daily meditation practices, which they had commitments to do every single day. After waking up, the nun thus did her first religious practices. These typically included morning prayers or meditation, setting up a shrine and doing a daily offering,[6] or making prostrations. After that, she freshened up and ate breakfast. Around eight o'clock or earlier, she went to the shrine room, or the temple (lha khang) to chant and pray together with other nuns. The temple ceremonies, which often continued until lunch time, were only interrupted by a tea break. In some nunneries, there were also classes in the morning (for example, from 10 until 12 o'clock). In their classes, nuns were taught, for example, certain Buddhist texts, meditation and calligraphy. The teachers were usually learned monks, but I have also seen, for example, an elderly layman teaching the nuns. In addition, many nunneries in the Tibetan regions in China are keen nowadays to teach their residents English. In exile monasteries and nunneries, it is very common to see (foreign) English teachers.

From midday until around two o'clock, the nun had free time. During the break, she did some household chores, cooked, slept, or mingled with her nun friends. Some also studied or did their homework. After the break continued classes, group chanting or both, until the evening meal. In the evening, the nuns again cooked, then studied and memorized the texts learned earlier that day. They also completed their personal practices or spent time with other nuns. In many nunneries, the nuns were not allowed to leave their houses at night, usually after 10 or 11 in the evening.

Ani Phuntsok from Kham described her typical day in a nunnery this way:

> In the morning, I get up very early and then I have to chant the daily prayer. I usually don't have breakfast; I don't have time for that. Then we have group chanting. In the afternoon, sometimes I go to my friends and sometimes visit my cousin or sister [at the nunnery]. Sometimes they come to my house. Then we eat together. We don't have much time in the afternoon; the program starts around two o'clock. We only have time to cook lunch and eat it. We don't have much time to study in the afternoon. In the evening, we cook dinner. Sometimes I chat with friends for a little while. Sometimes I chant the daily prayer that I was not able to finish in

---

6. Tibetans often start their day, for example, by burning incense and discarding the old water in small metal water bowls before a Buddha figure on their home altar and replacing it with fresh, pure water.

the morning. Then I stay with friends until it gets dark; after that, according to the rules of the nunnery, we have to stay in our own homes. So, I stay at home and study. Sometimes I get little sleepy and I try to practice writing. Like that.

Ani Lhatso's daily schedule was very similar to that of Ani Phuntsok:

First, I do *ngöndro*. After that, I say a little prayer that we have to chant every day. So, I chant that in the morning. Sometimes I get up at five, but usually it is six when I get up. I sit on the bed and think about the teachings by the lamas and *khenpos*. I try to meditate a little with those thoughts. Then I do some chanting. I have my breakfast around seven and then after that I have to go for group chanting. In the evening, after I come back, if I have to cook food, I cook. If I don't need to do that, I do a little chanting. Then, sometimes I review the dharma lessons, sometimes I have other nuns visiting me and we chat for a little while. It is like that in the evening. We should chant different scriptures in the late afternoon. If there are many requests by laypeople to chant scriptures, we should chant until 10 o'clock in the evening. In the winter, there isn't work to do, so we chant scriptures the whole day.

Ani Sherab, who left Tibet in order to enroll at a nunnery in India, told about the daily activities of her nunnery in this way:

In the morning at 5 o'clock, the bell is ringing and we have to wake up. After that we wash our face and then all the nuns go to the prayer hall and do prostrations for fifty minutes. And after that, all the nuns go to the prayer hall for about one hour for a *pūjā*.[7] And then we have breakfast. After finishing the breakfast, we have to clean our rooms and bathrooms in fifty minutes. Then, after that we have to gather to sing the national song. Every Tibetan school does this. Before starting a class we have to gather all children studying there on the big ground to sing a national song and after that you can go to your own class. [...] In the morning there are three classes: one English, one philosophy and one Tibetan language. We have a tea break in between. After the tea break, there are three classes again.
    This nunnery is not exactly Geluk. There are no sects. So, therefore, you can study according to the Sakya tradition, Kagyu tradition; you can study everything. So, sometimes they invite lamas from different schools and you can go to study with them. One teacher from Geluk, one from Sakya; we have teachers from the three different schools. Then there is a lunch break. After lunch until 2 o'clock, there is a break. You have free time. If you want to do homework, you can do whatever. After that we start a Tibetan class from 3:30 to 5 o'clock. [...] Then we have two hours of free

---

7. A religious ritual which in Hinduism includes expressions of honor, worship and devotional attention. For exiled Tibetans, it usually refers to a Buddhist *sādhana*.

time and we have to do our homework. We have to memorize. Then at 6:30, we have dinner. After 7, when the dinner is finished, we have to go to the prayer hall to pray for one hour. Then after that you have to study by yourself. At 10:30 at night, every nun has to sleep. At 10:30, a disciplinarian nun makes rounds. Until then, you can keep lights on or talk.

Every second Saturday of a month, we can go out. You can go outside at seven in the morning, eight or seven but you have to be back here exactly at five o'clock. If you are late even two minutes, they will punish you. You have to work in the kitchen. After 5 o'clock, you can't see anyone outside the nunnery. Sunday mornings we wash our clothes, clean our rooms and if you have a garden, you clean your garden. And, if you have time you can study, prepare for Monday. Sunday is very nice. We have TV in the nunnery but you can watch only one day for two hours. Sometimes the Dalai Lama's speech, which you can also listen. You can get some knowledge from that.

The nunnery that Ani Sherab was staying at in 2008 was a nonsectarian nunnery. The exile situation has brought along with it some changes for the nuns, compared to their traditional way of life in Tibet. The idea of admitting nuns from all of the various schools of Tibetan Buddhism into one nunnery was not that commonly practiced in Tibet. The discipline of the nunnery was strict and the daily schedule was tight, with plenty of classes and other activities. It should be emphasized, however, that not every exile nunnery is the same. The nunnery Ani Sherab was staying at was atypical in many ways. For example, the exile nunnery where I stayed for the longest period of time resembled the nunneries I visited in the Tibetan regions in China. The major outward differences had to do with the living conditions and facilities. While in the Tibetan regions in China the nuns usually live alone – or sometimes an older nun stays with a younger one – in separate houses, in exile the nuns do not usually have separate houses but live in a "block of flats." It is also very common for younger nuns especially to share their room with another nun, and sometimes with many nuns. In exile nunneries, there is often also a common kitchen where the nuns take turns cooking a common meal for all of the nuns at the nunnery. These kitchen duties are usually regarded as the least appealing part of monastic life. As Ani Sherab said, those who returned late to the nunnery were punished and this meant extra kitchen hours.

In addition to the daily routine, nunneries have monthly and yearly schedules. Certain days of the month are special days with common temple gatherings. In one nunnery I visited, the nuns were allowed to go into a retreat in the first, second, third and seventh month of a year. In this nunnery, the nuns also had three days of holiday per month: one after every ten days. In some other nunneries, Sunday was a holiday. In yet another nunnery, the nuns had two longer holidays every year: 15–20 days during the Tibetan New Year (Tib. *losar, lo gsar*) and 15–20 days in the summer. During their days off, the nuns were allowed to leave the nunnery for errands. During longer holidays, they often went to visit their families.

Even if the nun did not stay in a nunnery, she tended to follow the same routine every day. Ani Dikey, who lived with three other nuns in a small house in Amdo, explained:

> We follow the same routine every day. I get up early in the morning, around six. I recite prayers, do prostrations, make an offering and have breakfast. After that, I may take some rest and then again recite prayers and read texts. After dinner, I read Lamrim.[8]

Ani Lhamo, who also stayed in a nuns' community in Amdo, told that for the most part the nuns performed their personal religious practices in their rooms. For teachings, the nuns went to visit particular monks and lamas at nearby monasteries. Ani Lhamo said:

> There are only three occasions in a month when we pray together. Then, sometimes we also go to perform death rituals in the village. Apart from these things, most of the time we do prayers and perform rituals alone in the house. [...] There is a scholar monk at Rebgong Gompa. We go to him and receive his teachings. He asks us to study texts such as Lamrim by heart and do prostrations. We have to take an oath under him to complete our daily routine, such as "I will do this and I will do that and so on." I promised to do 500 prostrations a day and I am doing it now.

Even those nuns who did not stay at a nunnery or in a nuns' community tended to keep a daily routine. Ani Karma, a 60-year-old nun who had never stayed in a nunnery, told that her daily activities included chanting the *om mani peme hung* mantra and fasting.

The nunneries I have been to thus seemed to follow an observable daily schedule. However, even if the daily routine of the nunnery was generally the same, the individual nuns could perform different kinds of religious activities according to their knowledge and experience. In all the nunneries I visited, both in the Tibetan regions of China and in exile, the nuns were mostly leading a life related to their monastic path and status. Older nuns in India remembered their first years in exile as loaded with work as they built the nunneries. Many of the Tibetan nunneries in China have also recently been rebuilt, and it was not uncommon

---

8. The *lam rim chen mo*, or "stages of the path," is a Tibetan Buddhist text that presents the path to buddhahood in hierarchically ordered stages.

to see nuns working construction side by side with Chinese workers. It was also a duty of a nun or the nun's family to build living quarters for her in a nunnery's compound. However, the nuns I interviewed were not forced to take regularly part in other mundane work. The situation was different when they visited home. I once traveled to Ani Palkyi's home with her. As soon as we stepped inside, she started to wipe the floor, cook food and serve her parents and other family members.

"There Are Definitely Problems Related to Livelihood"

In historical Tibet, the economies of monasteries and nunneries were based on the monastic institution and individual monks and nuns. With regard to the former, most nunneries seem to have been economically autonomous institutions. Part of their income was based on donations from local people or from pilgrims (Havnevik 1989, 56–59). Individual nuns could provide for themselves, for example, by working as personal servants for wealthier nuns. Nuns also performed religious services for the laity. They either recited prayers in the nunnery or performed rituals at laypeople's homes. Nevertheless, nuns had very different ritual relationships with the lay community than monks. Unlike monks, they did not usually perform services such as divinations and chanting at various life events, especially funerals. Sometimes nuns also did farming and handicrafts. The most important provider for the nun, however, was her natal family. Because of this, Havnevik believes that most nuns came from middle-class families and either joined a nunnery because they wished to or because they were encouraged by their family (Havnevik 1989, 56–59; Makley 1999, 211).

According to Melvyn Goldstein, in traditional Tibet becoming a monk was believed to bring a great amount of merit both to the ordained person and his family, and monastic life was to ensure that the boy would never have to experience the hardship and poverty of village life (e.g., Goldstein 1997, 14; 1998b, 16–17). Kim Gutschow has stated, however, that nuns embody the ideals of voluntary poverty that the Buddha outlined, not because they choose to but because they must. Gutschow writes:

> Sending a daughter to the nunnery is akin to placing her in a community college without any scholarship. She may have access to ritual knowledge, peers, and pilgrimages which take her far beyond her provincial village life. Yet she is tied to an institution close to her natal village, so that she can work at home to earn her daily bread.
>
> (Gutschow 2004, 84)

Gutschow has argued that much of the inequality between monks and nuns is due to the concentration of wealth and status produced by merit-making practices. According to her, those with wealth and power, such as monks who are at the top of the system, are said to have accumulated more merit in past lives. Nuns, on the other hand, are seen as a "lesser field of merit" and thus supported less (Gutschow 2004, 3). Karma Lekshe Tsomo writes:

> Lack of support for women's practice has forced generations of female religious to remain at home rather than join an established religious community, as do the monks. An unmarried woman may shave her head, don monastic robes, and engage in spiritual practice, but in exchange for her upkeep, she is expected to perform the duties of a household servant – looking after the stove, fields, animals, and children.
>
> (Tsomo 1999a, 179)

The nunneries I studied in greater detail were under a monastery and thus administered by its head lama. In these nunneries, the nuns were given a certain amount of money each month. In one of the nunneries in Yushu, each of the nuns was given 70 RMB per month while the poor nuns were provided with the sum of 200 RMB a month. I was told that the head lama of the monastery-nunnery used to tour in mainland China in order to collect money for his monastic institutions.[9] In another nunnery that was also under a monastery, the nuns were given 50 RMB every month.

The most important source of personal income for an individual nun was the nunnery. Many also named both the family and the nunnery as their most important sources of livelihood. Offerings from the laity were not the main source of living for any of the nuns. It can further be noticed that in the Kham regions and in exile, nunneries more often took care of the livelihood of the nuns, while in Amdo the family was the most important provider. Besides the nunnery, the family's support was thus crucial for the nuns. However, those nuns who answered my question about the economic status of their childhood family considered it to be either poor or moderate. Not a single nun considered herself as having a wealthy family background. Not surprisingly, the nuns I interviewed had met with many financial problems. Ani Yonten said:

---

9. Despite some restrictions, some Tibetan lamas travel periodically to areas populated with Han Chinese or have Chinese disciples come to visit them. In this way, some of them can accumulate a considerable amount of wealth according to local standards (Costello 2008, 106).

> Being in a nunnery or in a monastery means that there are definitely problems related to livelihood. But from the Buddhist point of view, all these are trivial things to give that much importance.

Ani Changchub told about an unfortunate incident that led to the community of nuns losing one of their most important sources of income:

> Earlier, most of our needs were met by the offerings of money people give to the *stūpa*[10] here. But now we don't get anything from that. This stūpa was looked after by a monk and a nun who used to be here a long time back, but later another nun joined them. At that time, they were looking after the *stūpa*. But later, because some problems occurred between them, they decided to give the *stūpa* to the nearby monastery. The monks from the monastery once ordered us to leave this place, but we didn't listen to them because these houses were built by my niece. The monks took away from us the responsibility of looking after the stūpa, so the little income that we had received before stopped. Now they make an elderly man look after the *stūpa*. The local people here sometimes tell us to complain to the local government about this unfair treatment, but we don't want to raise havoc. After all, we are wearing the Buddha's robe and our main objective is to practice religion. So, we decided to leave things as they are. Today, although there are difficulties in terms of livelihood, by the grace of god we don't have to live with empty stomachs. The local people have been generous in giving us food and sometimes they pay some amount for the rituals that we perform for them.

A reciprocal relationship between the monastics and the laity has always been central for the survival of Buddhist monasticism. From the viewpoint of laypeople, the most important purpose of the monastic institution is to offer religious ceremonies and services for the laity. Nevertheless, while the money given by the head of the monastery to the nuns as regular "pay" originally came from lay followers, it was less common for an individual layperson to ask religious services directly from a nunnery. Among the reasons for less support seemed to be long-followed customs and the idea that the nuns' religious practices and spiritual capacities were different from those of the monks. In fact, previous studies of Tibetan monastics have noted the discrepancy between the religious functions of monks and nuns (e.g. Gutschow 2004). Havnevik, for example, writes that according to most of her informants, it was not the custom in Tibet for laypeople to ask nuns to perform ritual services in their houses, since it was believed that rituals performed by monks are more powerful (Havnevik 1989, 174–175). I asked my informants why they

---

10. Tib. *mchod rten*, "relic shrine."

thought less support was provided to nunneries by the laity. A 30-year-old laywoman from Amdo/Sichuan said:

> It is a long-followed tradition. Since this kind of disparity was there from the beginning, the same is followed by the next generations as well. As a matter of fact, both monks and nuns follow the same religion and do the same practices, but people say that there is a difference. That is the reason why people in my area don't really invite nuns to perform so many rituals, especially rituals like a funeral. This is how things work, even at a social level. For instance, boys are treated better than girls, so it is happening in the religious community as well.
>
> (IN2011/3)

While many of my lay interviewees thought that the monks and the nuns performed similar religious practices, some believed they were different. A 28-year-old layman from Amdo/Qinghai told me:

> The nuns don't usually do what the monks do. Studying Buddhist dialectics is done only by monks. Most of the time, nuns perform simple rituals like prayers, meditation, penance and so on. [...] I don't know the reason, but I think that it must be a kind of instituted tradition that some great lamas long ago created separate ways of lives for monks and for nuns.
>
> (IN2011/7)

A 75-year-old laywoman from Amdo/Qinghai also thought that monks were more knowledgeable:

> Nuns may not have the knowledge that monks have. Monks have greater knowledge, but being a nun is also good. They don't have to think about the family and can devote themselves to religious practice.
>
> (IN2011/11)

In order to attract laypeople, the nunnery has to be famous or at least well-known for its discipline or practice. Only a handful of the thirty-nine laypeople I interviewed had ever been to any nunnery. A 29-year-old layman from Amdo/Sichuan had been to a nunnery because there was a certain nun there who performed medical treatments:

> The reason for going to one of the nunneries was that I was suffering from some stomach illnesses at that time and there is a good nun who is a medical practitioner at the nunnery. So, I went there to consult that nun. The other nunnery I visited because my friend needed to get some herbal medicine from the nunnery and he wanted me to accompany him.
>
> (IN2011/2)

There was, however, one set of prayers that was considered as efficacious or even more powerful when performed by a nun: Tārā (Tib. Dolma). A 20-year-old layman from Amdo said:

> I think that nuns are reciting Dolma most of the time. Reciting prayers like Dolma is also done by most of the Tibetan women. I think that the essence of their practice must be the same. Just as monks practice Buddhism for all sentient beings, nuns do so in the same way. When it comes to performing rituals, there are lots of prayers that laypeople can't recite. Sometimes the lamas tell a particular individual or family to recite certain prayers, and in that case the concerned person goes to the monastery to request the monks to perform the ritual. For simple prayers like Dolma and such, people go to a nunnery to request the nuns to recite it for them.
>
> (IN2011/1)

The laity thus prefers monks for most rituals, leaving nuns to perform more basic tasks that accumulate merit. From the nuns' side, this has a very negative consequence vis-à-vis their economic situation: nunneries and individual nuns are supported less than monasteries and monks. The most important source of livelihood for a nun has traditionally been her family, which has customarily given food and nowadays also money. Help from the family is still crucial, because many nunneries do not give nuns a monthly allowance or otherwise support them, as is the case in some of the wealthier nunneries I visited.

"A Nun in a Family Makes the Whole Family Look Bad"

The lesser degree of support has to do with the different standing of monks and nuns. Generally speaking, monks are respected more than nuns. This disparity does not go unnoted by the nuns. The discussion with Ani Dawa, who was living in Amdo/Qinghai, provides the viewpoint of one individual nun, but it is very representative when it comes to the nuns' own impressions about their status:

> M.H.: How about laypeople? Do they respect monks and nuns equally?
>
> Ani Dawa: No, there is a difference. Being male, monks are respected more, whereas we nuns being female don't receive the same respect as the monks do.

Most of the laypeople I interviewed expressed their respect for both nuns and monks, but it was obvious that most of them valued monks over nuns. A 22-year-old female student from Amdo/Qinghai said:

> We talk about the nuns, but it's a different view. When we talk about monks we kind of feel respect toward them, but when we talk about nuns it's kind of great that these nuns keep the *stūpa* clean and do their daily offerings … [But] the feeling of respect is somewhat less, I think. I also feel

like that. That is because of the environment, the culture. Where I grew up, my parents taught me to do that, to do this.

(IN2011/14)

I then asked her if the nuns are respected less because of their gender or because of their lower education status. The female student said:

> I think because they are women. They are really educated, like, for example, the nun from my village, I heard that she is really educated. The nun's niece, who is my friend, went to learn Tibetan there [the nunnery] and the nun taught her. She [the friend] is actually a college student. She must be more educated than that nun, right? But she [the nun] could really teach her a lot. That means she is very knowledgeable. Because they are women, people feel like that.
>
> (IN2011/14)

The 30-year-old housewife from Amdo/Sichuan said:

> Since both the nuns and monks practice the same religion, there is a sense of devotion for both. In that respect, it is almost the same. But the intensity of respect these two categories receive is different. It is analogous to the difference that we generally find between girls and boys in the society. If a boy and a girl go to a family as guests, the boy is made to sit on the bed and the girl is made to sit lower than the boy. So, the same thing is happening at the religious level as well. For instance, we find more lamas in the monastery than in the nunnery.
>
> As far as my place is concerned, becoming a monk or having a monk in the family is something to be envied by everyone. But having a nun in the family makes the whole family look bad. Most people have the idea that someone becomes a nun only when she fails to do anything in society as a laywoman. There is a big difference in the way people in my area address monks and nuns. But I heard from others that in Ngawa, if a family has three or four girls, one has to become a nun. People give considerable respect to the nuns there.
>
> (IN2011/3)

There is, of course, some variation when it comes to the laity's ideas on nuns. This discussion with two laymen from Amdo was revealing:

> M.H.: Are you saying that becoming a nun is not as good as becoming a monk?
> Man 1: It is the same.
> M.H.: Even though they have a different ordination?
> Man 1: From a religious perspective it must be the same, but the way local people view and approach it is different.
> M.H.: What do you as a "local person" think?
> Man 1: The monk is better. Monks are good at analyzing, but nuns can't do such things.

> Man 2: No, I don't agree with his view. We can't generalize things in that way. To what extent one is respected completely depends on the circumstances.
>
> (IN2011/10)

According to Anna Grimshaw, she was frequently told that nuns "played" at being religious devotees, but in reality they were "frustrated, gossiping women." People regarded nuns as uneducated when it came to the Buddhist scriptures and esoteric meditative practices (Grimshaw 1994, 23, 41). Makley also noted that nuns in Labrang were subjected to scandalous talk and negative stories by the laity and the monastics. They were widely considered to be interlopers or compared to dogs and Muslims. In particular, nuns' bodies were the objects of especially intense contestation. Makley believes that this was because they were seen as challenging the gender ideals of the community and because the body of a nun was more visible than ever before. Unfortunately, gossip about nuns was more than idle talk; it had serious social consequences for young women (Makley 1999, 182–183, 194–195, 227–228, 239; 2005, 260). I rarely encountered such harsh talk about nuns. However, the 33-year-old government employee from Kham had a rather pessimistic idea about the future of nuns:

> Man: I generally think nunneries have no future path. First, the men usually have more social maturation and earn well. That's why the monk can dominate the monastery and make it rich. However, the women are unable to choose any lifestyle; they are unskilled. So, once they become nuns, they just become a burden for the nunneries.
>
> M.H.: Do you think the number of nuns has increased or decreased recently in Yushu?
>
> Man: From my point of view, it has decreased. Because I have witnessed a nun who came to a hospital for medical treatment and she said that something was wrong with her stomach. However, the doctors found her to be pregnant. I asked her why she had a kid. She answered that once she slept in a mountain, which was a god mountain [that made her pregnant]. She couldn't help it. But people have lost their faith in the nuns' future and refuse to become nuns. They judge nuns.
>
> M.H.: What do you think about nuns, aside from those few nuns?
>
> Man: In my view, I think the majority of them are doing well.
>
> M.H.: How about monks? Do they have the same troubles?
>
> Man: Of course they have. I heard a lot. I strongly believe no matter what religion you believe in, if you want to destroy it, only the believers have the right, not the outsiders.
>
> (IN2011/20)

It is often claimed that the position of women varies considerably in the different schools of Tibetan Buddhism. Women are seen to have a lower position in scholastic and hierarchical schools, such as the Geluk school, and more freedom in the less structural Nyingma school. This difference was also brought up by some of my informants. Here is a discussion with two laymen I interviewed in Amdo. One of them was a scholar and the other was a teacher.

> Man 2: Obviously that [the lower number of nunneries] is visible. Labrang alone has around 108 branches, but only one nunnery. There are 500 lamas but only one female lama.
> M.H.: So, why is that? What do you think?
> Man 2: The ultimate reason for this is that in Tibetan society, women don't enjoy the same privilege as men do. The reason for why there are more nuns in the Nyingma school is because in their tantric tradition, women are considered as *khandromas*. In the Geluk school, women have a very low position; they are the epitome of impurity as such. Since Geluk is a widespread school, it brings its influence to bear in the major part of the Tibetan regions.
> Man 1: May it be because of the strict discipline of the Geluk sect?
> M.H.: So, you are saying that Geluk has much power in Tibetan society.
> Man 2: Yes, of course. Geluk is the dominating school in Tibetan society.
> (IN2011/10)

According to the men, the primary reason for the small number of nunneries was the position of Tibetan women in general. Another of the men also brought up that the status varied between the different schools of Tibetan Buddhism. Interestingly, he nevertheless claimed that clearly most of the nunneries in the Tibetan regions belong to the Nyingma school of Tibetan Buddhism. He said:

> There must be around 100 or not more than 100 nunneries in the whole of Tibet. Once I came across something about the nunneries in Tibet in a magazine published by a women's association. It said there that out of 100 percent of the nunneries in Tibet, 90 percent of the nunneries are Nyingma.
> (IN2011/10)

In general, my lay informants mainly explained the gender differences in monasticism by referring to religious doctrines. Interestingly, the more educated they were, the more they tended to highlight gender differences. The 26-year-old male student from Amdo referred to religion when he explained the suffering experienced by women:

M.H.: Some Tibetans say that Tibetan women suffer more than men.
Man: Yes, from a religious perspective, due to attachment, anger, ignorance and a different biological formation, they are subject to more suffering. So, that is the reason for women suffering more.
M.H.: What is the reason for that? I didn't get you. Can you try to explain again?
Man: From a religious point of view, women have an intrinsically stronger impulse for lust, and the biological difference makes them carry the baby in their womb. So, these are certain conditions that make them suffer more than men. Being a layman and being a monk are different. Monks become monks because manhood gives them the best opportunity to learn.

(IN2011/8)

The following discussion with a 25-year-old monk from Amdo is also illuminating:

Monk: It is easier for a man to attain enlightenment.
M.H.: Why?
Monk: In terms of Buddhism, usually the girls have a bad heart. They are more moody, more narrow-minded. They get angry just because of small reasons.
M.H.: So (they are) more emotional somehow?
Monk: Not emotional. I mean, men have a big heart and they can accept more, but the girls become angry easily. They also have a dark heart. Black heart. If I say this, do you get angry?
M.H.: No, that's your opinion.
Monk: There are other reasons, too. There are many reasons. For example, if you go to a monastery or a temple, there are monasteries and temples that strictly forbid girls to go inside. You are not allowed to go. It's because you make the deities angry.

(IN2007/3)

Together with certain traditional ideas about female gender and its potential (discussed later), fewer encounters with nuns can reinforce negative concepts about them (see also Sonam Wangmo & Edo 2016). Importantly, the prejudices have serious consequences for nuns.

"But it Didn't Take Long for All the Beautiful Things to Deteriorate"

The Chinese takeover of Tibetan regions had tremendous consequences on monastic life. Ani Tsewang, a 95-year-old nun from Kham, had become a monastic before the advent of China and had lived in a nunnery in

Yushu. She had, however, been forced to leave her nunnery and had only returned to her old, reopened nunnery some years ago. This is how Ani Tsewang recollected the hardships faced after the Chinese occupation:

> After 1958, those [nuns] who still had families went back to their own homes. There were a lot of beggar nuns; they just wandered around. Some of us were poisoned in a few months. So we were like that. And we stayed like that. In 1958, when they said that the Chinese were coming, I ran home to my parents. [...] I had my parents. But my father was sick and my mother was jailed. At that time, a lot of women from our village were jailed. My father was sick and he died. My sister had a lot of small children and I helped her to take care of them since I had no place to go. [...] In 1958, the nunnery was destroyed and the nuns wandered around. I had my parents, so my life was good. But there were lots of nuns who were beggars. They collected barley heads in the autumn and then they ate them. [...] They [the Chinese] took most of our food and clothes, but we still had some left for the children. We sewed the worn-out clothes again and again. A lot of food was taken away, so we really suffered a lot because of starvation. Lots of people died from starvation at that time. But the children and I survived. We were not full at that time. We were never full. We just survived.

Ani Tsewang did not flee Tibet in the hope of happier and more peaceful life. However, many nuns have left, especially from Central Tibet. According to Karma Lekshe Tsomo, the flight of nuns from Tibet has occurred in two main waves. The first of these consisted of those nuns who fled in 1959 or soon thereafter. The second wave is comprised of nuns who fled more recently. Among them were, for example, more than 400 nuns who arrived in India and Nepal between 1989 and 1993. Tsomo estimated that there were about 1,290 Tibetan refugee nuns living in exile in India and Nepal in 2003 but the number must be much bigger now (Tsomo 2003, 346).[11]

Five of the nuns I interviewed for this research had also left Tibet. For them, the monastic life they had waited for so eagerly turned out to oppressive because of state policies. Of these nuns, two older ones – Ani Dolkar and Ani Dolma – decided to take part in the anti-Chinese demonstration in Lhasa in 1988. They followed the example of a group of monks who had initiated a protest in Lhasa in 1987, which started a series of demonstrations that continued until 1989 when martial law was imposed by China (see Smith 1996, 602–603, 616; Powers 1995, 181–184). Ani Dolma described her motives in this way:

---

11. For example, Tibetan Nuns Project based in Dharamsala in India supports seven Indian exile nunneries which have about 760 nuns. In addition, some individual nuns not living in a nunnery are supported by the TNP (see https://tnp.org/nuns).

> The authoritarian regime may have claimed to have given enough freedom to study and practice religion. But in reality there was no freedom at all, and seeing these injustices that were being done to our people I became politicized.

Ani Dolma and Ani Dolkar were detained, imprisoned and brutally tortured in prison. Ani Dolkar shared her story with me in India in 2008. I want to recount her story here at length, as she found it important to share. She recollected:

> Meanwhile, the Chinese oppression had taken a toll on every Tibetan life; our religious freedom came under major scrutiny. In 1988, Ani Dolma and I decided to take part in a demonstration against the Chinese occupation. Initially, we were twelve nuns and two monks. While I was in Lhasa, I used to listen to His Holiness the Dalai Lama's teachings with a tape recorder in secret. I realized how our own brothers were deprived of such privileges and I went back to our head nunnery to see if anyone was interested in joining the upcoming protest against the Chinese rule. Eleven nuns confirmed their participation and were later joined by two monks. We spent one night at a lhakhang and the next day left for the Main Temple[12] in pairs in order to avoid suspicion. We were pretending that we were there to do some offerings and give alms to beggars. To our surprise and disappointment, a large number of police officers were already posted there. We didn't know how they came to know about this protest. They arrested us, saying that we were there to protest against them. They ordered all the vendors to pack their belongings and closed the shops. Realizing our own helplessness, we decided to make two different groups and started shouting slogans and throwing pamphlets, shouting "Long live His Holiness the Dalai Lama," "Free Tibet," "China go back" and so on. In the meantime, more policemen were called and we were all arrested. I was captured by three policemen who took me to a van. One monk was shot and was bleeding. We were all put in the same army truck. Our hands were tied and they started hitting us with guns. But we still kept on shouting slogans.
>
> We were taken to a prison and there were already more than 30 prisoners, who were mostly criminals and murderers. We nuns and monks were kept in separate wards. They hung plywood around our neck on which our names and the nunnery's name were written. They took our photos and interrogated us. There were six interrogators, five Tibetans and one Chinese. One interrogator asked me why we were hell-bent on disrupting the normal lives of others and creating a rift between the Tibetans and the Chinese. "We know that there was someone who was behind all these problems. Do you have any contact outside Tibet? Do you have any

---

12. The Tsuklakhang (*gtsug lag khang*) Temple in Lhasa is also known as the Jokhang (*jo khang*).

relatives outside Tibet? It would be nice if you told us yourself, as otherwise we will find it out sooner or later."

"I did it myself, there was nobody who instructed me to do such things."

After hearing my rebuttal, they started hitting and kicking me. I was threatened that I would be shot dead: "You were lucky that I forgot my gun today."

"You have been killing our people for so long; I am not afraid to die. You can shoot me whenever you like." I was quite adamant with my statements. Another policeman came with a huge dog and directed the dog to bite me. The dog started biting me and they kept on asking the same question. My answer was the same. I saw my other friends interrogated, too, and the dog was directed again to bite [one of them]. Unfortunately, she tried to run away but the dog jumped and grabbed her. She was badly injured. I just had a few minor bruises. We were taken inside another room and our clothes were removed. Facing the wall with my hands on my head, they started interrogating again. Two Chinese policemen came up with electric rods and we were given electric shocks. I was told later that laypeople would fall unconscious immediately after receiving electric shocks, but it didn't happen with nuns and monks that easily. That remained a mystery.

Later we were moved to separate cells again and I was received by four policewomen with different torturing devices, mainly an electric rod, bamboo canes, braided ropes and so on. All my clothes were removed again, even my undergarments, and I was made to lay down on the floor. They started abusing me with a bamboo cane and inserted the electric rod into my orifices. I couldn't bear the pain and fainted. I didn't remember anything until they made me stand up. It seemed that they were quite enjoying the whole torturing scenario and started making fun of my huge breasts, as I was quite healthy at that time. "Look at your breasts! They are huge!" and "You must be a mother of two children! You must be a prostitute, falling for monks." They went on and on. They inserted the electric rod into my mouth, then into my vagina, and it would go on for a couple of times. I was beaten with bamboo canes when I refused to open my mouth. "Aren't you enjoying this rod in your vagina, you prostitute?" They yelled. I felt like the whole world was crushing my body. I was shaking and my teeth were on the verge of falling out.

I was taken to another cell and I was locked inside. I couldn't feel anything. It was more like the whole world was rumbling and I was standing upside down. My memory was fading and I had flashbacks once in a while of their torturing. One thing I kept hearing was the question about who was behind us, the mastermind. "You were too young to take such drastic steps and must have been brainwashed by the Dalai Lama's clique." These were the few repeated sentences I kept hearing.

After three days, when I regained enough strength, I realized how bad the bruises were and how deep the injuries were. The pain was unbearable. They used to interrogate us three times a day. The beating went on until the fifth day and then the torturing was considerably reduced. We were given the worst food, leftovers mostly prepared from the remains of vegetables and rotten ones. Our food was prepared by the criminals and murderers who were locked inside. The food was normally half-cooked, and the worst was that they spat in the food in front of our eyes, and they threw cigarette ash and butts [in it]. We were escorted by these criminals to the bathroom and toilets while the police on duty made lewd remarks. We were not supposed to look up and down or talk while we were taking turns in the toilet and bathroom. We were not given enough time in the toilet, too; they always made us rush and run. We were not given a mattress or enough food for three days. I slept on the floor for three days with open wounds and bruises all over my body. The cell where I was locked was so dirty, it looked more like a toilet, with human excreta, blood, mucus and purulence everywhere. The whole cell reeked of blood and human excrement.

We spent two months in this cell. The new rules for such protests were yet to be formulated. The longest imprisonment was for three months. The Panchen Lama[13] was alive and his charisma was such that they were unable to formulate any new rules and regulations. The new rules and regulations were formulated as soon as His Holiness the Panchen Lama passed away. We were released with other 83 prisoners and were given an elaborate description of the new rules and regulations. As soon as I was released, my brother was there to receive me. I was bedridden for weeks. I was too weak to visit a hospital and consult a doctor. My brother went to Lhasa every day on his horse, taking my urine and stool for check-ups. My mother bathed me every day, followed by massages with home-made oil. And she made me sleep in the sun. After I regained my health, she told me that she hadn't expected me to live. My mother couldn't eat and sleep while I was sick.

I went back to my nunnery after recovering and there were lots of security personnel, interrogating other nuns. We had three rounds of talks. Now the time had come to denounce His Holiness the Dalai Lama and blame him. Furthermore, we had to apologize for what had happened in Lhasa and accept our faults. They instructed us. "Otherwise, you will all go to prison again." We were further instructed not to leave our hometown and there was a routine check. Finally, we decided to flee Tibet. My family members didn't object at all. I came to Lhasa and we traveled for nine months in a van. My aunt, who is also my teacher, was also with us.

Ani Dolma was detained and imprisoned together with Ani Dolkar. This is how Ani Dolma described the protest and the imprisonment:

---

13. The Panchen Lama (*pan chen bla ma*) is the second highest lama in the Geluk school. Here she refers to the 10th Panchen Lama (1938–1989).

Life as a Nun

> A year after I became a nun there was this big revolution in 1987 and again in 1988, in which I took part in Lhasa. In May 1988, I went to protest because in 1987 many Tibetans were put in jail because of protesting. So we went to ask for the release of these prisoners. Because of this, I was detained and then imprisoned. But I was lucky. I was imprisoned for only two months. They could have sent us very far, to a remote jail, so that no one would have known where we were. But during that time, the Panchen Lama came to Lhasa and many prisoners were released because of him. Nevertheless, during these two months we were tortured every day. I was tortured a lot. You wouldn't have enough time to listen.

She continued:

> I can't finish telling the whole story now and there is not enough time to let me share [the story]. Sometimes I feel it's better to put it out of my mind, those black times I had in the prison. The experience I had in the prison is so similar to most of the Tibetan prisoners. An experience like that is beyond our human imagination. To make a long story short, we were tortured intermittently and mercilessly in the prison for two months. They used different methods to demoralize our hope to fight by sending dogs to chase us, by using electric tools inside our organs, beating us naked with our front side on the floor, playing with us like toys, forcing us to drink their urine and so forth. But luckily I was among the prisoners who were released in 1989 during the visit of the Panchen Lama.

After their release from prison, Ani Dolma and Ani Dolkar were expelled from the nunnery and forbidden to get involved in any political or religious activities. Ani Dolma recollected:

> One day, not long after my release, I was called to our nunnery to admit my faults. I refused to obey their demands. Eventually I was once again beaten badly and later in that same year expelled from the nunnery.
>
> More and more unrest took place in the nunnery because the nuns refused to accept their "faults." We were also told many times to jot down on a paper what we had done so far, that it was wrong and violated the constitution of China. We wrote them letters, admitting that we were in the protest, but we didn't accept what we did was wrong and against the national rules. [...] We were beaten badly during the interrogation session. 80 nuns were expelled from our nunnery for not admitting our mistakes. [...] The Chinese officials sent us home and told us that from that day onwards, we had lost our opportunity to study Buddhism and we had to lead a new life as a layperson. We would always be responsible if any unrest happened in our respective villages in the future. How could we become laypersons when our hearts were hungry to continue in the nun's life? Because we were not allowed to pursue life as a nun, I set out for India.

Because they did not want to live as laypeople, Ani Dolma and Ani Dolkar decided to escape to India where Tibetans under the leadership of the Dalai Lama and his exile government had created a refugee community (see Härkönen 2008). This is how Ani Dolkar described the escape to India:

> We were thirty people with six nuns. Our escape route was from Mount Kailash.[14] I couldn't walk, as I was sick. My mother had packed enough provisions for the whole journey. We walked on foot for almost one month. We ran out of food, begged for food during the rest of the journey, and finally reached the Nepalese border. I believe I would be in prison if I had stayed. They had handed me and my friend an official letter saying that we were the masterminds behind the protest. My friend escaped, too, but she couldn't make it to India and died during the escape. I could have died if my aunt and other friends hadn't helped me. I was bedridden in India for years and medication didn't help. I had almost given up my hope of regaining my health until I went to attend His Holiness's teaching in Manali.[15] I prayed that if there was any chance of recovering from this prolonged illness, to show me some sign. Otherwise, I would gladly accept my fate. Interestingly, I started feeling lighter from the very next day and in a year I had recovered.

Ani Dolma recollected her escape this way:

> It was not an arranged trip. Our journey to India inadvertently came to mind when we, three nuns, visited Mount Kailash. Since we didn't know the trail to India, we had to depend on a guide. But our guide fooled us and left us alone and helpless before even a week had passed after beginning our trip. He took our money and we had to sell our robes to earn money to continue our journey. Because of the financial problems and because we did not know our way, we were forced to stay in a remote place for almost a month. Luckily we met a kind lady who was on her way to Nepal and she helped to take us there. We didn't have anything to give her except our sleeping bags and things we didn't need. We also gave her money once we reached the Nepal reception center. [...] It took almost two months to reach India.
>
> A protest was going on in New Delhi under the supervision of and organized by the Central Tibetan Administration when I reached the reception center in New Delhi. Instantly I seized that opportunity to share the unrest and the violation of human rights in Tibet with the media. I was quite proud to be a spokesperson for my brothers and sisters who are still suffering under the five red stars in Tibet.

---

14. Mount Kailash (Tib. Gang Rinpoche, *gngas rin po che*) is an important pilgrimage destination for Tibetans.
15. Manali is a hill station in Himachal Pradesh, India.

In addition to nuns like Ani Dolkar and Ani Dolma, who were political prisoners and left Tibet, there were many other nuns who decided to escape. In 1996, China launched the "strike hard campaign" in Tibetan monasteries and nunneries. Work teams were sent to monasteries and nunneries to "reeducate" monks and nuns in their political and religious beliefs. During the campaign between 1996 and 1998, 492 monks and nuns are said to have been arrested and 9,997 expelled from their religious institutions (e.g., Schwartz 1994).

As noted at the start of this book, 32-year-old Ani Sherab from the TAR recollected the time when the Chinese implemented patriotic education in her nunnery: "it didn't take long for all the beautiful things to deteriorate". Like Ani Sherab, most of the women started on their hazardous journey either because of fear of political persecution or to seek educational and religious freedom and better social and economic opportunities outside Tibet (see Tsomo 2003). Many Tibetans I have talked to in exile name meeting the Dalai Lama as one of the most important motives to flee the Tibetan regions in China. One of them was Ani Dechen, who was finally able to flee in 1999. She recollected:

> The Chinese Communist government had been implementing patriotic education, especially inside the monks' and nuns' communities. And they even persecuted the monks and nuns. All this caused problems between the Chinese and the Tibetans. Our only way to get rid of this problem was to come to India. [...] Secretly, we made one big group consisting of forty-three people along with a Tibetan guide. Except for three nuns in our group, all the others were laypeople. Our journey to India started in 1996, but all of us except our guide were detained when we reached Mount Everest and we were sent back to a prison in Shigatse.[16] They took away all of our belongings and money. Luckily, we were released from prison after a month.
>
> After a year, I again tried to flee from Tibet. Unlike before, I was all alone in that ferocious journey. I submitted an application to the Chinese officials to allow me to go near our nunnery, stating that I was going to Dham[17] to meet my relatives. Eventually I got a permission letter to travel to Dham. I bribed a Nepalese [official] when I reached the Dham checkpoint. With our best endeavors, we managed to sneak through the checkpoint in the early morning. It was the most exhilarating experience in my life when I first felt the touch of Nepal's soil. I felt safe, and I knew a happy time would come soon: the time to meet His Holiness the Dalai Lama, the time to study Buddhism freely. I was picked up by an official from the Tibetan reception center in Nepal and later sent to Dharamsala. I stayed a year

---

16. Shigatse (*gzhis ka rtse*) is a city in the TAR.
17. Dham is in the border of China and Nepal.

outside the nunnery preparing for an entrance exam. Luckily I passed the exam and I was enrolled in the nunnery.

Ani Sherab escaped in 1995. This is how she told about her flight:

It was in 1995. I accidently met a Tibetan pilgrim from India and we exchanged words. I listened to her eagerly and at last I won her heart and she revealed the secret route to India. Instantly I thought I would escape to India to see His Holiness the Dalai Lama and to study Tibetan philosophy.

Months flew by. I took my younger sister to our nunnery and taught her texts. But my heart always yearned to go to India. All I was waiting for was a suitable time and company to begin my journey. I soon found a nun for company. One day, I called my younger sister to my room and disclosed to her that I was soon leaving to India. She cried a lot. I assured her I would also take her to India once I reached there. And I sent a message to my family saying not to worry about me and that I would take good care.

But running away from our nunnery was not a piece of cake. I discussed it a lot with my companion and decided to make a good and reasonable excuse that we both had to go to Lhasa to read the Kangyur[18] to some people we knew. Hence, we wrote an application to our nunnery kindly requesting them to grant us three months' leave.

We started our journey after a few days. We went to Lhasa to look for people going to India. My partner and I were under 18, and there was not any guesthouse we could stay in Lhasa unless we paid extra money to the owner secretly. That was the system implemented by the Chinese government, that a person under the age of 18 was not allowed to stay at a guesthouse in Lhasa. Soon we found a truck going to Mount Kailash. We each gave 400 RMB to the driver and he agreed to take us there. It took more than a week to reach there and finally we reached there safely. But it was a strenuous journey; sitting still in a truck day in and day out.

Things turned more difficult when it came to finding a good and trustworthy guide to take us to India. In addition, the security was tight and there was more control over there. No matter how tough it might be, we needed to be strong enough to get out of Tibet. At last we found a group that was going to India and we joined that group. We were around 100 people in total. It was a nicely mixed group of people of different ages and family backgrounds. We all knew it would be a very dangerous journey, but our determination and courage obscured all the danger and encouraged us to move forward.

We crossed rivers, mountains and cliffs in the harsh weather of the Himalaya range. Our feet swelled from walking, and our bodies smelled badly. And then an unimaginable thing happened as Nepal was just a gaze away from the mountain we were climbing: we were caught by the Chinese police.

---

18. Kangyur is the Tibetan translation of the collected scriptures.

Our bodies were checked and our money was taken, and some of us were beaten badly and mercilessly. They took all of our money and belongings. And then luckily they set us free without anything except our clothes and told us to go to India without money and told that the Dalai Lama would help us.

So, our big group dispersed into many [small ones]. My companion and I decided to go back to Mount Kailash. We survived because of donations we received for reading the scriptures on the roadside while many pilgrims passed the road to circumambulate Mount Kailash. Finally, we managed to flee to India with the help of local people in the Tibetan border area.

But during our second escape to India, we were again caught, [this time] by Nepalese police. They were ready to hand us over to the Chinese police. When we realized that, we begged them to kill us on the spot rather than letting us die in the hands of the Chinese police. So, they took pity upon us and set us free. But sadly they took away our money. We were checked by a female police officer. They checked all our body parts; they even checked our underwear. But they were not clever enough to check my cap! I had hidden enough money under my cap. That would be enough to use for five people to travel from Nepal to India. I sponsored three Tibetan people who were left there without any money. At last we reached the Tibetan reception center in Nepal.

The oppressive political situation and restrictions they faced in religious life, particularly in the TAR, caused some of my nun informants to flee their motherland. The flight is extremely dangerous and demanding, and many who set forth never manage to make it to Nepal or India. Nevertheless, these women made a decision to flee and managed to escape in spite of the tremendous difficulties and obstacles that they faced during the journey.

Part III

TIBETAN NUNS IN DOMAINS OF POWER

– 8 –

Oppressive Social Institutions of Tibet under Chinese Rule

In the previous chapters, the nuns related their motives for becoming a nun, the difficulties they faced during the process, and the hardships they kept encountering in their present life. The stories also revealed the various ways in which they coped with these difficulties and how meaningful they considered their life as nuns to be.

As noted above, for Patricia Hill Collins (2000) the term "interlocking systems of oppression" refers both to macro-level connections that are linking systems of oppression and to micro-level processes within interlocking structures of oppression. The first includes, for example, the connections of race, class, sexuality and gender, while the second describes the ways in which individuals and groups occupy a social position within the oppression. The focus in the previous section was on the micro-level. In this section, my aim is to take the analysis a step further and investigate how the macro-level connections of gender, religion and nationality are linked with systems of power in the context of Tibet under Chinese rule. In order to do that, I discuss and analyze the lived experiences shared by the nuns in light of previous studies, in the context of other material I collected during my fieldwork, and within the framework of intersectionality.

Following Collins, I focus on different domains of power and the ways in which the dimensions of oppression are constructed and maintained structurally, disciplinarily, hegemonically and interpersonally. As can be remembered, for Collins, any particular matrix of domination – or the general organization of hierarchical power relations in a society – is organized through these four interconnected domains of power. Each of the domains also serves a specific purpose. According to her, "individual biographies are situated within all domains of power and reflect their interconnections and contradictions" (Collins 2000, 306; see also Pelak 2007, 2).

The structural domain of power covers social institutions[1] that are organized to reproduce subordination. These wide-ranging, interlocking institutions include, for example, the polity, law, religion, family, legal system and economy.

The central motives given by the nuns for donning the robes included various social institutions or institutionalized practices that were seen as especially disadvantaging for Tibetan laywomen. In Tibetan society, traditional institutions such as marriage, family, the distribution of work, education practices and religious bodies have traditionally organized and continue to order the subordination of Tibetan women. Furthermore, in the context of contemporary Tibet under Chinese rule, the Chinese polity, its laws and economic systems can be seen as disadvantaging Tibetan women in multiple ways: as women, as Tibetans and as religious practitioners. In what follows, I look at these more closely.

Endless Work and Limited Opportunities for Education

The kind and amount of work done by women in traditional Tibet varied according to geographical location, the livelihood they practiced, and the social class they belonged to. In the urban noble families of Central Tibet, where the men were often government employees or practiced trade, the women stayed at home to take care of the family. In rural areas in southeast and northeast Tibet, where nomadism and agriculture were the main sources of livelihood, the women worked long hours doing household chores and agriculture, animal husbandry and trade (Thonsur 2003, 324–325).

The traditional modes of livelihood still seem to prevail. Therefore, for most of my informants, life before nunhood was filled with work. Their duties included household chores inside and outside the home, farming and/or herding. Women milk female yaks, produce and maintain the family's food supply, and do other housework (see also Wu 2013, 49). Many of the nuns mentioned that tending after the animals was particularly tiresome.[2] They also had to look after their younger siblings,

---

1. Social institutions are complex social forms that reproduce themselves. These include, for example, governments, the family, human languages, business corporations, legal systems, etc.
2. In the Tibetan regions, children usually start herding when they are eight or nine years old. Herders leave in the morning and only return in the evening. Herders are also often alone all day, and there is no protection against rain, sleet, hail and wind (Wang 2009, 71). The herding life is thus made more difficult by harsh natural

their siblings' children, or take care of their aging or sick parents or grandparents.

The nuns gave various reasons for the fact that they were mostly uneducated but the main reason seemed to be that their help was needed at home. In fact, their situation was reminiscent of that in traditional Tibet where women were not educated as often as men, since it was thought that women, whose main duties involved serving the husband and the children, did not need education. The sources of education in traditional Tibet were Buddhist monasteries and their affiliated colleges or institutions, which provided religious education and general literacy. While it was a common practice for a family to send one of their sons to a monastery, it was not that common to send a girl to a nunnery. In addition, secular schooling in Tibetan regions in the early twentieth century was mainly accessible by the children of aristocrats (Bangsbo 2008, 191–193; see also Thonsur 2003).

The situation changed after the Chinese takeover in the 1950s. The number of secular schools also increased in the rural areas, and particularly after the introduction of the new economic policy in the 1980s, there has been significant progress in the educational development of the Tibetan areas. With the passing of the Compulsory Education Law in 1986, China introduced an educational system that required every child from the age of six or seven to undergo nine years of schooling (Bangsbo 2008, 194; Wang 2009).[3]

While the Tibetan regions have received a modern educational system extending from primary school to higher education, most rural schools in Tibet have had a very low enrolment rate, especially of girls (Kalsang Gyamtso 2008; Wang 2009). There are various reasons for these low attendance rates. Among the most important reasons are the teachers' poor teaching skills, the scarcity of educational material, and school fees. Ellen Bangsbo also mentions that some parents regard the school curriculum as irrelevant or indoctrinating and prefer to keep their children

---

conditions. Whatever the weather conditions, nomads have no choice but to milk and herd (see Goldstein and Beall 1990).

3. Nevertheless, there is still a large gap between the educational attainment of Tibetans and ethnic Chinese, and even between Tibetans and most other minority nationalities in the People's Republic. For example, by 1990, less than 20 percent of Tibetans in the TAR had received a primary school education. This figure increased to 42.3 percent by 2005. Nevertheless, the illiteracy rate in the TAR was still as high as 44.8 percent in 2005. This is the highest among the Western provinces and regions of China and much higher than the national illiteracy rate of 11 percent (Kalsang Gyamtso 2008, 150; Wang 2009).

at home.⁴ The recently raised requirements for teacher qualifications in rural schools have resulted in the closing of village schools. This has obliged very young children in Tibetan rural areas to attend boarding schools at the township level located some distance from their homes (Bangsbo 2008, 202). Among the most important issues is language instruction. Officially the Central Government has always supported the policy of Tibetan-medium education, but in practice this has never been fully implemented (see Wang 2009).⁵

Thus, the Compulsory Education Law notwithstanding, most Tibetan women in rural Tibet are not educated for more than two or three years maximum, if at all, and many of them cannot read and write (Chertow 2008, 160). In the mid-nineties, Charlene Makley noted that despite central and provincial government efforts, illiteracy rates for Tibetan women were extremely high, reaching 80–90% in rural areas. According to Makley, among the reasons were families insisting on keeping girls at home to work and the number of women cadres being still small, compared to men (Makley 1999, 176–177). According to Wang Shiyong's estimation, at least 60% of Tibetan females in the Qinghai Province are illiterate (Wang 2009, 17). Despite compulsory education, the idea still prevails in Tibetan culture that educating a daughter is not as important as sending a son to school. While there is a new generation of educated Tibetan men and women who have been fortunate to attend school, after basic schooling only a few Tibetan students manage to continue their studies. There is very little vocational training currently being offered.⁶ One of the few available options is to train as a teacher. The university fees are high, however, representing a burden to many families (Hyytiäinen 2008, 116–117; Kalsang Gyamtso 2008, 151–152).

---

4. She also mentions that up to 500 Tibetan parents each year choose to send children between the ages of six and thirteen to attend Tibetan schools in India run by the exile Tibetan authorities, such as Tibetan Children's Villages (TCV) (Bangsbo 2008, 199, 202).
5. The language of instruction in most primary schools in the Tibetan areas is Tibetan but in secondary schools mostly Chinese. Secondary schools in Tibetan are present mainly in the Tibetan areas outside of the TAR, especially in Qinghai Province. According to Kalsang Gyamtso, there is no universal policy to assess which language should be the main medium of instruction for Tibetan speaking students. The choice of language is often made by the individual local leaders (Kalsang Gyamtso 2008, 152–154).
6. By 2005, at the national level, 38.3 per cent of citizens had a junior secondary education and 12.4 per cent had a senior secondary education, while in the TAR these numbers were only 8.4 per cent and 2.1 per cent respectively, the lowest level in the People's Republic (Wang 2009; Kalsang Gyamtso 2008).

Even if a woman is educated and has a career of her own, she normally continues to take care of family matters. I once interviewed a university teacher who, after the interview in her office at the university, had to run home to cook lunch for her husband and children. This pattern recurred in every family I visited: even if the woman worked outside the home, she also had to take care of her family and its needs.

New Economics and Tibetan Poverty

Aside from the new education requirements, the advent of the Chinese regime has brought considerable changes to the traditional Tibetan means of livelihood. The Seventeen Point Agreement signed in 1951 states that Tibet's agriculture, animal husbandry, industry and trade are to develop gradually in accordance with the actual conditions of Tibet. Because of this policy, the traditional economic pattern remained nearly unchanged between 1950 and 1959 (Wang 2009, 86).

The 1959 uprising, however, ended the relative internal autonomy of the Tibetan areas. The Central Government decided to implement a "democratic" reform, which mainly consisted of land distribution and abolition of what China called serfdom. The socialist transformation was soon accompanied by the Cultural Revolution (1966–1976) and the commune system. The introduction of communes drastically altered traditional economic and social patterns, which for Tibetans meant considerable poverty and misery (Wang 2009, 86–88).

In the early and mid-1980s, rural communes and state farms were dissolved and the household responsibility system was introduced. Land was generally divided equally among all the members of the commune on a one-time basis. As a result, living standards and general economic conditions improved (Wang 2009, 90; Goldstein et al. 2002, 34; Goldstein et al. 2003).

Despite the positive changes, the considerable gap between eastern and western China remained. In order to narrow the gap between poor western China and the rich eastern part of the country, China implemented the so-called "China Western Development Policy" (Ch. *Xibu Daikaifa*) in 1999. The policy covers six provinces including Gansu, Qinghai, Sichuan, and Yunnan, and five autonomous regions, including the TAR. The main mechanisms of the policy include the development of infrastructure (transport, hydropower plants, energy, and telecommunications), the enticement of foreign investment, efforts in ecological protection (such as reforestation), the promotion of education, and the retention of talent that would otherwise flow to richer provinces. As a result of these actions, Tibetan living standards and general economic conditions started to improve. The actual impact of these modernizing efforts is, however, subject to much debate (Lahtinen 2010, 119–121; Wang 2009, 93; 2008).

Thus, despite the improvements, compared to other parts of the People's Republic, there is still a massive difference in the Tibetan standard of living. In general, poverty in China is highly regional. The northern and western provinces, including Xinjiang and the TAR, are poorer than the provinces in the east. Poverty is also much more common in rural areas than in the cities. An average city dweller, for example, is three to six times richer than a person living in the countryside (Kallio 2005, 76–77; see also Wang 2009; Lahtinen 2010). When it comes to natural and energy sources, China's border area is among the richest in the country.[7] Despite this, in an economic sense they are the backwater. What has led to the poor economic situation is the fact that the regions are geographically and climatically harsh, sparsely populated and poorly educated. Chinese economic policy alignments are also among the reasons (Luova 1999, 137; Wang 2009).[8]

According to Wang, when the Tibetan regions are compared to other parts of China, the gap in the standard of living is enormous. Thus, while one of the main aims of the Western Development Program has been to diminish the gap between west and east, it has grown even wider. The gap not only exists between different regions and provinces, but also between rural and urban areas, particularly in the TAR. Given the fact that the overwhelming majority of Tibetans live in rural areas, only a limited number of urban Tibetans are able to enjoy the benefits of economic growth (Wang 2009, 33, 94, 96).

The Chinese government has moved millions of people to its frontiers. As a consequence, during the 1990s, the number of ethnic minorities in

---

7. In total, over one hundred minerals, including gold, silver, copper, iron, aluminum, antimony and lithium, have been discovered in the Tibetan regions (Wang 2009, 15).
8. Wang Shiyong's (2009) research focuses on the question of why the Tibetans do not effectively participate in the market in the context of China's economic development process. He comes to the conclusion that there are various political, social, cultural as well as environmental factors that explain the difficulties met by Tibetan communities. According to Wang, Tibetans face very similar problems and challenges when it comes to modern life despite the fact they live in five different large administrative regions in China. Wang is of the opinion that in order to promote local people's participation in the market, local conditions should be taken into consideration. This has not been done in the Tibetan areas but the economic development policy in these regions is nearly always an attempt to replicate the inland model and open up markets (Wang 2009, 16).

the labor market started to decrease in western China due to the migration of the Han Chinese. It has been argued that migration to western China has led to the marginalization of ethnic minorities, who have increasingly had to choose between non-profitable traditional livelihoods and unemployment (e.g., Luova 1999, 136; Luova 2005, 53, 65; Asikainen & Vuori 2005). The migration of Han Chinese has thus made the position of the ethnic minorities even more difficult, as rural Tibetans have to compete with tens of thousands of Han and Hui migrant laborers.

According to Goldstein et al. (2002, 36), two of the most constant complaints heard from Tibetan villagers they studied in Central Tibet were related to the difficulties they encountered when they tried to find work. Wang is of the opinion that the biggest challenge faced by Tibetans in the modern economic environment is their lack of a proper education. Despite the attempts to improve education, there is still a large gulf between the educational attainments of Tibetans and the Han Chinese majority, as well as between Tibetans and other ethnic minorities (Wang 2009, 18).

Even though China has attempted to bring wealth and well-being to the Tibetan regions, the nuns I interviewed considered their family background to have been poor or moderate at most. Not a single nun thought of herself as coming from a wealthy family background. My data is not extensive enough to offer wide-reaching conclusions on how economic status overlaps with other oppressive dimensions in the lives of my nun informants. Nevertheless, it can be noted that all of the nuns from the TAR considered their family background as poor, while those from the Amdo part of Sichuan, for example, estimated their family's economic status to have been moderate. There were no major differences between the nuns from the Kham and Amdo parts of Qinghai, but nuns from the Kham region more often considered their family background as poor.

In order to understand how the changes brought about by the Chinese state had altered their lives, I asked the nuns about any possible changes that had taken place in their birthplaces in recent years. Many of the nuns interviewed were unable to name any changes in their birth areas. The inability to name any changes may have to do with the fact that many of the nuns used to, and still tend to, have a highly localized lifestyle. Because they had not seen many other places, they were not able to compare the periods between then and now. Most nuns also came from remote rural regions typically populated only by Tibetans. Thus, their contact with the Han Chinese majority or other minorities was limited. While some nuns did mention that living conditions had improved the improvement in the living conditions has been more than anything else a result of digging and selling caterpillar fungus.

In addition to the improved living conditions, some of the nuns mentioned the growth of their birthplace and specifically the government-implemented changes to livelihoods. Environmental degradation has been a serious problem since 1950, when the government initiated modernization efforts in the Tibetan areas. Among the many reasons for this, including natural and human activities, overgrazing is a major problem (Wang 2009, 32). Accordingly, the state has the right to intervene in herders' livelihoods in order to protect the environment of the rangeland (Costello 2008, 82; Wu 2013, 51). Animal husbandry is limited today to certain areas, and trees have been planted to prevent erosion. Instead of moving four times a year, nomads now move twice a year, in winter and summer. Nomads have also been forced into settlements built by local governments, or they have moved into towns and cities on their own (Wu 2013, 50–51). According to Susan Costello, while the problems of population growth and environmental degradation are common everywhere in modern China, the Tibetan pastoral areas suffer more than other places. Among the reasons are the unsuccessful family planning policy, which is discussed below, and the lack of other work opportunities, as discussed above (Costello 2008, 82).

It can be suggested that traditional institutions that structure the distribution of work and educational practices still prevail in the Tibetan societies. Tibetan women have never been secluded from society and work, but have been an important labor force in the traditional livelihoods practiced by Tibetans. The fact that women's work is not limited to household chores, for example, has meant that women are burdened with multiple tasks. Interestingly, while women are qualified to work along with men, they have much more rarely been considered competent enough to be given an equivalent education.

The interviews with the nuns brought up various reasons why they were not sent to school: because of their gender; because they were the youngest or oldest and had to stay home to take care of family matters (especially if they were the oldest or youngest and also unmarried, their parents preferred to keep them at home); and because their family was poor (leading them to be withdrawn from, if they were sent there at all). Finally, the likelihood for them to be sent to school depended on the area they were from. Thus, the opportunity to attend school depended not only on their gender, but on how it intersected with age, family background, social status and place of origin.

The new educational opportunities and requirements imposed by China have advantaged the younger generation of Tibetan people. Nevertheless, the improvements have not always reached Tibetan women, because parents still prefer to send their sons, not daughters, to school. Distrust toward Chinese people is also among the reasons for not sending children to school.

While China has brought about many changes that have affected the traditional livelihoods and economics, traditional livelihoods still prevail. In addition, attempts to raise Tibetans out of poverty have not been successful for the various reasons given above. As a consequence, if we look at the status of Tibetan women, it can be seen that it depends not only on gender and traditional gendered practices, but also on the ways that traditional livelihoods and the new laws and economics intersect in their lives. In some cases, the intersection of traditional livelihoods and market economy, for instance, may have produced wealth and new opportunities, while in others they may have led to deeper poverty and marginalization. In general, among the nuns I interviewed, poverty and marginalization seemed to be more common.

Marriage and Motherhood

In Tibetan culture, the roles of wife and mother are the most acceptable social roles for women. Nevertheless, the interviews with the nuns revealed that a wish to avoid family life – and, chiefly, marriage – were among the most important motives to don the robes. Despite the fact that only two of my nun informants had been married before becoming a nun, all of the nuns I interviewed had a very negative view about marriage and family life. My lay informants also assumed that many women become nuns because they want to avoid marriage and motherhood.

Previous studies have often emphasized the flexible marriage conventions and high female autonomy of Tibetan society. Depending on the area, Tibetans have traditionally practiced, and still practice, monogamy, polygyny, and polyandry. Polyandry was mostly practiced among nomads, with a woman marrying two or more brothers from the same family.[9] The lineage of the family usually followed a patriarchal system, but in some areas, such as the Kongpo[10] region, the lineage of the family was arranged according to a matriarchal system, meaning that the mother was the head of the family and owned the property while the sons married outside. The marriage of widows and divorce were not uncommon and, according to Thonsur, women were not stigmatized by divorce or widowhood (Thonsur 2003, 326–327; Makley 1997, 14).

---

9. This practice does not indicate a high status of women. It was usually followed in order to avoid distribution of wealth outside the family.
10. Kongpo (*kong po*) was an area of southeastern Tibet in the premodern period.

While there are different marriage conventions in the Tibetan cultural area, ranging from monogamy to polyandry and polygyny, as well as patrilocal and matrilocal residence systems, the social arrangement mainly follows monogamy and patrilocal residence (on Amdo in particular, see Wu 2013, 106–107).[11] Traditions of marriage, particularly the preference for the patrilocal residence system, can be seen as putting sons and daughters into unequal positions.

Tibetan marriages were traditionally arranged by the families, and this practice is still followed, especially in rural areas. According to Wu Qi, for instance, self-determined marriage is gradually growing in Amdo regions, but it has not replaced arranged marriages in remote areas of Amdo (Wu 2013, 125). When choosing a suitable candidate, family reputation and social background as well as economic status are considered important. As I stated previously, my informants also mentioned that that a girl's outer appearance and personal reputation had a role to play. However, as one of my informants claimed, there are no such requirements when it comes to the looks of a man. According to Wu, many Tibetans in Amdo also continue to pay a bride price in arranged marriages, and the price is higher today than it was in the past. Giving a dowry is also a common practice in many regions of Amdo (Wu 2013, 104, 140).

Tibetan families are usually extended families with three generations living under the same roof. Following tradition, one of the siblings normally stays with the childhood family and takes responsibility for the aging parents, grandparents and the house, including the cattle and the fields. If the offspring is a boy, he usually settles down in his childhood home with his wife and children. However, if the offspring is a female she marries out or stays unmarried in her childhood home. My informants did not mention matrilocality as an option or as an actual practice among their families (see Wu 2013, 106, 111).

While Tsering Norzom Thonsur, for instance, has claimed that Tibetan women have not been subjected to harassment or abuse because of their gender, it should be acknowledged that physical violence is not unknown in Tibetan families. Makley has noted that it is difficult to measure the extent of violence against wives among Tibetans. Based on her observations in Amdo, she claims that actual violence against wives was fairly

---

11. Charlene Makley has noted the important fact that the main social and property-holding unit in Tibet has been the household, not the lineage. For this reason, less moral weight has been put on female chastity as a guarantee of paternity. A variety of marital arrangements were possible in order to preserve a household's holdings across generations (Makley 2002a, 60).

rare, particularly in the nomadic and more remote farming regions. It seems, however, that incidents of wife-beating have increased in urban settings (Makley 1999, 231; see also Wu 2013, 170).[12] Furthermore, many of my informants mentioned marital abuse and violence. My Tibetan female friends also talked often about infidelity. Without exception, husbands rather than wives were considered potential betrayers.

Divorce is not desirable, but it is not uncommon in the Tibetan areas. After divorce, both partners are free to remarry. Compared to nomads, farmers are said to be more conservative about a woman joining the family with children from a previous husband. According to Wu, a woman over 40 years of age has relatively slight chances of remarrying. Remarriage of widows and widowers is controversial because many Tibetans today assume that a widow is an unclean person and that her negative karma caused her to lose her beloved one in this life. According to Wu, this is probably because of Chinese influence on Tibetan culture (Wu 2013, 168, 171–174). As my informants stated, it is much easier for a divorced man to find a new wife than for a divorced woman to find a new husband. The same holds for widows: some thought that a female widow is a bad omen and thus cannot be married. It is not uncommon, therefore, for a widow to become a nun. It is thought that she does not have any other options, and this assumption has led to the oft-repeated notion that all women become nuns out of desperation.

In Tibetan culture, marriage is expected to lead to the birth of children. Tibetan families have traditionally been large, and despite the Chinese policy that restricts the number of children families still tend to be big (see Goldstein et al. 2002; see discussion below). The reasons for families having a large number of children are tradition, religion, and the limited use of contraception. Children have traditionally been an important part of the workforce in the family and a necessary bulwark for the aging parents. Contraception is not usually forbidden in Buddhist traditions and societies, and it can even be seen as a kind of "skillful means."[13]

---

12. Makley is of the opinion that this has to do with the fact that in urban families, women have found employment outside the home and thus expect the right to also participate in forms of public recreation, like men. For husbands, beatings have thus been a way to reassert male dominance in the family (Makley 1999, 231).
13. For example, the 14th Dalai Lama has stated that basically the purpose of sex is reproduction, but he has also stated that birth control measures should be adopted in order to "ensure the quality of life today in developing countries, and to protect the quality of life for future generations" (Keown 2005, 67). However, there can be reservations around certain types of contraception, such as those that prevent a fertilized egg from remaining in the womb.

Contraception that prevents ovulation or fertilization completely is, at least in theory, more acceptable (see Keown 2005).[14]

Goldstein et al. have shown in their study of the TAR, however, that more than 50 percent of the married Tibetan women they studied began to use contraception only after they had four or more children. The scholars thus noted that a somewhat paradoxical situation existed: both high fertility and the relatively high use of modern contraceptive methods coexist in rural areas. According to Goldstein et al., this is partly explained by the relatively short time that intensive family planning had been operative by the time of the research. The large number of children was also explained by women's attitudes towards having a big family. According to women, the number of children was based on income; thus, the more prosperous the household, the more children were welcome (Goldstein et al. 2002, 32–33).

Apart from practical reasons, ideological factors are important for the large number of children in a family. Abortion is considered a serious act lacking skillful means. This negative attitude toward abortion is based on the Buddhist doctrine of rebirth, the ideology of nonviolence, and the belief that being born as a human is very rare. According to the doctrine of rebirth, karma causes rebirth after rebirth. Consequently, conception does not mean the beginning of personal existence but its continuity. From the viewpoint of Buddhist ethics, therefore, there is no difference between an unborn fetus and an already born person and, at least in principle, the abortion of a fetus is karmically as serious as killing a child or an adult. In addition, abortion is thought to bring negative merit to everybody who is involved in the process (see Florida 2000; Keown 2005). While children are often desired and very much loved, mothers are seen as encountering endless suffering in life because of, for instance, miscarriage, infant mortality, and spousal abuse (see also Gutschow 2004, 137).

The nuns interviewed came from the families with 2 to 13 children, an average number being six children in a family. About half of the nuns studied had still two parents alive at the time of the interview but those who had lost a parent, a mother had been lost more often than a father. My nun informants thus clearly saw family life with children as causing a lot of suffering. In fact, two of the most common reasons for becoming a nun were the avoidance of marriage and motherhood. It can be noticed

---

14. The study by Goldstein et al. (2002) from the TAR shows that of 515 currently married women aged 25–44, 52.6 percent reported that they were using contraception, as were 58.1 percent of the currently married women aged 30–44. The most common method used by women aged 25–49 was an IUD (34 percent), followed by sterilization (tubal ligation) (31 percent), Norplant (19 percent), pills (13 percent) and injections (3 percent) (Goldstein et al. 2002, 32).

that many young girls become nuns just before they reach a marriageable age. The average age of becoming a nun of the nuns I studied was 27 years. However, a closer investigation shows that most of them had become nuns as teenagers between the ages of 14 and 20. The biggest group was those who had become nuns when they were 18 years old, followed by groups who had become nuns at the age of sixteen or twenty. The age of my informants becoming a nun is in accordance with previous studies, according to which Tibetan women become nuns before or during their twenties. When examining the age of becoming a nun and the place of birth, it can be noted that my informants from Ü-Tsang became nuns in their early teens, while girls from the Amdo region joined monastic life a little later in their teens. Girls and women from the Kham regions appear to have become nuns at different ages. The age of becoming a nun may be a strategy for avoiding the traditional marriage institution and motherhood, which are so clearly perceived as disadvantaging Tibetan women.

It can be concluded that while gender is important for the unequal distribution of power in marriage and family life, there are also other factors. The girls' desirability as a candidate for marriage depends, for example, on her family's social and economic status. Girls from poorer families have less say in choosing their husbands and less power if the husband becomes abusive. Her life as a married woman depends on her husband, of course, but also on the family she marries into. Aside from marriage, motherhood was seen as an important source of suffering. Interestingly, Goldstein et al. (2002) noted that the richer someone was, the higher the number of births in their family. In this way, economic status importantly converges with the number of children.

Unequal Buddhist Institutions

> In Tibet, men have a higher position than women. Girls don't find a job; they can't do anything. Tibet has this tradition. Monks have more power than nuns. If I was a monk I could go anywhere, to Lhasa or to India. But I'm a nun and I can't go. Monks should have a great dream. They can become famous and knowledgeable. As a nun I can't have this kind of dream.
> (IN2007/12)

Intersections of major institutional practices such as distribution of work in traditional livelihoods, marriages, and new institutions introduced by the Chinese state can be seen as disadvantaging Tibetan women in many ways. As a result, it is not surprising that nunhood that is ideally free from a lay life attracts some Tibetan girls and women. Nonetheless, when my informants finally became nuns they found themselves at the bottom of the hierarchy of the monastic institution. As Gutschow put it, "nuns do not flee society so much as join an alternative or transcendent form of society" (Gutschow 2004, 191).

As the interviews above show, for the nuns monastic ordination did not mean full-fledged membership in the monastic institution or getting away from a gender-based unequal distribution of power. The full monastic ordination is not available for Tibetan nuns, and the highest status they can acquire is that of a novice nun. Among others, Gutschow has argued that the most significant differentiating factor between monks and nuns is precisely their disparate levels of monastic ordination. Karma Lekshe Tsomo is also of the opinion that the status of nuns within the Buddhist traditions in general correlates with their ordination status. Thus, where the full ordination as a *bhikṣuṇī* is available, the nuns' level of education and status within the society also tend to be higher.[15] Where the novice ordination is available to nuns, women are recognized as members of the order but not treated equally with men. Where not even novice ordination is an option, as is the case in most Theravāda countries, nuns have a secondary and often subservient role, relative to the monks, in the religious sphere (Tsomo 1999b, 9; Carbonnel 2009; Bunnag 1973; van Esterik 1982; see also Harvey 2005).

After becoming a nun, it has to be decided where to continue monastic life. Ideally, it is actualized in a monastery or a nunnery. Despite the revitalization of monastic life in the Tibetan regions, there are still far fewer nunneries than monasteries. Since there are not many nunneries to enter into, many of the nuns had no other choice but to stay with their natal families. Staying at home usually meant that, despite her monastic status, the nun continued to work for the family as before.

Some of the nuns interviewed were lucky enough to join a nunnery or a nuns' community. Even if this was for many of them a much better option than staying in their natal home, living in a nunnery did not mean freedom from problems, especially those related to their livelihood. The biggest and wealthiest nunneries offered the nuns a monthly allowance, but many were dependent on their natal families and the benevolence of the laity. One of the problems was that the family often lived too far away to be able to meet the daily needs of the nun and the laity preferred donating to monks.

Many of the nuns shared the hope of receiving an education in monastic life. In fact, many of the nunneries I visited had just been reopened a few years previously and had started some sort of study program for

---

15. See, for example, Eichman's study on prominent Taiwanese nuns.

the nuns. Nevertheless, the education in the nunneries was still not something to be taken for granted. Partly because of the basic level of their religious and spiritual education, most nuns are not awarded the title of lama, and they are seldom recognized as the reincarnate tulkus of previous great teachers. All of the people I interviewed agreed that these religious authorities were extremely important for the Tibetans. Despite that fact, for most, a female lama or *tulku* was unheard of. A few, however, mentioned that significant female figures are not called lamas, but "khandromas" (*mkha' 'gro ma*, Skr. *ḍākinī*). Nevertheless, only a few had heard of or knew any khandroma. There are, nonetheless, some female incarnations recognized by a particular lineage, by a certain monastery or nunnery, or by the local community, such as the female incarnation I went to look for in Hainan (Havnevik 1989, 81; see above). Since monasteries were founded with the spiritual and administrative guidance of these religious authorities, the lack of female lamas means that nunneries are usually sub-branches of monasteries, where males are often their heads (Gross 1993; Havnevik 1989).

The nuns I interviewed were from all of the four main schools of Tibetan Buddhism. The nuns belonging to the Kagyu, Sakya and Nyingma schools lived in nunneries and received religious or at least some sort of elementary education in the nunnery. The nuns that belonged to the Geluk school, however, lived in nuns' communities. One also lived by herself and one with her family. The monastic status of the nuns thus seemed to also depend on the school they belonged to.

Finally, in addition to the crossing of gender and traditional institutions and practices in religious and monastic life, the status of the nuns in monastic life today depends on the Chinese state, as I clearly showed in the previous chapters on the nuns who left Tibet. From the Chinese point of view, monks and nuns are usually held in utmost suspicion, and the Chinese government restricts the number of monastic institutions and the number of monastics. In some areas, it also interferes with the religious and communal life of the monastic institutions. This is done, for example, through patriotic education.

– 9 –

Internalized and Forced Discipline

The disciplinary domain of power manages power relations through routinization, rationalization, and surveillance. According to Collins, the goal is to create "quiet, orderly, docile, and disciplined populations" (Collins 2000, 299). The disciplinary domain of power is also a form of surveillance which is internalized. For Collins, the disciplinary domain of power refers particularly to the organizational practices of social institutions, and it relies more than anything on bureaucratic hierarchies and techniques of surveillance. She claims that this realm of power has become more important with the growing significance of bureaucracy in modern social organizations. Nonetheless, I also see (traditional) cultural practices, beliefs and expectations as powerful means for disciplining people's behavior.

In traditional Tibet, power relations were mainly regulated by religious institutions and internalized cultural traditions. As is the case in many other Buddhist societies, the history of Buddhism, monasticism and politics in Tibet were closely intertwined (Kvaerne 1984, 255). According to Melvyn Goldstein, by the twentieth century, monasteries and monastic people had become inseparable from the idea of the prosperity of the Tibetan nation and civilization. The relationship between the state and the central monasteries was reciprocal: the biggest monasteries were expected to help the central government maintain its power in return for the support and protection given them by the government. It was believed that the real measure of superiority and uniqueness of Tibet as a nation was its number of monks, and it became the goal of the 13th Dalai Lama's government to recruit as many boys to monkhood as possible (Goldstein 1997, 14, 16; Goldstein 1989, 8–10, 23, 816).

By authorizing monastic and lama institutions, the state monitored power relations that were routinized and rationalized over time. The close relationship between religious and political power made it difficult to question the prevailing power systems. Tibetan traditional society was thus relatively homogeneous when it came to managing power relations.¹ The advent of the Chinese regime dramatically changed the disciplinary domain in the Tibetan society.

Tibetans as an Ethnic Minority

Today Tibetans are one of the 56 ethnic minority groups (Ch. shaoshu minzu) in the People's Republic of China.² This means that, on the one hand, as Chinese citizens, they fall under the institutional practices and organizations of the Chinese state.³ On the other hand, however, the Law on Regional Ethnic Autonomy (Ch. Minzu Quyu Zizhi), which was passed in 1984 and revised in 2001, gives them, along with other ethnic minorities, rights to administer their internal affairs within designated autonomous areas, practice their customs, speak their language, and follow their particular religious beliefs.⁴ The laws also guarantee minorities greater control over local economic development than allowed in non-autonomous areas, the right to manage and protect local natural resources, and the right to organize local public security forces to maintain public order. Nevertheless, the higher authorities must approve any measure or regulation to exercise autonomy, which means that the autonomous areas do not have independent self-governance (Lahtinen 2010 98–100; Luova 1999, 136).

The Chinese government's attitude toward ethnic minorities is highly ambivalent. On the one hand, ethnic minorities have quotas and other benefits. Ethnic minorities that live in the rural areas are entitled to

---

1. This is not to deny that there were different kinds of governance systems in different areas of traditional Tibet.
2. The term "ethnic minority" refers to all ethnic groups other than the Han. Comprising 106 million people and 8.4 percent of the total population, ethnic minorities are concentrated in the twelve western provinces. In particular, the autonomous regions have large populations of ethnic minorities (Lahtinen 2010, 50, 70).
3. The government system of the PRC includes the Constitution, the National People's Congress (NPC), the State Council and the Communist Party. The governing system is a top-down organization that involves both political and administrative functions, which are imposed by the central government on all lower levels of administration in China. The autonomous regions have their own local governments and more legislative rights; nevertheless, the Party Secretary, who is Han Chinese, has the real power in all autonomous regions (Lahtinen 2010, 50, 59).
4. The status of ethnic minorities in China has changed according to the political alignments of the central government from forced assimilation to moderate tolerance. The reformist politics started by Deng Xiaoping in the 1980s meant that ethnic minorities had more freedom to exhibit their distinct national features.

have two to three children, for example. There are also regulations that give minorities educational and economic benefits, such as quotas at educational institutions and loans at a low interest rate. With these prerogatives, the Chinese government attempts to keep minorities satisfied with their position and quicken the development of the minority regions (Luova 1999, 136–137; Lahtinen 2010, 71).

On the other hand, the separation of any territorial units from the nation is strictly prohibited. In order to promote the establishment of Han Chinese values, to strengthen the military and governmental grasp of the regions, and to intensify the exploitation of natural resources, the Chinese government has moved millions of people to the frontiers. The Communist Party of China (CPC), which is the ruling party, holds power at all levels and in all localities in China, including the ethnic autonomous regions. With some exceptions, autonomous governments rarely exercise their theoretical right not to implement the policies of the central government. Thus, regional autonomy is often seen merely as a political façade to disguise Han dominance (Luova 1999, 136; Lahtinen 2010, 73).[5]

Tibetan Women under Scrutiny

When the Tibetan nuns I studied are considered from the viewpoint of the disciplinary domain of power, it can be seen that they are governed and disciplined, but also surveilled as women, as Tibetans, and as religious practitioners.

According to Collins, the disciplinary domain of power relies chiefly on bureaucratic hierarchies and techniques of surveillance. It can, however, be argued that institutional practices of the structural domain of power define and "order" the ways in which individuals are expected to behave. In other words, individuals internalize cultural and communal expectations and shape their behavior according to the prevailing norms. Thus, a Tibetan girl is more often expected to take part in the domestic work in family life than to seek education. The multiple workloads of Tibetan women are not questioned, either. The role as a hard-working laywoman is expected to be internalized. Cultural practices such as marriage are

---

5. For criticism on this topic, see Zheng (2010), according to whom, "in the western world, the Tibet issue has been extensively discussed in the context of human rights and 'universal' constitutional principles, but rarely in the context of Chinese constitutional law."

accompanied with certain codes of behavior that are often put into practice without questioning.

It can be suggested that the shift from traditional Tibetan disciplinary practices to those managed by China through its bureaucracies has often been directed at Tibetan women and their bodies. The most obvious has been the family-planning policies. Serious accusations have been made about the Chinese government practices of coercive family planning in the Tibetan regions. It is claimed that China has imposed strict birth limits and has forced women to undergo abortions and sterilization. In the mid-1970s, when family planning was introduced in the TAR, it was targeted at Han Chinese couples and Han Chinese married to Tibetans. These couples were allowed to have two children, but the restrictions were not strictly enforced. In 1983, a family-planning policy that allowed a couple to have two children was also applied to urban Tibetan cadres and workers in government enterprises. Finally, in 1984, the birth limits were extended to rural Tibet, such that Tibetan farmers and herders in Central Tibet were allowed to have only three children (Goldstein et al. 2002, 27–28).

Beginning in the early 1990s, however, the government started to put greater emphasis on family planning in the rural areas as part of a program that attempted to alleviate poverty by the year 2000. It retained the previous 1983 limit of three births per woman for rural areas and extended the two-child birth limit to all Tibetans in the urban sector, as well as to rural township-level officials. For the first time, coercion was used in the rural areas in the form of disincentive programs. Fines and penalties were given to the households of women who exceeded the three-child limit (Goldstein et al. 2002, 28–29). Ani Sherab from the TAR recollected the birth policy this way:

> They [the Chinese] also implemented the three-child policy to all Tibetan women in our area. But luckily my mother had already given birth to eight children before this policy. The penalty would have been 1,000 RMB if more than three children were born to a family. [...] This was around 1990. They [the Chinese] had hired doctors from abroad and they did surgery for free. Since we are Buddhist, such a three-child policy was new in our world and we didn't dare to bear it. So, some of the women ran away to the mountains to avoid this policy.

While the central government's campaign increased family planning in the rural areas, it was not strictly enforced by Chinese standards.[6]

---

6. Goldstein et al. have argued that it is not sufficient to analyze family planning by only studying government regulations. At all levels (prefecture, county, rural township, work unit, etc.), there is considerable flexibility regarding how to

For example, a shortage of funds and personnel made it difficult to put into practice. Nevertheless, according to Goldstein et al., the new family-planning campaign was met with considerable voluntary acceptance by rural women and their families (Goldstein et al. 2002, 32). Either way, my research shows that apart from five nuns, the rest of the nuns interviewed came from families with more children than allowed by the official policy. The biggest group was that of nuns whose families had five children, while the following groups were those with four or eight children in the family. China's one-child policy was relaxed to a two-child policy in the end of 2015. In 2021, the government announced that all married couples were allowed to have as many as three children.

While "premodern" Tibet should not be considered a closed or unchanging entity, its first large-scale encounter with "modernity" only came with the new Chinese rulers in the second half of the twentieth century.[7] According to Jennifer Marie Chertow, women participate in the project of modernity by serving the needs of the cultural dominant. She claims that Tibetan women have been used as markers and participants in China's nation-building project within a Communist vision that aims to bring about "dialectical historical change through rapid modernization and industrialization of its 'backwaters.'" (Chertow 2008, 148–149, 156). Chertow writes:

> Public media, both state and non-state, construct a newly gendered, classed, and racialised subject-citizen: "Tibetan woman". She bears traditional culture and stands at the forefront of formations of Chinese modernity, signified by state socialism, and Western modernity, signified by neo-liberalism.
>
> (Chertow 2008, 151)

Tibetan women are thus increasingly made as an object of development initiatives in the present practices of the state and state-approved, international non-governmental health projects. Women hold a central

---

implement regulations. Individual prefectures and counties were given substantial autonomy in deciding how to proceed. Many factors, such as the distance from a county seat, the availability of medical facilities at county hospitals and the eagerness of county and rural township leaders, have influenced how the campaign has been implemented (Goldstein et al. 2002, 27–29).

7. Attempts by the 13th Dalai Lama to "modernize" Tibet in the 1920s with the introduction of Western-style education, the creation of a standing army, Tibetan currency and a postal service were largely unsuccessful, mainly due to the opposition of the powerful Buddhist monasteries (see Samuel 1993; Smith 1996).

position in these development projects, which aim to "modernize" the health care system (Chertow 2008, 156).⁸

While the Chinese state in particular has been seen as using Tibetan women to signify modernity and tradition, according to Charlene Makley, the Tibetans she studied had also renegotiated gender relations in post-Mao Labrang. Makley argues that as the Tibetans in the region had entered a new era of identity politics in which "authentic" Tibetanness was both highlighted and challenged, the gender difference had become particularly important. Thus, since the Tibetans were excluded from authority over land use and law enforcement within the political borders of the nation-state, gender difference had become a key arena for the (re)construction and contestation of a "cultural frontier" in Labrang (Makley 1999, 108). Makley suggests that these changing cultural politics of sexuality had different consequences for men and women. Tibetan women's bodies – their labor, reproduction and sexualities – became a site of resistance to and regulation of change. Women were, for example, expected to refrain from inappropriate heterosexuality and to show this in their discrete speech, dress, and physical distance from laymen and monks, as well as from monastics' spaces (Makley 2002b, 606). Thus, according to Makley:

> as Tibetan men's sexual agency expanded in unmarked ways to meet modernity, Tibetan women's sexuality was increasingly marked and curtailed in order to maintain the integrity of Tibetan households and sacred places.⁹
>
> (Makley 2002a, 91–92)

Tibetan Nuns under Inspection

According to Makley, it was precisely the body of a nun that was seen as challenging the gender ideals that structured the community under the threat of assimilation. She claims that the nuns' monastic androgyny ironically reminded of the Communist-imposed androgyny. This

---

8. NGOs play an important role in supplementing the inadequate poverty alleviation, health care, and education services of local governments, and they have therefore been accepted to some extent (Lahtinen 2010, 43).
9. Wu Qi interestingly writes that many Tibetan Amdo women are more conservative than men regarding clothing. Many of his research participants believed that this had to do with the tradition according to which a woman should have a sense of shame about whatever she does and says, and that this affects her choice of clothing. In other words, women should not expose their bodies as a man does (Wu 2013, 60).

is because both posed a threat to the household-monastery system by claiming that difference of sex was irrelevant and encouraging women to move out of the household. According to Makley, this explains why nuns who challenged the gender ideals of the community were the objects of particularly intense contestation and scrutiny (Makley 2005, 260, 278, 283).

My interviews with lay Tibetans and nuns showed that compared with monks, the morality of nuns was more under inspection. As I mentioned previously, parents expressed worries when a girl declared her wish to become a nun. One of the concerns was her reputation. In a citation above, a layman told how he had met a nun who was pregnant without even knowing it. Many other incidents implied that the nuns themselves tended to guard their reputation more carefully. While I often had lunch or dinner with some monks I knew, the nuns repeatedly refused to enter public restaurants with me. If they did, they often refused to eat anything. For me, this signaled the internalized discipline and modesty that they were expected to follow as female monastics.

The nuns were also surveilled in their monastic life. Five of the nuns I interviewed had left Tibet because of the Chinese control policies put into practice particularly in Tibetan monastic life. With their close connection to Tibetan nationalism (discussed below), some Tibetan monasteries and nunneries have become highly suspicious in the eyes of the Chinese, and the central government has taken tighter control of Tibetan monastic and religious life. The number of nuns and monks is restricted and candidates under 18 years of age are not allowed to join monastic life. The Chinese government has also attempted to regulate the Tibetan system of reincarnation.

The disciplinary domain of power manages the power relations that regulate the lives of Tibetan nuns as women, as religious practitioners and as Tibetans who live under the rule of the Chinese state. As Tibetan women, they can find themselves as representatives of both tradition and modernity. As female religious practitioners, they are observed by other Tibetans. And as Tibetan religious practitioners, they are monitored by the Chinese state.

– 10 –

Hegemonic Ideologies and Doctrines

The aim of the hegemonic domain of power is to justify practices in other realms of power. This field of power includes, for instance, ideology, culture, and consciousness. Collins argues that by manipulating ideology and culture, the hegemonic domain connects social institutions (structural domain), their organizational practices (disciplinary domain), and everyday social interaction (interpersonal domain) (Collins 2000, 302).

The hegemonic domain of power in Tibet has traditionally included particularly religious teachings. These, along with cultural conceptions, have forcefully shaped ideas about women and the feminine. Today, traditional ideas are competing with ideas of modernity and secularism promoted by the Chinese state. Consequently, contemporary concepts of gender in Tibetan culture are a complex mix of both religious and cultural beliefs, as well as Chinese and Western ideas concerning gender.

Four Doctrinal Layers of Tibetan Buddhism

Tibetan Buddhism is founded on the doctrines of early Buddhism, Mahāyāna and Vajrayāna.[1] Accordingly, in addition to the sūtras corresponding to those of the Theravāda Pāli Canon, the Tibetan Canon – the Kangyur (bka' 'gyur) and Tengyur (bstan 'gyur) – contains Mahāyāna sūtras, Indian commentarial literature and tantras developed later. In addition to the doctrines and practices of these three vehicles (Skt. yāna) of Buddhism, a wealth of folk beliefs and practices can be found in Tibetan Buddhism. Furthermore, the several orders and schools of Tibetan Buddhism have many particular doctrines, which give them

---

1. By early Buddhism, I loosely refer both to pre-sectarian Buddhism and to those schools into which the Buddhist monastic saṅgha initially split. Despite my generalizing use of the concepts, I acknowledge that "early Buddhism" along with the categories of "Theravāda," "Mahāyāna" and "Vajrayāna" are not unambiguous or homogeneous.

each a distinctive character (Samuel 1993; Powers 1995).² According to Georges Dreyfus (2003), the Tibetan Buddhist tradition contains four "layers" that interact and overlap.

The first layer, the "Hinayāna,"³ consists of the basic teachings of early Buddhism, including the *Four Noble Truths* (Skt. *ārya-satya*). According to these truths, suffering in cyclic existence (Skt. *saṃsāra*) is inevitable and caused by our craving. It is, however, thought to be possible to overcome suffering through Buddhist practices, such as morality, concentration, and insight. *Nirvāṇa*, the final spiritual goal of early Buddhism, is described both as the cessation of suffering and as a peaceful and supramundane state (Dreyfus 2003; Harvey 2005).

Along with most Buddhist traditions, Tibetan Buddhism emphasizes the impermanence of conditioned reality and the inevitability of suffering and death. Living beings who have not achieved nirvāṇa (Tib. *mya ngan 'das pa*), that is, the enlightenment of a buddha (Tib. *sangs rgyas*), are subject to a continuous, painful cycle of rebirth, or *saṃsāra* (Tib. *'khor ba*). This rebirth, whether as a human or in a divine or infernal state, is determined by the force of one's past meritorious and demeritorious actions, or *karma* (Tib. *las*). Rebirth and karma, as well as their associated moral systems, are important in Tibetan Buddhism and the Tibetan worldview. The initial stages of the Buddhist teachings strongly emphasize death and rebirth as motivations for practice. One must turn from worldly activities to religion by taking refuge in the *Three Precious Jewels* (Tib. *dkon mchog gsum*): the Buddha, his teaching (Tib. *chos*), and the religious community (Tib. *dge 'dun*). Often one's spiritual teacher, *guru*, is mentioned as a fourth refuge (Dreyfus 2003, 18; Powers 1995).

These fundamental Buddhist teachings and practices are combined with the second layer, the ideas and practices contained in the Mahāyāna (Tib. *theg chen*), which grew soon after the time of Emperor Aśoka, sometime between 150 BCE and 100 CE (Lamotte 1984, 60; Harvey 2005, 89). A massive body of texts was produced within the Mahāyāna tradition, but it is possible to define three main features: focus on the *bodhisattva* ("an awakening being"), new formulations about the doctrine of emptiness (Skt. *śūnyatā*), and a new cosmology that saw the Buddha as a glorified and transcendent figure (e.g., Harvey 2005). To elaborate on

---

2. The main schools of Tibetan Buddhism are Geluk, Kagyu, Nyingma (*rnying ma*) and Sakya. Sometimes Bön is counted as the fifth school.
3. Hinayāna, literally meaning the "Smaller Vehicle," is often contrasted with Mahāyāna, which means the "Great Vehicle." It is a pejorative term that should be avoided.

these, the ideal of the *arhat*[4] of early Buddhism was replaced by the figure of the *bodhisattva*, who forgoes his/her own enlightenment in order to lead others to liberation. To achieve this superior goal, the *bodhisattva* must develop particularly strong compassion (Skt. *karuṇā*) and enter the path described as "the perfection vehicle" (Skt. *pāramitāyāna*). This consists of the gradual and extremely long cultivation of six perfections (Skt. *pāramitā*): generosity (Skt. *dāna*), ethics (*śīla*), patience (*kṣānti*), effort (*vīrya*), concentration (*dhyāna*), and wisdom (*prajñā*) (Dreyfus 2003, 18–19; Powers 1995; Samuel 1993, 224–225).

One of the primary qualities that *bodhisattvas* train is the direct realization of emptiness, or the "perfection of wisdom" (Skt. *prajñā-pāramitā*). The philosophical view of emptiness (Skt. *śūnyatā*) was first formulated in the early *Abhidharma* literature. The early doctrine of emptiness stated that all phenomena lack an essence or self and are dependent upon causes and conditions. The Mahāyāna further developed the concept of emptiness by stating that all phenomena are said to be empty because they are "dependent arisings" (Skt. *pratītya-samutpāda*; Tib. *rten cing 'brel bar 'byung ba*) (e.g., Harvey 2005, Dreyfus 2003).

The new understanding of emptiness that denied the inherent existence of any object of mental attention implied that to understand the true nature of samsaric phenomena was to attain *nirvāṇa*. It was declared that the early "Hinayāna" understanding of nirvāṇa was based on a "category mistake," because due to the emptiness of all phenomena there is fundamentally no real difference between *samsāra* and *nirvāṇa*. Instead, the state in which one lives is a result of one's perceptions. Accordingly, if suffering is the result of false perception, enlightenment indicates that a person has "awakened" from the sleep of ignorance which keeps beings trapped in the cycle of birth and death (Powers 2006, 40, 153). According to the Mahāyāna, there is no fundamental difference between the Buddha and other sentient beings because everyone possesses the same capacity for enlightenment. Thus, whereas earlier Buddhist texts state that most people lack the ability to follow the path to nirvāṇa, the later Mahāyāna texts contain the idea of the buddha-nature of all beings (Harvey 2005, 95, 121; Mills 2003).

This Mahāyāna view led to several further developments in the presentation of buddhahood. According to the Mahāyāna, the historical Buddha Śākyamuni was not the first buddha, nor will he be the last. In the Perfection of Wisdom literature of the Mahāyāna, the Buddha became a cosmic figure whose wisdom surpasses that of all humans and gods. The

---

4. A person who has destroyed all mental defilements and afflictions and has thus become freed from cyclic existence.

new *sutras* also contained passages that provided the foundation for a theistic and devotional interpretation of Buddhism, centered on the cult of deified buddhas and bodhisattvas (Harvey 2005).

The Mahāyāna sūtras, along with Indian commentarial literature, form the primary source of philosophy in Tibetan Buddhism.[5] These emphasize the buddha-nature (Skt. *tathāgata-garbha*, Tib. *de bzhin gshegs pa'i snying po*) of all beings, the altruistic motivation of a bodhisattva, and the emptiness of all things (Tib. *stong pa nyid*), including *samsāra* and *nirvāṇa*. Tibetan Buddhists, both laypeople and monastics, are thus encouraged to cultivate compassion (Tib. *snying rje*) for all living beings. One is to embark upon the path of a *bodhisattva* (Tib. *byang chub sems dpa'*) and to develop the *pāramitās* (Tib. *pha rol tu phyin pa*), including wisdom (Tib. *shes rab*) of emptiness (Dreyfus 2003; Samuel 1993; Powers 1995).

The third layer of Tibetan Buddhism consists of esoteric texts and the ideas and practices found in the tantras (Tib. *rgyud*) (see Dreyfus 2003, 19–20; Samuel 1993, 224–225). Around the seventh century CE, a form of Indian Mahāyāna Buddhism developed which saw itself as a new, more powerful "vehicle" to salvation. The new vehicle, Vajrayāna, was based on a large body of texts called tantras, which were said to have been taught by the historical Buddha to a select group of disciples, who then passed them on (Harvey 2005, 133–134). Tantras adopted the same basic structure as the Mahāyāna *sūtras*, but presented a complete worldview with its own philosophy, cosmology, and practices (Powers 2006, 215). Often referred to as the "Diamond Vehicle" or "Mantra Vehicle" of Buddhism, tantric Buddhism uses rituals, symbols, mantras and visualizations, both for the realization of enlightenment and for the creation of supernormal ritual powers (Mills 2003, 12).

According to the tantric worldview, reality is essentially pure but this fact is hidden from ordinary sentient beings. Suffering is a result of fleeting delusions which do not affect that purity. The aim of tantric practice is to reveal and actualize reality's pure potential. One begins the practice through a relation with a tantric teacher, a guru, who plays a particularly important role. The guru is seen as a fully enlightened being who introduces his disciple to the pure nature of reality through an act of empowerment.[6] Tantric practice is organized into two distinct stages. The first is that of *generation*, consisting of practices involving identification with a tantric deity (Tib. *yi dam*) in order to actualize the qualities of the buddha in oneself. The second is the stage of *completion*,

---

5. For a detailed description of Mahāyāna doctrine, see Williams (1989).
6. Empowerments are usually understood as consecrations through which one enters into tantric practice.

consisting of yogic practices aimed at manipulating and controlling subtle physical energies in order to produce the luminal state of awareness. It is assumed that under these conditions, the mind is free from its usual conceptualizations and is able to remain in a non-dual state (Dreyfus 2003, 19–20; Mills 2003, 92–93). It is also believed that the tantric methods of the Vajrayāna offer the possibility for a more rapid attainment of enlightenment, perhaps within this present lifetime. Hence, a "serious" Tibetan religious practitioner will normally undertake Vajrayāna practice (Samuel 1993, 204, 275). Tantra may also be practiced for worldly and instrumental purposes in order to develop various miraculous powers (Dreyfus 2003, 20).

The fourth layer found in the Tibetan Buddhist tradition is a non-canonical layer of folk religion. It consists of practices such as possession, exorcism, divination, healing, retrieving life force, the worship of mountain and lake deities, and so forth (Dreyfus 2003; see a more elaborate presentation in Samuel 1993). Particularly important in the formation of the fourth layer has been Bön. It has now absorbed many Buddhist practices and doctrines, and it is sometimes considered as the fifth main school of Tibetan Buddhism today (Samuel 1993). The fourth layer – or folk religion – is relatively similar in many traditional Buddhist cultures (see Spiro 1970). In Tibet, the relationship between doctrinal Buddhism, based on sūtras and tantras, and folk religion is considered especially close because of the importance of tantra in folk religion (Dreyfus 2003, 20).

Buddhist Ideas of Female and Feminine

Various ideas about women and their religious potential and opportunities can be found in the interviews. Becoming a monk is believed to bring a great amount of merit, both to the ordained person and to his family (see also Goldstein 1997, 14–15; 1998a, 16–17), but the lived experiences of the nuns showed that the family was often highly suspicious when a daughter expressed her wish to join monastic life. Many laypeople also assumed that the nuns somehow had dubious motives to join monastic life. Their possibilities to advance on the religious path were seen to be limited. Furthermore, in monastic life, the nuns were less often asked to perform religious services and thus were less supported by the laity. As argued by Gutschow, the status of the nuns in a Tibetan society implies that nunhood is not seen as an important field of merit.

Because religious traditions and doctrines are seen as justifying the submission of women, feminist research on religion has often focused on religious doctrines in order to explain women's "lower" status. The most important set of beliefs that has shaped the conceptions of femininity and masculinity in Tibet since the seventh and eighth centuries is Tibetan Buddhism. Consequently, explanations for the lower empirical position of Tibetan nuns have been sought particularly in the Buddhist texts (e.g., Horner 1975 [1930]; Paul 1979; Falk 1980; Gyatso 1987; Willis 1987; Gross 1993; Harris 1999; Hae-ju Sunim 1999; Wilson 2001).

The conceptions of woman and the feminine in Tibetan Buddhism reflect both the doctrines of the *sūtras* and the tantras, which inherited many prevailing ideas about the female sex from Indian culture. For example, the erotic goddess who tempts the male ascetic is a common theme in Indian mythology (Havnevik 1989, 23-24). According to I. B. Horner, the first Buddhist texts were mostly written down by men at the time when the position of women had already started to decline after the time of the Buddha (Horner 1975 [1930], 50). In the Vedic period (c. 1900-550 BCE) and around the point that Buddhism was born in India, women were relatively independent. By the beginning of the Classical time (550 BCE-550 CE) and as brahmin priests gained in power, however, the independent status of women had started to decline (Havnevik 1989, 22-23).

Elizabeth J. Harris (1999) has examined female images in five Nikāyas, or Sūtra-Piṭaka collections, from the Pāli Canon. According to her, women and the feminine are presented on two levels: one is symbolic and the other is as real, living women. Symbolically, a woman is presented as a temptress, as a mother and as divine or sacred. First, the impurity of women is emphasized. Her biological processes, such as menstruation, are seen as polluting. A woman symbolizes impermanence, suffering and an obstacle to renunciation. The Buddha is reported to have said: "Womenfolk are uncontrolled, Ānanda. Womenfolk are envious, Ānanda. Womenfolk are greedy, Ānanda. Womenfolk are weak in wisdom, Ānanda" (Harris 1999, 50).

Lorna Amara Singham (1978) has noted that the first step in renunciation is to disengage oneself from the sensual pleasure embodied by women. Women thus represent something that is at the same time the most wanted and the most rejected. Their capability to give birth and perpetuate the karmic cycle is connected to a lay life, which in Buddhism symbolizes grasping. Accordingly, the female gender is connected to sensuality, desire and attachment, and it implies suffering, death and rebirth. The Buddhist cosmogonic myth about gender differentiation and the formation of society in the Pāli Agañña-sutta ("Knowing the Beginning") illustrates how previously androgynous, asexual and identical beings were polarized into two different sexes when they ate soil

– the symbol of the feminine. Consequently, the return to monastic life implies returning to an androgynous and asexual state (e.g., Gross 2005).

Second, according to Harris, a woman is presented as a mother. As a mother she symbolizes birth, reproduction and mature, self-sacrificing love. In particular, she is praised when she gives birth to a son. Nevertheless, motherhood is not idealized in early Buddhism; it is most of all connected with suffering. Occasionally, virtuous laywomen are idealized as caring wives and mothers, and their female beauty and fertility are celebrated (Harris 1999, 53–55).

Third, a woman represents a mystic or a goddess, who has acquired spiritual knowledge and wisdom. Such women who have rejected stereotypical female roles as mothers and as the objects of desire are therīs, or female saints, in early Buddhism (Harris 1999, 60–61). An early Buddhist collection on the *therīs*, the Therīgāthā, is a collection of short poems that was supposedly recited by members of the Buddhist saṅgha in India around 600 BCE. It is believed to have been written mainly by women. The Therīgāthā is seen to contain various sections that support the idea of similar possibilities for men and women to advance on the spiritual path (see Hallisey 2015).

Among the most central questions related to the female gender is the question of enlightenment in the female body. Harris (1999) and Nancy Falk (1980), for instance, argue that the suttas in the Pāli Canon regard the woman-man dichotomy as irrelevant because of the fundamental oneness of everything. Early Buddhism thus emphasizes the insignificance of gender in spiritual matters and contains an idea of their equal opportunity to reach enlightenment. In canonical texts such as the Therīgāthā, there are various examples of women achieving *nirvāṇa*. Nevertheless, the early Buddhist texts are also ambivalent when it comes to the spiritual capacities of women. They include, for example, lists of obstacles faced by women. For this reason, buddhahood is considered to be possible only for men. Even the possibility of becoming a *bodhisattva* is sometimes denied women because one of the physical marks of the *bodhisattva* is the male organ (e.g., Gross 2005).

Liz Wilson (2001) has researched stories found in the hagiographical literature of early Buddhism. In the stories, monks use the female body metaphorically in order to portray the consequences of sensuality. Being more corporeal, the nuns function as a means for creating monastic institutional androgyny. According to Wilson, the nuns in the texts who rejoice as they count the imperfections of their bodies have learned to see themselves from the male point of view (Wilson 2001, 42, 58).

The Mahāyāna literature varies widely in its portrayal of the female sex. It includes highly negative attitudes toward women's spiritual potential, but also sections that grant her a religious role equal to that of a man. The Mahāyāna includes all of the previous ideas of the female found in early Buddhism. In short, three main ideas can be found. First, women are presented as temptresses and as the daughters of the Buddhist demon, Māra. As mysterious, sensual and destructive, they need male control. Second, women are viewed as mothers. In this role, they symbolize pain, suffering and grasping, but also compassion. Third, the feminine is symbolically connected with *prajñā-pāramitā* (perfection of wisdom), which is represented by the female goddess Prajñāpāramitā (Paul 1979; Gross 1993).

In principle, the bodhisattva path is seen as being available for both men and women. The texts are no consistent, however, in their treatment of the question of the level of bodhisattva a woman can achieve before becoming a man. Diana Paul (1979) has classified the Mahāyāna texts into three different types: 1) those texts that deny women the opportunity to enter the buddha-fields (such as the Pure Land Sūtra); 2) the majority of *sūtras*, in which a woman is a lower-stage bodhisattva; and 3) those few texts in which a woman is a spiritually advanced *bodhisattva* and close to buddhahood (Paul 1979, 169).

The question of the woman's capabilities is further complicated by the episodes of gender transformation found in the Mahāyāna texts. Gender transformation episodes have been explained in many ways. In the simplest, they can be seen as an attempt to refute the traditional idea of a woman not being capable of achieving buddhahood or even the state of a higher-stage *bodhisattva*. Alternatively, the episodes have been translated in light of the Mahāyāna philosophy of emptiness, according to which "male" and "female" are only conventional categories (e.g., Gross 2005). Hae-ju Sunim, for example, is of the opinion that the Mahāyāna texts where a woman transforms herself into a man do not reflect sexism, but are examples of the skillful means by which the absurdity of gender discrimination is demonstrated (Hae-Ju Sunim 1999, 138).

The negative conceptions of women found in early Buddhism, as well as in the Mahāyāna, are often contrasted with the Buddhist tantras, which are filled with positive ideas and symbols of the body and the feminine. The Buddhist tantric texts share the idea of the possibility of enlightenment in this life, regardless of a person's karma and gender (see Havnevik 1989, 32; Ray 1980, 228–229). While the *sūtras* present grasping and desire as the primary reason for suffering, in the tantras the energy of desire is harnessed in the striving for higher spiritual goals. According to the tantras, the body, sexuality and emotions are the key components in this effort. Sexual symbolism, and occasionally sexual intercourse,[7] therefore have a central role in tantric practice, in which union of the masculine (representing method/skillful means) and the feminine (standing for wisdom) is pursued. This union is believed to lead to the realization of the emptiness of all phenomena. The union of the masculine and the feminine is often depicted in Buddhist iconography by the sexual union of a buddha and his consort. As the physical body becomes the vehicle for enlightenment, the female principle is no longer conceived of as something to be transcended (e.g., Gross 1993).

According to Reginald A. Ray (1980), for example, the image of female *siddhās*[8] presented in the traditional tantric literature is highly positive. They are depicted as "insightful, dignified, courageous, independent, powerful, and creative." This is the case, even in spite of the fact that there were always far fewer women tantric practitioners than men and that only occasionally were great teachers female (Ray 1980, 228, 241). Miranda Shaw (1994), who has investigated the position of women in Buddhist tantric texts, commentaries and oral tradition, claims that a striking feature in the tantric literature is its respectful attitude toward women. She criticizes the view that the role of women in tantric sexual practices was merely as partners and passive objects. On the contrary, she claims that women actively created tantric doctrines, rituals and yogic practices from the beginning of the tantric movement. Consequently, she argues that while tantric Buddhism emphasizes gender polarity, this should not be taken as evidence of the exploitation of women. Instead, this should be seen as promoting the complementary nature of men and women, as well as the view of women as the source of spiritual power. She further claims that the appearance of female buddhas in tantric iconography had a positive impact on the position of women because it showed that buddhahood could be reached in the female body (Shaw 1994).

Rita Gross (1993) agrees with Shaw and claims that the fundamental doctrine of tantric Buddhism is that there is ultimately no difference between female and male, and both are equal in their capacity to attain enlightenment. This becomes evident, for example, with the enlightened female protectors and spiritual guides, *ḍākinīs* (Tib. *khandroma, mkha' 'gro ma*), and popular female *bodhisattvas*, such as the gentle Tārā and the esoteric, wrathful Vajrayoginī (Tib. Dorje Neljorma, *rdo rje rnal 'byor ma*), who is visualized in the highest form of yoga tantra (Gross 1993).[9]

---

7. The rite is carefully controlled through yogic techniques.
8. Those practitioners of tantra who have attained realization.
9. It is difficult to judge how much these active and dynamic female images in fact serve as examples and a source of positive inspiration for Tibetan women.

Tsultrim Allione (1984), however, has claimed that the gender relations in the Indian tantric tradition changed radically when it arrived in patriarchal Tibet: the dynamic female aspect of Indian tantrism became a male character, whereas the female became associated with emptiness and wisdom. June Campbell (2002) puts forward a particularly negative view of the gender ideology in Tibetan Buddhism, claiming that the emptiness associated with women led to their transcendence in terms of fulfilling the social and psychological needs of men. She claims that ideas of the Buddha and the divine lama-king replaced the symbolic female subject and female goddesses, who became merely mothers or spouses of the buddhas. The existence of the female gods and symbols does not, in her view, guarantee a living female tradition or a positive symbolism for living female practitioners.

Ulrich Timme Kragh (2011) has argued that because the tantras were primarily written by men, they reflect an androcentric view. According to Kragh, the tantric biographies are most often about men, while women are depicted as ethereal *dākinīs* encountered by men in dreams and visions. He claims that female tantric partners are elevated as *dākinīs*, who are above the patriarchal norms and outside prevailing, conventional gender relations. Furthermore, in tantric Buddhism, the breaking of conventional rules is sacralized. In other words, the aim is to transcend dualistic thinking by transgressing social taboos and conventions (for example, by means of intercourse, eating meat and drinking alcohol). Kragh thus asks if exalting women as pure and divine is forceful precisely because it inverts conventional expectations, according to which women are inferior and impure.

Previous textual studies have often characterized the conceptions of women in Tibetan Buddhism as contradictory, ambivalent, or as Alan Sponberg (1992) has argued, multivocal.[10] These characterizations bespeak the heterogeneity of the historical textual material, but can also be seen as a reflection of the great variety of theories, methods, and approaches brought to bear on its analysis. It may be asked, then, to what extent the perceived ambivalence of these conceptions is, in fact,

---

10. According to Sponberg, multivocality does not necessarily mean conflict or doctrinal confusion within the tradition, but rather tells about social, intellectual and practical challenges encountered by the early Buddhist community. Sponberg (1992) names four different orientations toward female and feminine that can be found in the Buddhist texts. First, *soteriological inclusiveness* indicates that everybody (i.e., men and women) can reach enlightenment; second, *institutional androcentrism* places nuns below monks in the monastic hierarchy; third, *ascetic misogyny* can be found in the texts that see women as threatening the spirituality of men; and finally, *soteriological androgyny* refers to tantric Vajrayāna.

ultimately a result of the efforts of finding a definition for a complex phenomenon, which in itself is not amenable to exhaustive assessment. Here, too, intersectionality could offer a framework by which the potential pitfalls of such over-arching approaches could be avoided

Cultural Conceptions of Women

Above, Makley argued that religion should be seen as completely integrated into the everyday workings of social life. (Traditional) Tibetan gender beliefs are also a complex combination of religious doctrines and cultural ideas concerning gender. To start with, female rebirth is widely considered as a lower birth in Tibetan Buddhist societies. This is evident in the common Tibetan word for a woman (skye dman), which literally means "lower birth." According to the Tibetan scholar Tsering Chotsho (1997), the etymological examination of words such as *pho* (referring to male) and *mo* (referring to female) shows that these words were not coined with discriminative perception and that both men and women in early Tibet enjoyed the same rights and equality. Tsering Chotsho is of the opinion that discrimination against women originated only during the time of King Songtsen Gampo, when the geographical and cultural expansion of Tibet led to interracial marriages and cultural exchanges with Nepal and China. As a consequence, terms were coined with a tone of comparison based on gender, and women were denoted by words such as *skye dman* and *nag mo* (the black one) (Tsering Chotsho 1997, 59–63).[11]

Barbara Nimri Aziz (1987) has claimed that being "born low" is institutionalized from the beginning of a girl's life in Tibet. According to Aziz, parents are not happy about the birth of a girl, and girls fare worse than their brothers. A girl must start working at an early age, while her brother is sent to school. A teenage girl is often sent to help a needy relative, whereas a boy is sent to serve a monk uncle and thus has a much better chance of becoming educated (Aziz 1987, 81–82). The notion that parents are not happy about the birth of a girl is not fully supported by my informants who largely agreed with the idea that differentiation between boys and girls starts only after they have grown up. I once talked with a 22-year-old female college student from Amdo about gender differences in Tibetan culture. She claimed that Tibetans prefer having a son because they think that compared to boys, there will be more suffering in a girl's life. The reason for this is that girls have menstruation, they have to give birth, and they have to do all the housework. I asked if

---

11. A common word that refers to woman is *bud med*, "absence of protuberance."

Tibetan boys do any housework at all. The female student said no, men and boys go to work. She also mentioned her mother, who sometimes asked her husband to help her with housework. In practice, however, the mother had to take care of the housework in addition to her own paid job outside the home. The female student thought that this was not fair, and she hoped to find a husband who would do housework. "It's our shared home, after all," she said.

A young Tibetan female friend of mine, who came from a nomadic family but was educated and is working as a teacher, once said to me:

> We consider women's life very difficult and pray that whenever someone dies he or she will be reborn as a male. If a lama predicts that the person who died will be reborn as a female, people cry. When I think of the word "woman," I feel sad because women are so low and they have so much work. There's never time for a nomad woman to relax, to sit down and chat with relatives. There's always some work to do, to serve other people ... So no one wants to be born a woman.[12]

My friend's comment is very similar to that of a female informant given by Gutschow (2004, 214-215). The woman stated:

> Oh yes, women are sinful and impure. We are more miserable than men because, as we say, wherever you look, men seem to be having a better time than women. Most men work less than women do, the men's work is easier, and men can spend all day sleeping while women hardly get a chance to rest for an instant. We women have to cook the meals, do all the housework, wash clothes and things, take care of the kids, and then go to the fields, and again in the evening cook another meal. We women are just plain unlucky because, as they say, we still have not removed prior bad karma.

According to Gutschow, female birth is thus considered a punishment by Tibetans, and the suffering experienced by women is explained by their bad deeds in previous lives. The limited possibilities of women to improve their position are also attributed to negative actions carried out in their prior lives. According to Gutschow, Tibetan proverb states that women lag seven lives behind men, in other words, they have to accumulate seven lives more merit before they can be born as a male. According to this view, women need more merit than men because they are more likely to fall into lower rebirth in their next life. Most Tibetans also believe that a woman has to born as a male before she can progress on the Buddhist path (Gutschow 2004, 16, 212; see also Makley 1999, 116).

---

12. Personal discussion. My female friends and assistants were very eager to share their own ideas about Tibetan culture and gender.

According to Gutschow, purity and impurity are also gendered in Tibetan discourse. Whereas the "solid" male body represents purity and sacredness, women who menstruate and are capable of giving birth are potentially polluting and also prone to pollution themselves. Having a female body is considered a misfortune because it is more vulnerable to sickness, misuse and rape. The bodily impurity is also considered to reflect the mental capacities of women: they are said to be envious and greedy and to be obsessed by anger and lust (Gutschow 2004, 202, 208–209). Tibetans argue that women are not excluded from reaching enlightenment, but their physical and social suffering makes it desirable for them to be reborn as men (Havnevik 1989, 29, 146–147).

While it was common for my Tibetan informants to consider women's life as more difficult, the 36-year-old highly educated woman from Amdo, Qinghai told me that she did not agree with this idea. She said:

> Maybe for some people it's really difficult, but usually... I really don't understand that... I've heard some foreigners saying that Tibetan women's life is very difficult or men are like this, but we don't think so. We are in this society. So, we don't feel that many difficulties or that it is hard. Maybe we are already accustomed from a young age. In general, maybe in some places – of course, like in nomadic areas or in farming areas – sometimes women are ... but they still enjoy their lives in their position. If you think about yourself, as you become this person, this position, I don't think you think, "Oh, my life is so hard." They still make jokes and enjoy their lives. Maybe nuns always say that they don't want to get married or that life is so hard, but of course they don't have a child and they don't have a family and they are more independent and it's easier. In the nomadic and farming areas, women also enjoy their lives. So, I think every people have their own ideas. With their family, of course, it's sometimes very difficult and sometimes it's happy ... I think like this.
>
> (IN2011/12)

It can be suggested that the intersection of different religious and cultural conceptions promotes very negative ideas of Tibetan women as females and as religious practitioners. As argued by Havnevik, these ideas mean that, for example, the moral integrity of nuns is doubted. Some Tibetans believe that women are more emotional and because they are therefore unstable, they are unable to keep their monastic vows or advance on their religious path (see Havnevik 1989). While such perceptions are very common, they are not shared by everyone, of course. The quotation of the laywoman I just presented, for example, shows that social, economic and educational status may play a considerable role in perceptions of Tibetan women.

State-Controlled Programs of Modernity and Secularism

> Domination operates by seducing, pressuring, or forcing African-American women, members of subordinated groups, and all individuals to replace individual and cultural ways of knowing with the dominant groups' specialized thought – hegemonic ideologies, that in turn justify practices of other domains of power.
>
> (Collins 2000, 306)

In political terms, China is a one-party state whose power rests with the Communist Party of China (CPC). Since the Communist party came to power in 1949, Marxism and its Chinese interpretation in the thought of Mao Zedong (1893–1976) have been the essence of the ruling ideology (Lahtinen 2010, 31).

A central aim of the Chinese minority politics has been to lead minorities toward the state of development of the Han Chinese. According to Communist theory, reaching a common state of development would lead to the assimilation of different nationalities into one Chinese nation.[13] (Luova 1999, 137). China has thus justified Tibetan occupation by its modernizing efforts, which are believed to bring wealth to the Tibetan people. According to the official Chinese discourse, agreements were made in the 1950s between the 14th Dalai Lama's government and the central government of the PRC for the peaceful liberation of Tibet and "for bringing Tibet to the era of the state-controlled programs of modernity" (Adams 1996, 516). The invasion was largely justified by the idea of Chinese cultural and social superiority, as well as the belief that minor nationalities could not develop culturally or economically without the assistance of the "advanced nationality," the Han Chinese. Radical socio-economic reforms were introduced to help "backward" Tibet progress (e.g., Wang 2009, 41–42; see also Smith 1994, 1996; Samuel 1993).

In 1966, Mao began the "Great Proletarian Cultural Revolution" in order to hasten the elimination of all the traditional values of the "old" society – old ideas, old culture, old customs and old habits.[14] Religious

---

13. Western scholars have found similarities between Western colonialism and Chinese regional politics. The Western Development policy is seen as an attempt by the central government to promote the prosperity of the underdeveloped frontier for the benefit of the whole country. Migration is thus part of China's internal colonialism (Luova 2005, 67).
14. According to Ronald Schwartz, Chinese assumptions about Tibetan backwardness reflect China's own ambivalent relationship with modernity. In China, "constructing itself as a nation has involved overcoming its own perceived backwardness, while at the same time regarding political and economic domination by imperialist

institutions became a key target. Following traditional Marxist theory, religion was seen as a flawed worldview, which was produced in response to certain external forces. These forces kept religion alive and had to be removed through "revolutions, education, and science" (Yu 1971, 49). Traditional religion and culture were thus seen as remnants of the old feudal society that needed to be destroyed in order for Tibet to fully embrace Maoist socialism. Communist attitudes toward religion continue in official views. Thus, traditional culture is labeled as problematic because it represents all that was "backward" about the old, feudal China and because Buddhism continues to be seen as the principal source of the "exploitation of the masses."

The attempts by China to bring Tibet into the era of "modernity" had considerable implications for Tibetan traditional society, which was predominantly based on religious institutions. The Chinese government considered the Tibetan monasteries as a great obstacle to modernization. As secular officials removed religious rulers from power, monasteries became politically and economically insignificant institutions. Furthermore, the religious training given by monasteries was largely replaced by the modern Chinese educational system. Furthermore, increasing tourism has meant that Tibetan cities such as Lhasa have been transformed from religious centers into commercialized tourist attractions with shops, restaurants and karaoke bars. As governance, education, welfare and community organizations are taken over by secular agencies, traditional religion has fewer social functions in Tibetan society and religion is increasingly being relocated into private spheres of life. Also, improved communication, urbanization, and Chinese migration have destabilized local Tibetan communities, where religion has traditionally been located. The lives of the Tibetans have become increasingly dominated by the Chinese nation state (Lam 2006; Härkönen 2009).

It could be safely argued that many of the processes associated with "secularization" have occurred in Tibet.[15] Some scholars have also interpreted this forced institutional secularization as signifying a decline

---

      outsiders as chiefly responsible for its retarded development in comparison with the West" (Schwartz 2008, 3–4).

15. Whereas scholars of secularization do not agree on whether religion is in decline or not, most accept that macro-level social changes in modernizing societies give religion a different social role than it once had. Thus, ideological changes, along with the rise of modern science and technology, capitalism, industrialization and urbanization, are seen as altering the place and nature of religious beliefs, practices, and organizations, while also reducing their relevance for the lives of nation-states, social groups, and individuals (Bruce 1996, 362; Bruce 2002, 2; Eriksen 2001, 297–298; Casanova 1994, 21).

in Tibetans' engagement in religious practices and beliefs. For example, the anthropologist Vincanne Adams (1996) suggests that Lhasa Tibetans today are more interested in social mobility and economic security than in their religion. It is also claimed that the younger generation of Tibetans has become "less attached to the lamas and other religious figures," thanks to a new education system that supports the learning of Mandarin Chinese and values compatible with CPC ideals (Adams 1996, 530; Lam 2006, 2).

While secularization, at least to some extent, seems to have occurred at the institutional level, religion appears to have maintained its importance in the lives of individual Tibetans. This is evident in Tibetan nationalism, where religion plays a central role. Its importance was also emphasized by all of my informants.[16] The confusion of institutional secularization with the anticipated consequences that the process has on religion largely appears to be behind the dispute between the Tibetans and the Chinese. Thus while China expects that modernization and economic development will make religious practices irrelevant in the lives of Tibetans, economic development and improving living standards have not won over the hearts of Tibetans and have certainly not eroded the significance of religion (see Schwartz 1994, 228; Wang 2008, 29).[17]

When Tibetan women and nuns in particular are viewed in the (Chinese) hegemonic domain of power, it can be suggested that they live in the crossfire of different and competing hegemonic ideologies. As religious women, they are sometimes considered as embodying Buddhist ideals but nevertheless less capable than monks when it comes to practicing Buddhism and advancing on their spiritual path. As Buddhist nuns, they represent the "backward" Tibetan traditional culture for Communist and modern China, but as Tibetan women, they are used by China to also signify modernity. As religious Tibetan women, the nuns are in an awkward position between traditional Tibetan beliefs, which value religion but disparage nuns as religious practitioners, and Chinese modernization efforts, which trivialize religion and traditions and promote the principle of equality between the genders.

---

16. I look at the modes of Tibetan nationalism below.
17. Tibetans are not unanimous on this point, of course. While there are traditionalists who would like to see Tibetan language, culture, and religion preserved, even at the expense of modernization, there are also so-called "New Thinkers" who believe that Tibet's "backwardness" is the reason why Tibet fell to China. They thus believe that Tibet should become a modern nation, even if that means abandoning its traditional culture and religion (Wu 2013, 181).

-11-

Domination in Everyday Practices

While the structural domain of power arranges the macro-level of social organization with the disciplinary domain managing its procedures, the interpersonal domain functions through routinized, day-to-day practices of how people treat one another (e.g., the micro-level of social organization). Such practices are systematic, recurrent, and so familiar that they often go unnoticed (Collins 2000, 306–307).

The chapters presenting the interviews and lived experiences of the people I studied dealt specially with the micro-level practices, or micro-level social organizations, that had a strong impact on the lives of the Tibetan nuns. The lived experiences shared by the nuns revealed that day-to-day practices often oppressed them as women, as Tibetans and as female religious practitioners. The analysis of different domains of power also showed that the nuns had different strategies for adjusting to and coping with the unequal distribution of power. Consequently, my aim here is not to repeat what was already presented above or to list everyday practices, such as the ordinary seating order of Tibetans, the exclusion of nuns from many religious activities, or the different expectations and requirements faced by male and female Tibetans that can be seen as disadvantaging Tibetan women in particular. Instead, my objective, following Collins, is to point out how internalized the discrimination at the interpersonal level actually is.

According to Collins, most of us have little difficulty identifying our own victimization within some major system of oppression, be it race, social class, religion, physical ability, sexual orientation, ethnicity, age, or gender. However, what we usually fail to see is how our thoughts and actions perpetuate someone else's subordination. For example, a black heterosexual woman may discriminate against lesbians without giving it a second thought (Collins 2000). Accordingly, it can be noted that while a Tibetan laywoman I interviewed might recognize her own lower status as a female when compared to a male, she might discriminate against nuns without hesitation. For example, above I quoted two young laywomen talking about the gender inequality of Tibetan culture. While clearly acknowledging the unequal distribution of power between Tibetan men and women, they said that they themselves also felt less respectful toward nuns as religious practitioners.

Because of their ethnic status as a minority, many Tibetan men consider themselves as subordinate to the Han Chinese majority. Despite this fact, they do not often question the cultural practices and conceptions that subordinate Tibetan women because of their gender. Quite the contrary, they may actively maintain and promote gender inequality. Tibetan Buddhist monks usually recognize that their status as religious practitioners has been repressed under Communist China's rule, yet they are commonly unable to see how traditional monastic practices put Tibetan nuns at the bottom of religious life and hierarchies.

And what of the nuns themselves? Do they discriminate against others? It is probable that they also have their blind spots, as everyone does. The causes for this may be due to their social background or because of their status in the religious hierarchy. However, I am unable to answer this question because the interviews did not include aspects of discrimination.

Part IV

OPPORTUNITIES IN MONASTIC LIFE

– 12 –

Freedom in Monasticisim

In the previous chapters, I discussed the structural, disciplinary, hegemonic, and interpersonal domains of oppression faced by Tibetan nuns in the intersection of their gender, nation and religion. Nevertheless, I suggest that when analyzing intersectionality it is also important to discuss empowerment (e.g., Pelak 2007). Collins writes:

> Shifting the analysis to investigating how the matrix of domination is structured along certain axes – race, gender, class, sexuality and nation – as well as how it operates through interconnected domains of power – structural, interpersonal, disciplinary, and hegemonic – reveals that the dialectical relationship linking oppression and activism is far more complex than the simple models of oppressors and the oppressed would suggest. [...] Just as oppression is complex, so must resistance aimed at fostering empowerment demonstrate a similar complexity.
>
> (Collins 2000, 308)

Power structures are not static. The interplay of social structures and human agency creates oppression, but it can also produce opportunities. According to Collins and some other theorists of intersectionality, we are all disadvantaged in some ways but privileged in others. For example, I might be subordinated in Finnish society because of my gender. However, as a white Western female I am privileged in many ways when compared, for example, to the Tibetan people I studied. And yet, from the standpoint of the Tibetan nuns, I am definitely disadvantaged when it comes to religious and spiritual knowledge and experience. As Collins argues, "each individual derives varying amounts of penalty and privilege from the multiple systems of oppression which frame everyone's lives" (2000, 306).

As a consequence, despite the fact that African American women have been victimized by intersecting oppressions, representing them as completely passive victims obscures the fact that they can actively work to change the prevailing circumstances (Collins 2000). The nuns I studied are not "prisoners" of social structures, but can rather be seen as "agents" or the "subjects of action." If we agree that agency is the capacity of individuals to act independently and to make their own (free?) choices, what kinds of agencies can we find among Tibetan nuns? What is it that the nuns want to accomplish? What are their aims? What are the changes they wish to bring about? In what follows, I will investigate how the intersection of gender, nation and religion can be seen as producing opportunities and providing nuns with agency.

We can start by asking why my informants chose to become nuns, even though doing this meant acquiring a lower status in the monastic institution and in the wider society compared to monks. There are undoubtedly various reasons for becoming a nun in the contemporary Tibetan regions. Some of the motives are more conscious than others. Furthermore, many made a rational choice to become a nun, acting as intentional agents, while some believed that they became nuns as the result of their karma.[1]

Nevertheless, the nuns and the other Tibetans I interviewed commonly thought that there were generally two types of motives behind nunhood: spiritual, or "purely" religious motives, and secular motives, which were accordingly not regarded as "genuine" reasons. In practice, however, the two types of motives were often closely intertwined.

When the motives are examined more closely, they reveal different kinds of agencies and opportunities. First, I would argue that monastic status offers a nun not only freedom from the prevailing female state, but also opportunities that would not be available to her as a laywoman. Second, the status of a nun might provide her with chances to act for the emancipation of the Tibetan people by participating in Tibetan religious nationalism openly or by acting in a more subtle way.[2] Third, by acquiring the status of the compassionate bodhisattva she can benefit not only others but also herself through her actions.[3]

In order to appreciate why some Tibetan women still become nuns in the twenty-first century, it is important to know the society that they

---

1. While many of the nuns emphasized that becoming a nun was their own decision, it is important to understand that it is not so much their acts (or agency) in this life but their action in previous lives that made them nuns in this life. In other words, becoming a nun is caused by one's karma. (It can of course be asked if agency exists if the intentionality of the action and the change bear little or no resemblance to each other.)
2. I have discussed the open and more subtle nationalism of Tibetan nuns in a paper, "Tibetan Nuns: Gender as a force in a culture under 'threat'" (Härkönen 2013).
3. I have studied the question of compassion highlighted in monastic life in a paper titled "(Com)passionate Enlightenment: On the Soteriological Significance of Tibetan Monasticism" (Härkönen 2010).

are renouncing. The gendered suffering encountered by Tibetan women should be taken especially into consideration. Furthermore, to understand why they become nuns, it is also necessary to identify what nunhood offers them.

It is evident from the interviews, and particularly from the motives given by the nuns, that monastic life means freedom from many of the disadvantages experienced by laypeople. A lay life was seen as filled with work with few chances for free time or education. While the traditional livelihoods of pastoralism and agriculture have prevailed, the modernization reforms introduced by China seem to have made the life of rural Tibetans even more difficult. This is because of the growing economic gap and their impoverishment and social marginalization.

It can be assumed that the social changes have specifically deprived Tibetan women, who have traditionally been in the margins of society. Despite the new education policies, for instance, Tibetan women are in general still poorly educated. Furthermore, those who are lucky enough to have some schooling face challenges when it comes to receiving higher education and finding permanent jobs. In addition to being engaged in the traditional livelihoods, women take care of the household chores, children as well as aging parents and relatives. By taking nuns' vows, Tibetan women are mostly freed from the hard work experienced by laywomen.

Changes in the traditional society have not overridden the importance of marriage in Tibetan culture. Many traditional customs of marriage are still practiced. The fair appearance of a girl, as well as the prosperity and reputation of her and her family, seems to play a key role in her finding a suitable husband. Marriages are still often arranged by families, and the bride usually moves in with her husband and in-laws. Many women find that these practices are disadvantaging for Tibetan women. The marriage arrangements also make women more vulnerable, especially if the husband turns out to be abusive, the parents-in-law are nasty, or divorce takes place. By becoming a nun, a woman can avoid marriage and the disadvantages brought by marriage practices.

In Tibetan culture, marriage is expected to lead to the birth of children. Children are an important source of happiness for Tibetan people, as they are to anyone else. However, the prevailing conditions and realities of the society, including limited access to healthcare during pregnancy and childbirth, the tendency to have a large number of children, and high rates of childhood mortality and poverty can, among other things, make motherhood very hard. For mothers, freedom of movement is also much more limited. Furthermore, the Chinese child policy that have restricted the number of children, for example through sterilization, in a family is most concretely felt by Tibetan women. As nuns, they are free from the suffering that motherhood is thought to create.

In addition, it should be acknowledged that life as a nun offers women privileges that they could not enjoy as Tibetan laywomen. According to Yolanda van Ede, for example, by taking monastic ordination, Sherpa women strive to reject the restrictions and subordination imposed on them. In addition, monasticism is seen to offer economic independence, freedom, and opportunities to fulfill oneself in changing social conditions. Accordingly, in the middle of the twentieth century, the nunnery studied by van Ede seemed to function as a refuge for orphans and widows, whereas in the 1970s, it became a symbol of the modern lifestyle and offered improved chances for women to study (Van Ede 1999, 23–24, 104, 108–112, 167, 170).[4]

In fact, nunhood can function as a refuge for some disadvantaged women. In the nunneries I studied, there were, for example, some sick and extremely poor nuns. In one nunnery, there was also an old and blind nun who was taken care of by the other nuns. However, these nuns clearly formed the minority in the nunneries I visited or stayed. What life as a nun, and particularly life in the nunnery, offered for the nuns I interviewed was more than anything religious life with some education. Women who were mostly not educated and who were often illiterate before entering monastic life now had more opportunities for studying. Moreover, they could study in their mother tongue, Tibetan. While the possibilities for monastic education vary (for example, between geographical regions and schools of Tibetan Buddhism), they also depend on the prosperity of the nunnery. In general, however, there were increased chances to receive education in most of the nunneries I visited.

Furthermore, whereas laywomen are often occupied by their duties and responsibilities, especially toward their families, nuns have more opportunities for freedom of movement. The nunnery offers autonomy and an independence of which wives and mothers can only dream. For example, many of my nun informants had gone on a pilgrimage. Ani Palkyi, for instance, had made a pilgrimage from Yushu to Lhasa, doing full prostrations the whole way.[5] Sara Shneiderman has also stressed the communal aspect of monastic life. Nunhood thus represents a source of

---

4. Nevertheless, according to van Ede, "abandoning" feminine and female roles was not always welcomed by the Sherpa community, which at first found it difficult to respect the celibate nuns with their bald heads and asexual robes. The long hair of Sherpa women symbolizes their femininity, and cutting it means separation from their socially and culturally accepted roles as wife and mother.
5. See also Lhundrub Dorji (2010).

positive communal life defined by the women themselves (Shneiderman 1999, 233–234).

The nuns I interviewed wanted to eradicate the suffering that they thought Tibetan laywomen in particular encounter. Being free from the heavy work of lay life and especially that of family life, the opportunity for these women to study and practice Buddhism meant that they were taking positive actions to better themselves not only in this life, but also those to come. By choosing monastic life, the nuns as members of subordinate groups – meaning poor village girls and women with few choices – retained the power to act despite their subordination. Many of them, however, believed that leading a monastic life not only benefited themselves, but that life as a nun also offered them opportunities to act for the benefit of their fellow Tibetans.

– 13 –

Agency as Resistance and Cultural Maintenance

In research on women and religion, women's agency is often understood as resistance to the prevailing norms. In fact, the most obvious and visible mode of agency of the nuns I interviewed was that of resistance. The nuns' resistance did not focus on religious norms, however, but on the Chinese government. It was precisely in the intersection of religion and nation where their agency became the most visible. Two of the nuns I interviewed for this research had openly taken part in the Tibetan nationalist struggle, but there are also many others who are actively supporting the Tibetan cause.

Nationalism[1] is usually understood as a relatively recent development in Tibet. It has been suggested that Tibetan nationalism is only an outgrowth of encounters with the Chinese and that the idea of the Tibetans having a nation-state did not emerge until the early twentieth century and especially after the Chinese occupation and Tibetan exile (e.g., Anand 2000; Butler 2003; Lopez 1998, 200; Yeh 2007). Tibetan nationalism is thus seen to have grown only under the conditions of foreign rule, which is a phenomenon typical of colonialism.[2] The Chinese invasion of

---

1. Nationalism can mean many things – a movement, an ideology, and even a discourse of nationhood (see Delanty and Kumar 2006). It is also often described as a sense of national consciousness, which exalts one nation, holding its culture and interests above all others. In anthropology, nationalism is perhaps most often used to refer to an ideology that asserts that the cultural boundaries of an ethnic group should correspond to political boundaries (Eriksen 2001, 275).
2. Emily Yeh (2007, 650), for example, has traced the emergence of Tibetan nationalism to the escape of the 13th Dalai Lama to India and Mongolia after the British and Chinese invasions. In the early twentieth century, when China attempted to transform its previous "suzerainty" into direct sovereignty, the British displayed imperial interest in Tibet. The ruling 13th Dalai Lama responded by establishing some of the institutions typical of a modern state. A notable degree of national unity was achieved within Central Tibet, and Tibet declared its independence (Smith 1996, xi, 229, 262; Samuel 1993; Goldstein 1989).

the Tibetan regions in the 1950s signified a change in Tibetan nationalism, which for most Tibetans had previously been an "unfocused and localized ideology" (Smith 1996, xi, 448).

Contrary to Chinese expectations that the economic reforms and social liberalization of post-Maoist politics in the 1980s would remove the basis for Tibetan discontent, the relaxation of social restrictions led to a revival of Tibetan civil and cultural life – and to a resurgence of Tibetan nationalism. Given the traditional relationship between Tibetan religion and politics, the revival of Tibetan Buddhism signified for Tibetans a communal mode of life with political consequences. In fact, the revival of religion and the restoration and reconstruction of religious monuments were central to the revitalization of Tibetan social and political life (Smith 1996, 577, 582, 595; Kapstein 1998, 146; Slobodník 2004).

The fact that the revival of religion brought about a revitalization of Tibetan nationalism, which was threatening to China's territorial integrity and its political control in Tibet, led to the reestablishment of political control over Tibetan religious life. The resistance of the Tibetans against political control as they experienced it found expression in various demonstrations often initiated by monastic people, as shown above. The first documented protest started by monks was the demonstration in Lhasa in 1987 (see Smith 1996, 602–603, 616; Samuel 1993, 574; Powers 1995, 182–184). There were minor demonstrations in the 1990s, but only the demonstrations in 2008 managed to capture the world's attention again.

The resistance expressed by Tibetan women against Chinese rule has existed from the beginning of the occupation and even before that. Some women from Amdo and Kham were known for their leadership qualities during the resistance movement against the occupying Chinese forces (Butler 2003; Thonsur 2003, 329). The Tibetan women's demonstrations in Lhasa in 1959 and the political activism of some individual women before and during the Cultural Revolution are the most widely known instances (e.g., Pachen & Donnelley 2000; Thonsur 2003; Härkönen 2013). However, the women's nationalistic struggle became more visible only through a series of street protests in 1987–1996 staged by nuns in Lhasa.

As discussed above, two of the nuns I interviewed took part in the protests in 1988 when about fifteen women, inspired by the example of the demonstration by some monks in October 1987, marched from their nunnery to Lhasa and then to the Barkhor, the ring road surrounding the Jokhang temple at the heart of the city. Over the following six months, the nuns organized five similar protests. There were nuns' protests just before the anniversaries of the 1959 Tibetan uprising in 1989, 1992, 1993 and 1994, and around 27 September in 1989, 1990 and 1991. It is estimated that during this period, about 325 nuns from twenty-eight nunneries were arrested (see Barnett 2005, 323; Havnevik 1994).

According to Robert Barnett (2005), who has studied the street protests of 1987–1996, the protests differed from earlier ones in consciously relying on mainly non-violent methods. In addition, they became highly ritualized and symbolic; they imitated the traditional religious practices of circumambulating the Barkhor. Barnett suggests that the protesting nuns thus seemed to turn the practice of demonstrating in the Barkhor into a symbolic mode by means of which modern Tibetan resistance has been performed ever since: a politicized and non-violent circumambulation of the temple (Barnett 2005, 325–326).

Nuns continue to protest today. In March 2008, unrest broke out in Lhasa. The demonstrations also spread to other Tibetan inhabited areas in western China. The Chinese crackdown on the protestors sparked protests against the Beijing Olympic torch relay, for example, in London, Paris, San Francisco, Tokyo, Seoul and New Delhi.

The most dramatic way of protesting since 2009 has been self-immolation by Tibetans. At the time of writing this, 157 self-immolations have occurred since September 2009. Most of the protestors have been male, with "only" 28 women. Interestingly, taking into account their active role as protestors, only two of the self-immolators were nuns.

In addition to open resistance, there is also more subtle opposition. This type of agency exists even if it is not necessarily visible and its influence goes unnoticed (see Härkönen 2013). A 29-year-old nun originally from Kham but living in India in 2004[3] explained her motives to become a nun this way:

> If laypeople have a lot of knowledge and they know about politics, they can help the government. But ordinary laypeople, they can't do anything for the government. A nun's life is better than this kind of life. Even if we nuns can't do anything to help the government, we can be good nuns. If we can't help the government, at least we can read scriptures well and pray well. We can help by praying.

This is how Ani Dechen, who was born in Ü-Tsang but escaped to India in the year of 1999, described her future plans:

> I thought I will study well and in the future, I want to take a strong role as a spokesperson for the voiceless in Tibet. Sometimes I think I would like to go back to my nunnery to teach debate to the younger nuns. And I want to devote the rest of my remaining life to the preservation of our religion and the Tibetan identity. [...] I think a nun can do more for one's

---

3. I interviewed her for my master's thesis (Härkönen 2005).

community and for the country. You have more time to help others and think about others' welfare if you are a nun. On the other hand, if you are a laywoman, you are obsessed with your family life and you have less time to help others.

It may be suggested that for some of my informants, an important motive for leading life as a nun was the wish to conserve Tibetan traditional religion and culture, which they believed was at risk of being eradicated. In fact, the interviews I conducted in 2007 among Tibetans in Amdo and Kham in the Qinghai province suggested that Tibetans have both made use of their Tibetan Buddhist religion to defend their assumed ethnic identity and culture and negotiated the transitions of modernization to remain aligned with and promote the traditional religion and modes of life (Härkönen 2013).

First, religion appears to be involved in cultural defense. The following two excerpts reveal how religion is linked to Tibetan ethnic identity. The first excerpt is from an interview with a 42-year-old male painter from Kham:

M.H.: Why are there so many monasteries in Tibet?
Man: Under the seventh-century king, Tibet was a very rough place. The king thought that this problem had to be solved and invited two teachers [from India] to Tibet. Because there were no roads, accessibility was a problem and many monasteries had to be built. A monastery can change our minds. So after the monasteries had been built, people changed. For example, if Western people see a dying dog on the road they go away. But Tibetan people pray for the dog; they chant mantras. That is the reason for monasteries.
(IN2007/26)

The story mentioned by the man refers to the well-known story of how Tibet became a Buddhist country. According to the legend, an Indian-born teacher, Padmasambhava, tamed the local gods and spirits of Tibet and bound them to the service of Buddhism during the reign of the second "great religious king," Trisong Detsen, in the eighth century. According to the Tibetan view, this act enabled both Buddhism and "civilized" life to be established in Tibet (Samuel 1993, 220).

In addition to signifying the beginning of Tibetan civilization, Buddhism is seen as separating the Tibetans from both the Chinese and Westerners. As discussed above, Buddhism in particular traditionally separated them from non-Tibetans. "Tibet" thus referred to a certain territorial entity that was united by the Buddhist religion, while the idea of Tibet as a nation was a later development (see Kolås 1996; Samuel 1993; Smith 1994). The founding of the first Tibetan monastery thus marks the establishment of Buddhism in Tibet – and the beginning of Tibetan civilized culture. This is how a 32-year-old male teacher from Amdo described the importance of monastic life in Tibet:

> M.H.: What are the benefits of monastic life?
> Man: Many religious practices have been destroyed and the opportunities to study Tibetan are few. Tibetan traditional culture is in the monastery. It is the resource of Tibetan culture and life. That's why many monasteries were destroyed; they have become central places to spread Chinese culture. The Tibetan monastery has thousands of years of history and knowledge. It is a resource of our culture. In monastic life, religious practices, such as positive deeds, can be incorporated into daily life.
>
> (IN2007/20)

By the beginning of the twentieth century, Buddhism and the monastic institution had become inseparable from the idea of the prosperity of the Tibetan nation and culture (e.g. Samuel 1993). Besides their spiritual and ritual functions, monasteries provided a basic education for (mostly) young boys and maintained a Tibetan Buddhist scholastic tradition (see Dreyfus 2003). Interestingly, the idea of the monastic institution as a symbol of Tibetan culture and civilization is still held in the twenty-first century. The monastic institution provides resources for maintaining and promoting Tibetan ethnic identity and culture, as a 20-year-old male student from Amdo said:

> Monks can help Tibetan culture. They can preserve it. They know the language. In big monasteries, monks study the Tibetan language. They can preserve Tibetan culture. Some monks want to help Tibetans. Monks are important. We respect them and need them.
>
> (IN2007/20)

Monasteries also provide resources for the defense of the national culture. According to a 62-year-old layman from Kham the purpose of the monastery is to spread Tibetan culture and to save Tibetan culture (IN2007/27). It is conceivable that the oppression of religion by the Chinese was counter-productive and served only to strengthen Buddhism as a symbol for Tibetan ethnicity (see Smith 1994; Wang 2008). As the monastic institution lost its previous political power in society, it became an important symbol and locus of the Tibetan ethnic and nationalist struggle.

Steve Bruce has argued (in the modern Western context) that in addition to its role as a cultural defender, religion may provide resources for negotiating major cultural transitions or asserting a new claim to a sense of worth when social identity is threatened by rapid social changes (Bruce 1996; Bruce 1999). While the secular ideology of Chinese Communism has not replaced Buddhist religion, some of its ideas have been adopted by the Tibetans interviewed. This is how a former trader, a 68-year-old man from Kham, described the similarities and differences between Chinese Communism and Buddhism:

> In Tibet, we consider Tibetan monastics as very important for our nation. Why is that? It is because we are the followers of Buddhism, which came from Siddhārtha. That's why in Tibet we have lots of monasteries. And Buddhism has a very important relationship with science and also with Chinese law. In terms of Chinese law, for example, the Chinese have this theory: they say "serve the community." And in Buddhism, the main practice is also to serve the community, wellness for other people. So when we compare these two, they have differences in terms of range. Buddhism is wider. When we say "serve other people" it includes all six realms of sentient beings. But according to the Chinese policy, when they say "serve the community" it only includes the Chinese themselves, the people, only human beings. They are related, but there are also big differences. [...] Once you decide to be a monk, then you are really committed to dharma. You are also saying, "I'm a follower of Siddhārtha, Śākyamuni [Buddha]. I will serve the community, the goodness of the community." Monastics have these two motivations. One is to help themselves first, and then help others, to bring them happiness.
>
> (IN/2007/5)

Interestingly, promoting monastic life is thus justified by the idea of its communal good. A 25-year-old laywoman from Kham said:

> Monastic life benefits the community. After you die, if you know about Buddhism you don't need to go to hell. As monastic life develops, it also supports the Tibetan tradition, language and education. [...] In the old days, monastery buildings were old. The monasteries now are new and fancy. In the old days, there were few monks but now there are more and Buddhism has also developed. For example, in the old days, there were no nuns in my village, but now there are many nuns, monks and lamas. [...] In my opinion, when monastic life develops it also benefits the community.
>
> (IN2007/23)

It is evident that whereas the modernizing reforms by China have in many ways been disastrous for the traditional functions of the Tibetan monasteries, the higher standards of living resulting from the reforms have made the revitalization of monastic life possible. The higher standards of living and promotion of monastic life for the communal good are also brought up in the following two excerpts. The first is from a discussion with a 42-year-old laywoman from Kham:

M.H.: Do you think monastic life has changed somehow?
Woman: The monastic life has grown and developed, so it's getting better in our place in Kham. It's getting better.
M.H.: What are the benefits of monastic life?
Woman: If the monastery is economically developed, it is helpful for the community as well.
M.H.: Why is that?
Woman: It depends on economics. If you have support, financial support, then many things will be done. Then you can make monasteries bigger. The number of monasteries can be increased.

(IN2007/2)

Another layman, the 68-year-old from Kham, saw the number of monasteries increasing due to economic development:

M.H.: Do you think monastic life has changed somehow?
Man: It's a big change and the present monastery is better than in the past.
M.H.: How is it better?
Man: Because the government, the Chinese, made normal peoples' living conditions better. So, the present monasteries are really developing and progressing. It doesn't matter whether it is outside people or inside people; they can both support the construction of the monasteries, to increase the number of the monasteries. So, at present the monasteries are really developing and progressing.

(IN2007/5)

Not everybody sees the "progress" of the monasteries in such a positive way. A 36-year-old female university teacher from Amdo considered tourism the main reason for building new monasteries:

But, you know, tourism is booming. The government needs more money. So they also give some money for construction, to build new [monasteries]. [...] Then many tourists come and take pictures of us. But inside the monastery the education is really very, how to say, serious, how to preserve tradition, the culture. Before, in traditional society, the monasteries were the center, the heart of our area. There was a high level of knowledge. [...] From the outside, it's very beautiful ... [but] the monks and the nuns cannot focus on their practices and studies. So it's really a problem for the future.

(IN2007/1)

The interviews suggest that the Tibetan monastic institution has maintained its significance for the Tibetans interviewed because it is used on behalf of "cultural defense" and "cultural transition." When trying to understand the enduring significance of religion at the individual and communal levels in the modernizing Tibetan society, the counter-trends of secularization presented by Bruce thus seem convincing. The implication is that traditional religion provides resources for the defense of a Tibetan national and local culture in the face of extensive social changes, as well as resources for negotiating those changes meaningfully. First, the monastic institution, which traditionally marked the superiority of Tibetan culture, has become the source of Tibetan ethnic identity and value, as well as the symbol of the Tibetan nationalist struggle (see Smith 1994; 1996; Samuel 1993). Second, when religion is not used openly in cultural defense efforts, it is negotiated to fit the changing realities.

Furthermore, for the Tibetans interviewed, the monasteries represent Tibetan ethnic identity and culture, which are seen as differing considerably from those of the Chinese. Tibetan nationalism is thus mainly built on the idea of an ethnic identity that is distinctive from Chinese identity, because of Tibetan language and the history of the country, as well as its culture and religion.[4] Non-violence has also been the primary value and strategy espoused by the Tibetan nationalist movement (see Anand 2000; Butler 2003).

According to Havnevik, it can be assumed that in addition to religion, nationalist motives are involved when some contemporary Tibetan women choose to join and lead a monastic life. The growing interest in religion among young Tibetan women may thus be understood as part of a process of revitalization and conservation of Tibetan religion and culture. Through their choice to join monastic life, young women can be seen as choosing what for centuries has been the most highly respected way of life in Tibet – a way of life that has become crucial for conserving traditions (Havnevik 1994).

---

4. Typical of nationalism in general, Tibetan nationalism involves the glorification of presumed ancient cultural traditions, overemphasis of the cultural continuity of an "imagined" Tibetan Buddhist nation, and underemphasis of internal differences and change (Eriksen 2001, 276, 291–292).

– 14 –

Compassionate Agency

The modes of agencies presented above suggest that religion provides a nun with opportunities to influence her own life as a woman while the intersection of religion and nationality offers her chances to act for the good of her Buddhist religion and the Tibetan nation. The first of these emphasized the personal benefits gained in monastic life; the second stressed the communal aspect of monasticism. Is it possible to bring these modes of agencies together?

It appears that scholars of Tibetan monasticism have found it difficult to reconcile the conflicting ideals of personal renunciation and communal salvation. I would like to review this discussion in more detail here in order to make my following argument more intelligible. To start with, in early Buddhism, monastic life was ideally oriented toward a personal religious goal. For example, Étienne Lamotte (1903–1983), one of the greatest authorities on Buddhism in the West in his time, wrote about a Buddhist monk in this way:

> Personally, he confines himself to the passive virtues of renunciation and imperturbability which alone lead him to holiness in this world and, in the other world, to the destruction of suffering, to the end of saṃsāra, and to Nirvāṇa.[1]
>
> (Lamotte 1984, 58)

---

1. The otherworldliness of Buddhist monasticism was already emphasized by Max Weber, whose characterization of inner- and otherworldly asceticism aimed to capture the important distinctions between the world-transcendent ideal of Buddhist monasticism and the practical activism of Protestant asceticism. According to Weber, Christian monastics were not expected to leave the world behind in contemplation as much as Hindu or Buddhist monks. According to Georges Dreyfus, Weber goes too far in presenting otherworldliness as entailing an almost complete lack of interest in the world. Dreyfus claims that Weber's description does not hold for Buddhist monks, who have always been closely connected with the concerns of the laity and who act as the fields of merit and as ritual specialists for the laity (Dreyfus 2003, 343).

In practice, however, the world-transcending ideal and the ascetic separation from worldly life poorly capture the full reality of Buddhist monastics. A system of interaction between the monks and the laity emerged already during the lifetime of the Buddha, and nowadays the patterns of interaction are institutionalized and connected with the salvation of the laity (e.g., Harvey 2005). Thus, although it was generally considered impossible for a layman to completely put an end to "unease" or suffering, the laity could build up a spiritual bank account and in so doing attain better rebirth.

The tension between the contradictory requirements of being "out-of-the-world" and being "in-the-world" has also been raised by some scholars of Tibetan monasticism. Like for other Buddhists, celibacy and withdrawal from lay life are regarded as highly desirable. How are these different doctrines reconciled in Tibetan monasticism? According to some scholars, Tibetan monasticism should be understood as an individualistic pursuit, the goal of which is personal liberation. Others, however, have stated that renunciation alone is insufficient for attaining enlightenment, and that it must be joined with the compassionate wish to attain enlightenment for the sake of all sentient beings (see Härkönen 2010).

The distinctive social status and atomistic and anti-relational religious practice of Tibetan Buddhist Sherpas in Nepal has been emphasized by Sherry Ortner. According to Ortner, the religion in its highest ideals proposes only one solution to the problems of human experience: to break all social bonds, to refuse to form new ones, and to concentrate all one's energies on seeking enlightenment (Ortner 1978, 52).

Melvyn Goldstein and Paljor Tsarong also see Tibetan monasticism as one of history's most "radical psycho-social experiments," in that it has for centuries attempted to produce an atomistic social and cultural structure whose foundational building block is a solitary individual detached from the intimate attachments of the temporal world. However, while the monastic institution exists to provide an environment where monks can avoid attachments and worldly desires and be "out-of-the-world," at the same time, because of the Mahāyāna teaching of communal salvation, they are morally obliged to attend to the spiritual needs of the laity and be enmeshed "in-the-world." Despite this dual role of the monks, Goldstein and Tsarong come to the conclusion that the foundational goals of monasticism were successfully realized by the Tibetan Buddhist Ladakhi monks whom they studied. The monks had begun to move out of the "blinding web of attachments and desires" (Goldstein & Tsarong 1985, 14–15, 21–29).

However, Martin Mills, among others, has challenged the notion that Tibetan Buddhist monasticism is characterized by an evident move toward individualism, systematically detaching monks from relational social life. Mills argues that the image of a monk as "an isolated karmic individual" simply does not fit in with the ethnographic facts of Tibetan monasticism. The life of a monk is far from being socially atomistic, for through monastic ordination the monk enters a world that is comprised of kin-like teaching lineages. Furthermore, his renunciation of productive and reproductive activities forces him into daily reliance on householders to supply his physical needs. Mills claims that the disciplines of Tibetan Buddhist monasticism are aimed at systematically transforming the social identities and ties of household life into universalized religious aspirations of compassion, rather than replacing or repressing them (Mills 2000, 19–20, 29).

Gutschow has also criticized Ortner for not taking the reciprocal relationship between the monastics and the laity into account. Gutschow sees Buddhist asceticism as being based as much on reciprocity and communality as on withdrawal and individualism (Gutschow 2004, 6, 88–89). Georges Dreyfus has further claimed that the vast majority of Tibetan monks provide religious services for the laity, while only a small minority devote themselves to meditation in the solitude of hermitages. For many, being a monk or a nun no longer involves "a transcendental calling," but is simply a better means to the same end sought by the laity: the accumulation of merit (Dreyfus 2003, 34–37).

The discussion presented above reveals the difficulty in reconciling personal and communal salvation. Yet, my interviews show that there is no contradiction between the goal of personal liberation and the altruistic motivation of communal salvation in Tibetan monasticism. The key to understanding this can be found in the doctrine of compassion and in the figure of the bodhisattva.

The ideal of practicing religion for the sake of others was one of the most often mentioned principles of the nuns interviewed. We may recall Ani Changchub and Ani Tsomo, for example, who had lost their loved ones. Both of them wanted to become a nun in order to get rid of suffering, but also to do religious practices for their deceased relatives and spiritually benefit themselves. We can also remember Ani Yongtsen, who told how she first thought that being a nun merely meant being free from worldly hardships. Only after attending religious teachings had she realized the true purpose of monastic life. She said:

> We should practice dharma in order to benefit all sentient beings. We should have this way of thinking, right? After I listened to the teachings

of khenpos, I realized that as a nun I can't just eat the food I have, or drink the water I have, and then sleep. I realized that I must practice the dharma. After we become nuns, we should think about other living beings. In order to benefit them, I should practice the dharma, isn't that right? At first I thought that being a nun is very good, you don't have to work. All you need to do is just chant. Then, after I became a nun, I realized that I have to practice the dharma for all beings, isn't that so?

In the quotation as well as in the quotations, for example, by Ani Yonten, Ani Dawa and Ani Gyurmey, the importance of leading the monastic life for the benefit of others is emphasized. For Ani Yonten, too, the most important reason to be a nun was to help others. According to her, "the only expectation for a nun is to study religious texts and help those who are in need." Moreover, the life of the nun is contrasted with that of a laywoman. It is thought that a laywoman is only able to think of her family, while nuns with their broader perspective can work better for all sentient beings. Ani Dawa is of the opinion that the altruistic attitude is easier for nuns because they are not bound to family. Ani Gyurmey, who suffered from various health problems, claimed that merely practicing selfishly for her own benefit would not help her but could lead to her taking birth in a lower realm. Her idea further suggests that while only practicing for the sake of oneself would not be beneficial, it nevertheless becomes appropriate if others are included.[2]

The citations remind me of the interview with a monk whom I call here Thupten Sherab (see Härkönen 2010). Thupten Sherab, a 33-year-old monk from Amdo, had been ordained for almost half of his life. As a smart and extroverted man with good skills in Chinese, he had already become the personal attendant of a high reincarnate lama at his monastery. I met Thupten at his monastery in Qinghai in the autumn of 2007. During our meeting, he shared his life story with me and told about his reflections on monastic life. The following excerpts are illuminating in that they bring up the conflict between the motivations of personal liberation and altruism discussed above, as well as a solution of how to combine the two. Thupten first told why he became a monk:

> My family is poor and I have many brothers and sisters. My parents' income was limited and my further studies would have put pressure on them. When I was 16 years old, in order to decrease the burden, I decided to become a monk.

---

2. Sentient beings are believed to take birth in different realms of existence. In Tibetan Buddhism, the lower realms are the animal realm, the *preta* or hungry ghost realm, and the hell realms.

> Also, according to our religion, life is suffering. One day when I was 16, I met someone I know and he said that he was getting married. Three days later, he passed away. I realized that today you are happy and you only think of this day. But even if you accumulate wealth in this life you cannot take anything with you when you die, not even your body. No matter how wealthy you are, you won't bring anything with you but Buddhism. I thought of this and I was scared. When I experienced this I didn't understand it. I was puzzled and confused. I realized that there is only one method, Buddhism, for making this clear. So with my family's permission and in accord with my own wishes, I became a monk.
>
> (IN2007/11)

As was the case with the nuns I interviewed, monasticism for Thupten represented freedom from suffering. The three types of suffering detailed in the Tibetan Buddhist doctrine are present in his story. The suffering of misery was experienced through the poverty of his family and the unfulfilled dreams of further education. The suffering of change was actualized in the untimely death of his friend, who was about to get married. These experiences led Thupten to ponder the compositional suffering of the unsatisfactory nature of cyclic existence and to realize that Buddhism – and, more precisely, monasticism – was the answer to the question of suffering. Thupten continued:

> In general, people become monks or nuns because they are tired of their lives, unsatisfied with their lives. For example, if you are married and your husband beats you, of course you want to find peace. Women are very vulnerable and that's why they want to become nuns.
>
> (IN2007/11)

After this he revealed what he thought was the most important reason for being a monastic:

> There is another motive, too, a higher one. Those people see other people's suffering and want to help them. The most important monastic practice is to practice for the next life, for better rebirth. We think that each and every sentient being has at some point been our mother. So when we pray for our mother, we include everyone.
>
> (IN2007/11)

In the second excerpt, Thupten broadened his own experience to include others and discussed the motives of monastics in general. According to him, the most important motives are to put an end to the suffering of oneself and the suffering of others. The first motive is still the selfish goal of personal happiness. Interestingly, according to Thupten, it can be gendered because of the vulnerability of women. The second motive is a higher one. It is the altruistic attitude of a *bodhisattva* who sees the misery of others and strives for buddhahood for their benefit. These two motives are also the basis for monastic practice, the most important part of which is the practice for better rebirth. However, Thupten quickly added that all sentient beings are mentally included in this practice. All sentient beings are represented in Tibetan Buddhism by the mother, because it is believed that during countless eons of rebirths, everybody has been a mother for everyone else at least once.

Based on the views presented above, it can be claimed that the aim of Tibetan monasticism is to practice the altruistic mind and the behavior of the bodhisattva in order to accumulate merit and ensure favorable rebirth. Despite the "selfish" goal of personal liberation, the "higher" altruistic motivation (Skt. *bodhicitta*, Tib. *byang chub kyi sems*)[3] is included in monastic practice. As put by Wang, Tibetans know that their practice is ineffective and yields little merit if they perform religious actions solely to benefit themselves. It is thus crucial to pray for the benefit of all sentient beings (Wang 2009, 65). Nevertheless, the altruistic mental motivation does not hinder the personal benefit gained in monastic life and practice; in fact, it multiplies the merit of the monastic. Besides their status as defenders of Tibetan culture and religion, the nuns have thus acquired a role of the *bodhisattva*, who progresses on the religious path by helping others.

I argue that this mode of agency acquired by the nuns comes close to the modalities of agency discussed by Saba Mahmood. Saba Mahmood (2005) proposes alternative ways of thinking about agency. In her ethnographic study of urban women's involvement in the Islamist piety movement in Cairo, Egypt, she explores how women's active support for a socio-religious movement that sustains female subordination is problematic for feminist analysts. Mahmood questions the "secular-liberal" way of thinking according to which all human beings have an innate desire for freedom and that everyone seeks to claim their autonomy when allowed to do so. Furthermore, she criticizes the assumption that human agency primarily consists of acts that challenge social norms but not those that support them. Mahmood argues that the stress laid on politically subversive agency in feminist scholarship has led scholars to ignore other modalities of agency "whose meaning and influence are not captured within the logic of subversion and resignification of hegemonic terms of discourse" (Mahmood 2005, 2–5; see also 7; 153). Mahmood writes with regard to Egyptian women:

---

3. *Bodhicitta* is the compassionate wish to attain enlightenment for the benefit of all beings.

> The kind of agency I am exploring here does not belong to the women themselves, but is a product of the historically contingent discursive traditions in which they are located. [...] The women are summoned to recognize themselves in terms of the virtues and codes of these traditions and they come to measure themselves against the ideals furbished by these traditions, in this important sense, the individual is contingently made possible by the discursive logic of the ethical traditions she enacts.
>
> (Mahmood 2005, 32)

For Mahmood, agency is thus not only a synonym for resistance to relations of domination, but also a capacity for action that specific relations of subordination create and enable. She proposes keeping the meaning of agency open and "allowing it to emerge from within semantic and institutional networks that define and make possible particular ways of relating to people, things, and oneself." In other words, agency cannot be understood outside of its ethical and political conditions, but only from within the discourses and structures of subordination that create the conditions of its acting out. What appears from a progressivist point of view like shocking passivity and obedience may actually be a form of agency (Mahmood 2005, 9; see also 14–15, 18; 34).

While the context and the tradition are very different, both Tibetan nuns and Egyptian women take part in religious life that seems to disadvantage them as women. However, both also seem to gain modes of agency and opportunities that become intelligible only in a specific socio-cultural and religious context. For Tibetan nuns, monastic life means the possibility to transform one's position and status in this life, but it is also believed that monastic life can lead to a better rebirth (namely, release from a lowly female rebirth in the future). Thus it is a path, if not toward immediate enlightenment, at least toward a better rebirth.

Apart from allowing the women to earn religious merit for their own spiritual benefit, the agency of the nuns also enables them to engage in political activism, and assume a prominent role in the Tibetan nationalist struggle. Moving beyond the discursive context highlighted by Mahmood in the case of the Egyptian women's piety, the Tibetan nuns' agency is thus first and foremost defined by the complex intersection of religion, nationality and gender. It is from this same intersection, I would argue, that their opportunities can also be seen to arise.

– 15 –

Increasing Opportunities

As suggested above, the interaction between social structures and agency can change both. Nevertheless, as argued by Mahmood, "any social and political transformation is always a function of local, contingent, and emplaced struggles whose blueprint cannot be worked out or predicted in advance" (2005, 36).

Karma Lekshe Tsomo notes that over the last two decades, the situation of Tibetan nuns living in India and Nepal has changed primarily due to exile. Today, nuns participate in the Great Prayer Festival (Tib. *smon lam chen mo*), study philosophical debate, construct sand maṇḍalas (Tib. *dkyil 'khor*), perform sacred dances (Tib. *'cham*), and chant at public gatherings. The most notable changes have been in the field of religious education, particularly with the introduction of philosophical studies (Tsomo 2003, 348, 357; Mann 2009). The Tibetan Nuns' Project in India has been active in promoting monastic education for the nuns. I interviewed a co-director of the project in 2004.[1] She said:

> For many centuries, monks have really played a great role in the Tibetan society. That's why they are more respected. That's why, what I'm saying, to earn respect you have to do something to earn it. Not that you just say that people don't respect me, you know. So, for many centuries monks have been doing very good things for the society. And they've been learning and they've been debating. That's why they are highly respected. Now, we [nuns] also try to follow them. [...] The future goal of the project is to produce highly educated nuns so that they can serve this society and they can go back to Tibet. In Tibet, they can educate other nuns. And then we want some of the educated nuns to go to schools since they can really help young people.

Since 2012, there have also been Tibetan Buddhist academic degree of geshe ma exams for Tibetan nuns in exile (LeClear 2013).

---

1. I interviewed the co-director in English for my master's thesis (Härkönen 2005).

There are various factors that have contributed to the status of nuns in exile and in the Tibetan societies in China today. According to Tsomo, one factor is wider access to secular education, which has enhanced the educational qualifications of women in general. Another factor is that there are more chances for women to receive Buddhist teachings from renowned teachers. The third factor is that the perception of women's capabilities has changed. The media, personal contacts with Buddhist practitioners, and women from foreign countries and cultures have had an important role to play in this (Tsomo 2003, 356; Härkönen 2016).

An important element has thus been contact with the West and Western people. In particular, Western-born women taking the Tibetan monastic ordination in exile communities has played a central role in changing views on gender and religion (Swanepoel 2014, 2016; Mrozik 2009). For example, when Western nuns in the Tibetan tradition began considering full ordination in other traditions, Tibetan scholars raised inquiries about the origin and content of the Chinese and Korean Bhikṣuṇī Prātimokṣa texts. It emerged that the possibilities for establishing a *bhikṣuṇī saṅgha* within the Tibetan tradition depended on verifying both the texts and the living lineage. In other words, it is thought to be possible to reestablish the order by transmitting the lineage from an existing *bhikṣuṇī saṅgha* in certain conditions (Tsomo 1996, x.; Mann 2009; Heirman 2011).[2]

Many high-ranking exiled Tibetan lamas and lineage-holders have also shown their support for the full ordination for Tibetan women. In response to requests that he personally establish the *bhikṣuṇī saṅgha* within the Tibetan tradition, the 14th Dalai Lama, for example, has said that creating such an institution is not within the power of a single *bhikṣu* such as himself, but must be the decision of the *bhikṣu saṅgha* in accordance with *vinaya* procedures. He and some other high-ranking lamas have, however, publicly given their permission for nuns to travel

---

2. More research is being done on the possibility of taking the *bhikṣuṇī* ordination. I heard that Acharya Tashi Tsering from the Central Tibetan Administration's Department of Religion and Culture has been especially active. He has participated in international seminars that deal with Buddhist nuns, and he has written three volumes on the *gelongma ordination*. His research has been sponsored by the private office of the Dalai Lama.

   In the autumn of 2013, under the authority of the Central Tibetan Administration's Department of Religion and Culture, a group of ten monks (two from each of the four Tibetan traditions and two representing the nuns) met to do intense research on the *bhikṣuṇī ordination*. It is known that they prepared a 220+ page report, but I am not aware if it has been published or what the findings were.

to Hong Kong, Korea or Taiwan to participate in the full ordination (see Tsomo 1996, xi).

Recently, one of the most high-ranking Tibetan lamas, the 17th Gyalwang Karmapa, the head of the Karma Kagyu lineage, has also been active in promoting the equal status of Tibetan nuns and monks. He made a historic announcement at the Second Arya Kshema Gathering in January 2015, expressing his intention to take concrete steps toward restoring nuns' full vows in the Tibetan Buddhist tradition.[3] In the end of 2015, together with another distinguished lama, the Gyalwang Drukpa, the head of the Drukpa Kagyu lineage, he also stated that nuns should be addressed as tsunma instead of ani. Literally, tsunma means "nun," while *ani* means "aunt." Nevertheless, the question of the full ordination of (Tibetan) nuns seems to be still fervently debated question both within local and global Buddhist communities as shown for example by Swanepoel (2010; 2016). Furthermore, there still seems to be a huge gap between exile nunneries and Tibetan nunneries in China when it comes to Western feminism and its influence. This is, of course, due to better accessibility when it comes to exile nunneries.

Nevertheless, when asked about the reason for the emergence of nunneries in Yushu, a monk friend of mine stated that Tibet was also becoming more equal these days. According to him, there were not many nuns in Yushu earlier because the opportunities for religious studies were few. Now, he said, the situation for nuns was much better. As can be remembered, the changing status of nuns in Kham was also brought up by the nun I interviewed in 2007. According to her, previously nobody cared about the nuns, but now lamas build nunneries. A male head-lama of one of the monasteries in Yushu also emphasized that monks and nuns were equal and that I, as a researcher, should see it this way, too. The nuns in the nunnery under his supervision received religious education, as did the nuns, for example, in all the nunneries I visited.

Like anywhere else in the world, there is a generation gap between older and younger people in Tibet. This fact is highlighted by the ideas of the 30-year-old layman from Kham, Qinghai, according to whom the number of nuns has become bigger because of increased gender equality in the society. He thought that the idea of gender equality came first from the West to China and by the medium of television from China to the Tibetan regions (IN2011/15).

Among the factors that seem to have improved the standing of the Tibetan nuns has been their participation in Tibetan nationalism.

---

3. See http://kagyuoffice.org/the-gyalwang-karmapa-discusses-nuns-ordination-teaches-on-bodhisattva-vow (accessed 3.8.2016).

According to Robert Barnett, the issues that nationalist nuns raise in their protests and discussion in general are not gendered, apart from the distinctive ways in which they carry out their politics. This seems to be because of the urgency of the national question, which so far has overridden other issues. Nevertheless, the political activities of the nuns seem to have somewhat changed the way in which nuns are perceived in the Tibetan community. According to Barnett, the politically active nuns have come from two groups traditionally regarded as inferior in Tibetan society: women and nuns. In addition, they are from poor, usually rural, backgrounds from the lower class and with little education. Barnett suggests that because their motivations have more likely been considered pure, paradoxically this has inversely increased their standing when viewed as protestors. In their role as protestors, these women have thus acquired a relative degree of respect, which may have led to them being seen as models of nationalist courage and religious principle within their community. Through their "ritual of disobedience," they may thus have changed the general narrative about their position in Tibetan society (Barnett 2005, 288, 327–328; see also Butler 2003).

It has thus been suggested that the participation of Tibetan women in the nationalist struggle is not a women's liberation struggle, but an aspect of the Tibetan nationalist movement (Butler 2003). As suggested above, however, it is too narrow a view that women and gender relations are simply tools to further a nationalist project. Women are not only passive symbols, but they may have their own interests which they promote in national processes (Walby 2006). Thus, while a nationalist ideology draws from "invented" or constructed ideas of the ancient traditions of an old culture which is to be preserved and defended, it can simultaneously change the gender relations of the society and provide women with new, less traditional roles.

The relationship between gender and nationalism is thus complex and ambivalent. Nira Yuval-Davis and Floya Anthias (1989) have identified five major ways in which women have tended to participate in ethnic and national processes. These are: (1) as biological reproducers of members of ethnic collectivities; (2) as producers of the boundaries of ethnic or national groups; (3) as participating centrally in the ideological reproduction of the collectivity and as transmitters of its culture; (4) as signifiers of ethnic/national differences; and (5) as participants in national, economic, political and military struggles (Yuval-Davis & Anthias 1989, 7, 9). Apart from the first, Tibetan nuns can be seen to have been participating in all of the other processes of modern Tibetan nationalism.

Thus, it can be argued that the Tibetan nationalist movement has opened up new opportunities for nuns in Tibet and in exile. Meanwhile, nuns have adopted the role of culture guardians or "preservers," which has been made possible by the Tibetan nationalist movement; they have changed their traditional status (see Jayawardena 1986, 14). Havnevik has put this aptly. According to her, the nuns who are intensely concerned with the preservation of their religion, language, and culture are, at the same time, initiating changes in their status and traditional gender roles (see Havnevik 1994, 362, 265).

When looking at the structural, disciplinary, hegemonic and interpersonal domains discussed above, many changes can be found. Changes in the structural domain are the most obvious. There are changes particularly with the increasing number of nunneries and the nuns' improved chances for higher religious education. The new roles of the nuns as non-violent freedom fighters, their increasing numbers, and their mission as culture "preservers" seem to have changed their status and the ways in which they are viewed by society. There have thus been changes in the hegemonic and interpersonal domains as well. As expressed by the monk above, Tibet is becoming more equal when it comes to gender. Chinese occupation and its modernization efforts have also had an important role in promoting the ideas of equality through the media and via encounters with Chinese and Tibetans. Finally, globalization and Western contacts have been central. As the status of the nuns in Tibetan culture and nationalism becomes more visible, it is possible that it is also changing Chinese ideas about nuns, such that increased surveillance is directed toward them.

Part V

CONCLUSION

– 16 –

Between Oppression and Opportunities

Ever since the first encounters with the West, Tibet and Tibetan Buddhism have fed the imagination of Westerners. Those Westerners who had been influenced by the theosophical movement in the nineteenth century traveled mainly to the southern and western border areas of Tibet to study under Tibetan teachers. By the nineteenth century, Tibet had also become a source of political contention for some Western countries, prompting it to close its borders and isolate itself from outside contacts for almost a century. This further fed the idea of the enigmatic Tibet (see Baumann 2001; Lopez 1998).

The Western imaginations of Tibet have been forcefully criticized by some Tibetologists. In particular, the idea of a religious (premodern) Tibet has been dismissed as nothing more than a Western projection (e.g., Lopez 1998; Adams 1996; see also Dreyfus 2003).[1] Yet, while Tibet and its religiosity may in many ways be a construction of Western fantasies and Tibetan responses to these fantasies, Tibetan Buddhism and its monastic institution had important functions in historical Tibet. This still seems to be the case in the twenty-first century as also my research has demonstrated.

Social and political changes brought by China have had tremendous consequences on traditional Tibetan society, culture and ways of life. This is particularly the case with aggressive secularism, which nearly destroyed the monastic institution and permanently changed its role in Tibetan society. Nevertheless, the monasticism has been revitalized in recent decades. The revitalization of monastic life has also brought along with it the revival of female monasticism.

The aim of the book has been twofold: first, to give voice to a marginalized group of Tibetan Buddhist nuns, and second, to apply

---

1. These ideas of Tibet evoke Edward Said's (1978) famous argument according to which Western culture has produced a view of the "Orient" that is based on a particular imagination, which was popularized through academic Oriental studies, travel writings and a colonial view of the "Orient."

intersectionality by analyzing the dimensions of oppression and opportunities in the intersection of the nuns' gender, their Buddhist religion, and Tibetan nationality.

The first of the goals arose from the fact that Tibetan nuns have often been ignored, or have gained less attention, both in Tibetan societies and traditional literature and in academic texts. Consequently, relatively little is known about nunhood in historical Tibet. Furthermore, extensive field studies and research on contemporary Tibetan nuns, their experiences and life stories are still somewhat few in number.

Nevertheless, the existing studies of Tibetan Buddhist nuns in China, in exile and in other culturally and ethnically Tibetan areas have shown that compared to monks, nuns still tend to have a lower status in the monastic institution and in wider society. Consequently, whereas monks can receive the highest monastic ordination, full ordination is not available to nuns. This is despite the fact that during the time of the Buddha, nuns could receive full ordination. It has also been shown that the formal status of nuns provides them with limited opportunities for ritual or scholastic advancement. Accordingly, while monastic life is seen to offer men opportunities for education and upward social mobility, most nuns have neither been able to pursue advanced philosophical studies nor gain any official positions in the religious or lay hierarchies. Partly because of the elementary level of their religious and spiritual education, nuns are not usually awarded the title of a high religious teacher, and they have rarely been recognized as the incarnations of enlightened teachers. Since monasteries are founded on the spiritual and administrative guidance of these religious authorities, the lack of female lamas means that nunneries are usually sub-branches of monasteries typically run by men. The status of the nuns has also had considerable consequences for their social and economic situation. Due to lacking the full monastic ordination and their more limited scholastic knowledge and ritual capabilities, nuns are supported less than monks by the laity.

Interestingly, while the nuns' "lower" position is often acknowledged by Tibetan society and by many scholars, the "high" status of Tibetan women has frequently been emphasized. When the high status of laywomen has been highlighted, it has nevertheless been suggested that despite their lower prestige, life as a nun provides women with opportunities she could not enjoy as a laywoman. These conflicting views suggest that Buddhism is not only important in legitimizing the inequality encountered by the nuns, but it can also be seen as simultaneously empowering them.

The debate on the suppressing versus emancipating aspects of religion can be situated within a wider discussion of power and agency in feminist research. Power and agency are also two central themes running through this whole book. Power is a central concept for feminist theory and yet, according to Amy Allen, it is a concept that is not often explicitly discussed in feminist works (2011, 1). Allen argues that existing feminist accounts of power tend to have a one-sided emphasis either of power as domination or of power as empowerment, and these conceptions of power neglect the fact that women can at the same time be both dominated and empowered. They also miss the fact that some women subordinate other women and that individual women are differently empowered by particular practices, norms and institutions (Allen 1998, 21–23, 26, 31–32; see also Collins 2000, 2015).

Allen argues that feminists need a theory of power that takes domination and empowerment, as well as feminist solidarity and coalition building, into consideration. She suggests a threefold understanding of power: power-over, power-to, and power-with. Of these, "power-over" is the "ability of an actor or set of actors to constrain the choices available to another actor or set of actors in a nontrivial way." Allen is of the opinion that power-over should not be understood as intentional because much of the power is exercised "in routine or unconsidered ways" by people who do not necessarily consciously intend to do so (Allen 1998, 31–33). "Power-to" is the "ability of an individual actor to attain an end or series of ends." An interest in power understood as power-to focuses on how members of subordinated groups preserve the power to act despite their subordination. However, Allen argues that "power-to" or "empowerment" cannot be considered equivalent to "resistance"; resistance represents a particular application of power-to or empowerment, it is the "ability of an individual actor to attain an end or series of ends that serve to undermine domination." Finally, to fulfil the feminist interest in solidarity, Allen talks about "power-with," the "collective ability or capacity to act together so as to attain some common or shared end" (Allen 1998, 34–35).

The discussion on power outlined above shows that the concepts of agent and agency are closely related to that of power. According to Helena Kupari and Salome Tuomaala (2015), in feminist research, female agency is customarily understood through the concept of emancipation. This means that only resistance and the sort of agency that aims at social change have been considered noteworthy. Yet, understanding agency merely as social emancipation, the aim of which is social change, is not sufficient when it comes to studying women's religious agency. In fact, presuppositions can hinder us from seeing particular modes of agency that can be found in religious traditions (Kupari & Tuomaala 2015, 166; Ahonen & Vuola 2015, 19–20).

Conclusion

There has thus been tension between feminist studies and religion. According to Castelli, for example, there has been a tendency among many feminists to see religion in negative terms merely as an ideological and institutional form of constraint, and religious attachment solely as a sign of false consciousness. Castelli notes that this negative interpretation of religion is, ironically, a relic of feminism's own Enlightenment heritage (Castelli 2001, 5; see also Vuola 2010).[2] Johanna Ahonen and Elina Vuola (2015) have also pointed to the conflicting relationship between feminist studies and religion. On the one hand, religion has been seen by many feminist scholars as reactionary and religious women as oppressed by patriarchal control. On the other hand, religious women have often simply been ignored in feminist research (Ahonen & Vuola 2015, 7–8). Vuola has also noted that when religious women are taken as a subject of study, they are too often misconstrued merely through a religious paradigm. In other words, religion is seen as the only, or at least the primary, explanation for their status (Vuola 2010, 172).[3]

I have attempted to avoid this juxtaposition by applying intersectionality in accord with the second goal of my research. Intersectionality, which asserts that gender is not an isolated concept but works in conjunction with other social categories, has enabled me to take into consideration the complex relationship between domination and privilege. In order to apply intersectionality for my analysis, I thus first asked what kinds of dimensions of oppression and unequal distribution of power the nuns experience in the intersection of their gender, religion and nationality. Second, following Patricia Hill Collins, I asked how the dimensions of oppression are constructed and maintained structurally, disciplinarily, hegemonically and interpersonally. Finally, I questioned what kinds of opportunities and agencies the crossing of gender, religion and nationality offer to the nuns.

The interviews I conducted with the nuns, monks and lay Tibetans brought up the unequal distribution of power in contemporary social and religious life in the Tibetan areas of China. Nevertheless, they also revealed opportunities and agencies taken by the nuns.

When the oppression of the nuns I studied is subjected to a more detailed analysis, it can be seen that power structures and relations are constructed and maintained in different domains of power. If we

---

2. See also Vuola (2017). In her article, Vuola argues that for a long-time feminist research ignored religion as a significant difference and shows how intersectionality was a part of feminist theology already in the 1970s.
3. Today, this seems to be the case especially when it comes to gender and Islam (e.g. Jacobsen 2011; Gemzöe et al. 2016).

investigate the crossing of gender, religion and nationality of Tibetan nuns in these domains of power, the following conclusions can be drawn: First, in the structural domain, traditional but still dominant social institutions – such as traditional livelihoods and the distribution of work, educational practices, the arrangement of marriage and family life, and religious institutions – place Tibetan women and men in different positions. Thus, Tibetan women are burdened with far more work than their male counterparts and yet they have fewer opportunities for education. Family life with arranged marriages and motherhood also disadvantages women. While monasticism is perceived as offering freedom from the suffering encountered by laywomen, monastic hierarchies and practices can be seen as advantaging monks and disadvantaging nuns. Various institutions of traditional life can thus be seen as disadvantaging Tibetan women as women, as Tibetans, and as religious practitioners.

The advent of Chinese rule in the 1950s meant a new polity and law for Tibet in addition to new modes of economics. It seems that the Chinese modernizing efforts have had only limited (positive) impact on the lives of Tibetan women. As suggested above, the traditional nomadic and agricultural ways of life are still dominant, and gender relations and a gender-based distribution of work prevail as before. In fact, the modernization reforms introduced by China appear to have led to many socio-economic evils, which mainly affect Tibetan women. Thus, multiple processes – such as the Han Chinese population influx into the Tibetan areas, the impoverishment of rural Tibetans, the growing economic gap between Tibetans and Chinese, and the social marginalization of Tibetans – have exacerbated the life of Tibetan women who traditionally already existed on the margins of society. The changes brought by China have improved possibilities for education, but most of my informants had not benefited from these changes. One of the reasons is that it is still often not considered important to educate women. Chinese institutions, polity, law and the economy thus disadvantage many Tibetan women, both as Tibetans and as religious practitioners.

Second, in the disciplinary domain of power, the nuns find themselves monitored by traditional culture and Chinese rulers. Chinese governance brought with it new institutions of modern society that organize and manage the lives of Tibetan people and have displaced traditional religious rulers. In these administrative organizations, men and women, Han Chinese and minorities, poor and rich, educated and uneducated, rural people and city dwellers are put in hierarchical positions. These relations and practices are monitored in the disciplinary domain that on the one hand maintain internalized ways to act, and on the other, govern direct surveillance. As one of the Chinese minority ethnic groups, the Tibetans are given certain privileges, but they also face various restrictions. This is especially the case when it comes to their religious life. The nuns are expected to embody their religious status in certain, traditional ways and yet their monastic and religious life is controlled by the Chinese authorities. It can thus be suggested that Tibetan nuns are disadvantaged in the disciplinary domain of power as women, as Tibetans and as religious practitioners.

Third, the unequal distribution of power in these domains is justified by hegemonic ideas of religious and cultural beliefs, ideas of religion and modernity, and religion and gender. Accordingly, in the hegemonic domain of power, the Buddhist conceptions of female and the feminine, as well as cultural ideas of gender, are used, consciously or unconsciously, to justify subordinating practices in the structural and disciplinary domains of power. Hegemonic ideas are also promoted, for example, by efforts of Chinese modernization and its secularism. These hegemonic ideologies disadvantage Tibetan nuns as women, as religious practitioners, and as Tibetans.

Fourth, these domains of power culminate and find their expression in the everyday life of people and in their lived experiences. What is important here is to understand how oppression is internalized. The everyday practices clearly put Tibetan nuns as women below Tibetan men, as religious practitioners below Tibetan monks, and as Tibetans below Chinese men and women.

The interviews thus show that many oppressive power structures and relations limit the lives and choices available to the nuns I studied. Nevertheless, they also reveal that many of the nuns were highly active in choosing and determining the courses of their lives. I argue that the intersections of gender, religion and nationality also produce opportunities and provide nuns with different modes of agency. I suggest the following:

First, monastic life offers Tibetan women freedom from the suffering faced by laywomen. They are free from the responsibilities of heavy labor and family life with marriage and children. As nuns, they have more opportunities for freedom of movement, chances to study, and engagement in religious practices. Religious life thus offers them opportunities that they could not enjoy as laywomen.

Second, the juncture of their gender, religion and nationality offers nuns agency that can be understood in terms of resistance. This becomes most evident in their nationalism. In addition to open resistance, there is also a more subtle way in which nuns take part in the nationalist cause. By becoming nuns, some of them aim to keep Tibetan religion and traditions alive. As suggested in the interviews, one of the reasons why the Tibetan monastic institution has gained significance in the Tibetan nationalist struggle is because of its role as a conserver of Tibetan traditional culture.

Third, the final modality of the nuns' agency can be understood only in the context of Tibetan religion. Tibetan Buddhism is founded on the doctrines of early Buddhism, Mahāyāna and Vajrayāna. While all of these are important, both laypeople and monastics are encouraged to cultivate compassion for all living beings and to embark upon the path of a bodhisattva.

For many nuns, the primary motive to live as a nun is to practice for the sake of "all sentient beings." Monastic life thus represents for the nuns a method of fulfilling the most central goal of Tibetan Buddhism: to benefit others. Any attempt to embody the limitless and altruistic compassion of the bodhisattva, which is pervasive in Tibetan Buddhist doctrine, is meant to benefit others but also oneself. This is because by practicing compassionately for the sake of others, one accumulates personal merit. Positive merit is needed for a better rebirth in future lives. When looked at from this point of view, nuns can be seen as taking action toward influencing their present life but also future rebirths.

It is precisely in the intersection of religion, nationality and gender that Tibetan nuns are provided with opportunities. First, they have acquired a role as defenders of the Tibetan nation and religion. Second, as compassionate bodhisattvas that serve the community, they earn religious merit that advances them spiritually.

Despite the fact that they are not fighting for a higher status, participation by nuns in Tibetan nationalism appears to have provided them with new opportunities and roles in the monastic institution. Nuns who were inferior to monks in traditional Tibet, mainly because of their invisible position in Tibetan politics, have started to gain a new status through their involvement in the Tibetan nationalist struggle. Western and Chinese ideas of gender equality, as well as the support of some remarkable Tibetan lamas, have also been important. The most significant shifts in the status of nuns have, in fact, been in the field of religious education.

It can be seen that different aspects of power, as presented by Amy Allen, are at play in the life of nuns: power-over or power as oppression, power-to or power as agency, and power-with or power to act together in order to attain a shared end. Furthermore, while agency as resistance and emancipation can be found, there are particular modes of agencies – as suggested by Saba Mahmood – that become intelligible only in the religious context of Tibetan Buddhism.

Conclusion

In the light of my research, it can hence be suggested that when trying to understand the relationship between women and religion, it is not enough to focus merely on gender and religion. Apart from religious doctrines and practices, gender intersects many other dimensions. Religious women are not merely women and religious practitioners; they are also women with a certain social and economic position, women with a certain ethnic background and nationality, and women of different ages, social backgrounds, sexual orientations and ideologies. When the intersections of these are investigated in different domains of power, the question of "status" becomes extremely complex and multifaceted.

In this book of Tibetan Buddhist nuns, I have focused on their reflections on their lived experiences of oppression and opportunities from the viewpoint of intersectionality by taking the dimensions of gender, religion and nationality under investigation. There are many other aspects that could and should be taken into account. Because of the politically sensitive nature of the Tibetan "field," which did not allow long stays in one site, I conducted the field research by means of multi-sited ethnography. In my research, the field was thus constructed out of various geographical and spatial locations. These different locations were united by the notion of shared Tibetanness defined especially by Buddhism, Tibetan monasticism, Tibetan culture and, to some extent, a sense of Tibetan nationalism. Applying a multi-sited approach to the study of Tibetan Buddhist nuns proved to be illuminating. Among other things, I could witness some dramatic changes that took place in the Tibetan regions during the course of my research project.

In the future, it would be elucidating to focus more on the internal heterogeneity of the nuns, for example, in relation to their social backgrounds. If the political situation allows, their everyday lives should be studied more closely. It will also be very interesting to see if full ordination will become available for Tibetan nuns in the future, and what kinds of practical consequences this may have for their status.

Nevertheless, in this research I have focused on the nuns' stories and the three dimensions that I find most enlightening in the context of Tibet under Chinese rule. For while there are manifold studies of intersectionality as a theory and a method, there seem to be fewer studies that have actually applied intersectionality. This study is one way to apply intersectionality, and it is my hope that it illuminates one way to do it.

Appendix

Short Biographies of the Nuns

Ani Sherab was a 32-year-old nun and originally from Ü-Tsang in the TAR. Her family was poor and practiced agriculture for a living. The family had eight children. The father was previously a monk, but was imprisoned and forced to disrobe during the Cultural Revolution. Ani Sherab never went to school. She became a nun without her parents' permission when she was 14 years old and joined a nunnery near Lhasa. She escaped to India in 1995 and lived in a nunnery there. I interviewed her in 2008.

Ani Dechen, 29, was also from Ü-Tsang. Her family was semi-nomadic. She was the sixth of ten children in the family. Ani Dechen became a nun as an 11-year-old. Her sister was also a nun. She stayed in a nunnery in Tibet until she escaped to India in 1999. She was interviewed in India in 2008.

Ani Tenzin was 25 years old. She came from Kham, TAR. Her family was semi-nomadic with nine children. She did not go to school and became a nun when she was 18 years old. There was no nunnery she could have joined and she escaped to India in 2002. She was staying at a nunnery in India when I interviewed her in 2008.

Ani Dolma was 37 and originally from Ü-Tsang, TAR. She was from a family practicing agriculture. She was the youngest of eight children. She went to school for nine years before she became a nun at 14 years of age. She took part in a demonstration in Lhasa in 1988 and was detained and severely tortured. After her release she was expelled from the nunnery by the Chinese authorities and escaped to India in 1990. She lived in a nunnery during the interview in 2008.

Ani Dolkar was a 40-year-old nun from Ü-Tsang. She grew up in a semi-nomadic family with four siblings. She went to school for less than one year. Her aunt was a nun and inspired her to become one as well. She became a nun when she was 15 years old and with her aunt she helped to rebuild a destroyed nunnery near Lhasa. She participated in a demonstration in 1988 and was detained and tortured. She was also expelled from the nunnery and escaped to India, where I interviewed her in 2008.

Ani Rinchen was a 35-year-old nun from the Kham part of Qinghai. She was from a pastoral family and the oldest of three siblings. Her mother died when the children were still young, and they were taken care of by the father. Ani Rinchen was one of the most educated nuns I interviewed. Altogether she had studied

Appendix

more than ten years (for example, medicine at a university) and she sometimes practiced as a doctor. She became a nun when she was 21 years old. When I interviewed her in 2011, she lived in a newly built nunnery in Kham, Qinghai.

Ani Jamyang was 44 years old and from Kham, Qinghai. Her family was a semi-nomadic family with two children. She never went to school. Ani Jamyang donned the robes together with her mother after her father died when she was 22 years old. She meditated in the mountains for twenty years and earned a rare ordination called "tsulme." Her extraordinary ordination level was marked, for example, by her long hair. She lived in a newly built nunnery in Kham, Qinghai when I interviewed her in 2011.

Ani Karma was 60 years old and from Kham, Qinghai. Her parents used to be nomads with moderate economic conditions. The family had five children, of whom she was the oldest. She went to school for one year. Ani Karma became a nun when she was around six years old. She had never lived in a nunnery, but stayed at her natal home. She was interviewed in 2011.

Ani Samten, a 41-year-old nun from Kham, Qinghai, came from a family practicing agriculture. Her family was poor with five children. The mother had died. She did not go to school and became a nun when she was 16 years old. She was staying at a nunnery in Kham when I interviewed her in 2009.

Ani Palmo was 27 years old and from Kham, Qinghai. Her family's livelihood was pastoralism and she described their economic situation as moderate. The family had seven children. The mother had passed away. Her brothers went to school, but she did not. Ani Palmo became a nun when she was 25 years old and lived in a nunnery in Kham, Qinghai, where she was interviewed in 2009.

Ani Gyurmey was a 22-year-old nun from Kham, Qinghai. She described her family conditions as poor with everyone suffering from some kind of sickness. As a child she suffered from a mysterious illness with swoons, but got better as she grew up. The family had seven children and their livelihood mainly came from digging caterpillar fungus. She went to school for four years and became a nun when she was 19 years old. Two of her brothers were also monks. She lived in a nunnery in Kham, Qinghai. I interviewed her in 2009.

Ani Tashi was a 38-year-old nun from Kham, Qinghai. Her childhood family subsisted on pastoralism and their living conditions were moderate. The family had eight children and both of the parents had already passed away. She never went to school and became a nun when she was 20 years old. Her brother was a monk. She lived in a nunnery in Kham, Qinghai. She was interviewed in 2009.

Ani Yongtsen was 21 years old and from Kham, Qinghai. Her family was poor without any permanent source of livelihood. She had one sibling. She went to school for seven years and became a nun when she was 16 years old. She lived in a nunnery in Kham, Qinghai. I interviewed her in 2009.

Ani Phuntsok was a 31-year-old nun from Kham, Qinghai. She came from a poor family practicing agriculture. There were six children in her family. The mother had passed away. She went to school for eight years. Ani Phuntsok became a nun as a 27-year-old and lived in a nunnery in Kham, Qinghai, where I interviewed her in 2009.

Ani Choedron, a 32-year-old nun, came from Kham, Qinghai. Her father worked for the government and there were five children in the family. She went to school for thirteen years and became a nun when she was 22 years old. Her niece and uncle were also monastics. She lived in a nunnery in Kham, Qinghai. I interviewed her in 2009.

Ani Gyaltsen was 44 years old. She was from Kham, Qinghai, where her family led a semi-nomadic life style. The family was poor with eight children. She did not go to school and became a nun at 11 years old. One of her brothers was a monk. She lived in a nunnery in Kham, Qinghai, where she was interviewed in 2009.

Ani Kalsang, 37, was from a semi-nomadic family in Kham, Qinghai. There were ten children in her family. She went to school for two years and became a nun when she was 17 years old. Her brother was a monk. Ani Kalsang lived in a nunnery in Kham, Qinghai. She was interviewed in 2009.

Ani Lhatso was 37 years old and from Kham, Qinghai. For a living, the family rented apartments. Their living conditions were moderate. The family had five children. Ani Lhatso went to school for one year and became a nun when she was 20 years old. She stayed in a nunnery in Kham, Qinghai, where I interviewed her in 2009.

Ani Ngawang was a 39-year-old nun from Kham, Qinghai. Her family earned their living mainly by collecting caterpillar fungus and their living conditions were poor. The family had five children. She never went to school and became a nun at 37 years old. She lived in a nunnery in Kham, where I interviewed her in 2009.

Ani Palden was a 22-year-old nun from Kham, TAR. Her family were pastoralists. She was the oldest of four children. Ani Palden went to school for three years and became a nun when she was 20 years old. Her sister was also a nun and they both lived in at the same nunnery in Kham, Qinghai. I interviewed her in 2009.

Ani Palkyi was a 32-year-old nun from Kham, Qinghai. When she was a child her family earned a living by doing various menial jobs. One of her brothers was taking care of the family. There were five children in the family and one of them lived as a monk in India. Ani Palkyi never went to school and became a nun when she was 18 years old. She lived in a nunnery in Kham, Qinghai, when I interviewed her in 2007 and 2009.

Ani Samdup was 44 years old and from Kham, Qinghai. Her family was semi-nomadic. She was the youngest of four children. The mother had passed away. She went to school for less than one year and became a nun when she was 18 years old. During the interview in 2009, she lived in a nunnery in Kham, Qinghai.

Appendix

Ani Sangye was 20 years old and from Kham, Qinghai. The family's income came from nomadic work and caterpillar fungus. There were nine children in the family. She never went to school and became a nun when she was 18 years old. She lived in a nunnery in Kham, Qinghai. I interviewed her in 2009.

Ani Sonam was 30 years old. She came from Kham, Qinghai. There were four children in the family. The father had passed away and one of the brothers had a small business and was taking care of the livelihood of the family. Their living conditions were poor. She never went to school and became a nun when she was 29 years old. She lived in a nunnery in Kham, Qinghai. I interviewed her in 2009.

Ani Tsering was 22 years old and from Kham, Qinghai. Her family led a semi-nomadic life. There were five children in the family. She went to school for three years and became a nun as a 20-year-old. Ani Tsering lived in a nunnery in Kham with her sister, who was also a nun, during the interview in 2009.

Ani Tsewang was a 95-year-old nun from Kham, Qinghai. She became a nun before the Cultural Revolution and joined a nunnery soon after that. During the dark years of the Cultural Revolution, she had to leave the nunnery. She had joined the newly built nunnery a few years before I interviewed her in 2009.

Ani Wangchuk, 35, came from a poor agricultural family in Amdo, Qinghai. She was the second oldest of four children and went to school for two years. She became a nun as a 14-year-old and lived in a nunnery in Amdo, Qinghai, when she was interviewed in 2011.

Ani Yonten was a 36-year-old nun from Amdo, Qinghai. She was from a family practicing agriculture. She was the youngest of five children in the family. Her mother had passed away. She went to school for eight years and became a nun when she was 16 years old. She was staying at a nunnery in Amdo, Qinghai when I interviewed her in 2011.

Ani Dawa, a 41-year-old nun, was from an agricultural family in Amdo, Qinghai. There were ten children in the family. She went to school for nine years and became a nun when she was 17. She lived in a nunnery in Amdo, Qinghai. I interviewed her in 2011.

Ani Dikey, 44, was from a poor pastoral family in Amdo, Qinghai. There were nine children in her family. The mother had passed away. She never went to school and became a nun when she was 15 years old. She stayed in a nuns' community in Amdo, Qinghai. She was interviewed in 2011.

Ani Pasang was 32 years old. She was from a family subsisting through pastoralism in Amdo, Qinghai. She was the youngest of eight children in the family. She never went to school and became a nun at 16 years old. She lived in a nuns' community in Amdo with her aunt, Ani Dikey, who was also a nun. I interviewed her in 2011.

Ani Pema was 68 years old and from Amdo, Qinghai. She was married and had a family before she became a nun as a 64-year-old. She had practiced agriculture with her husband. She never went to school. When I interviewed her in 2011, she lived near a big monastery in Amdo, Qinghai.

Ani Lhamo was 23 years old and from Amdo, Qinghai. The family was semi-nomadic and the father worked for the government. She had two brothers. She went to school for four years and became a nun when she was 18. She lived in a nuns' community in Amdo, Qinghai. I interviewed her in 2011.

Ani Sangmo, a 23-year-old nun from Amdo, Qinghai, was from a pastoral family. She was one of the youngest of thirteen children in the family. The parents were dead. She never went to school and she became a nun when she was 19 years old. She lived in a community of nuns in Amdo, Qinghai. She was interviewed in 2011.

Ani Tsomo was a 40-year-old nun from Amdo, Qinghai. Her family's livelihood was based on agriculture. She was the oldest of the seven children. She had lost her parents when she was young and had taken care of the younger siblings. She became a nun when she was 28 years old. She lived in a nuns' community in Amdo, Qinghai. I interviewed her in 2011.

Ani Changchub, 53, was originally from the Amdo region of Gansu. She never went to school. She had practiced agriculture for living. She became a nun a year after she lost her husband at the age of 44. She stayed in a nuns' community in Amdo, Qinghai. Ani Tsomo was her niece. I interviewed her in 2011.

Ani Norzom, 31, was from a pastoral family in Amdo, Sichuan. There were six children in the family. Two of the brothers were monks. She never went to school and became a nun when she was 17 years old. She lived at home in Amdo, Sichuan. I interviewed her in 2011.

Ani Palzon was a 33-year-old nun from the Amdo region in Sichuan. She was from a pastoral family with four children, and her parents were still alive. She never went to school and became a nun at 19. Her sister and a niece were nuns and her brother was a monk. She stayed at a big nunnery in Sichuan. I interviewed her in 2011.

References

Interviews

Life Story Interviews

Ani Sherab, Ani Dechen, Ani Tenzin, Ani Dolma, Ani Dolkar: interviewed in Dharamsala, 1–30 June 2008

Ani Sonam, Ani Sangye, Ani Samdup, Ani Palden, Ani Palkyi, Ani Lhatso, Ani Ngawang, Ani Gyaltsen, Ani Kalsang, Ani Samten, Ani Palmo, Ani Gyurmey, Ani Tashi, Ani Yongtsen, Ani Phuntsok, Ani Choedron, Ani Tsering, Ani Tsewang: interviewed in Yushu, 24–31 July 2009

Ani Wangchuk, Ani Yonten, Ani Dawa, Ani Palzon, Ani Dikey, Ani Pasang, Ani Sangmo, Ani Pema, Ani Tsomo, Ani Lhamo, Ani Changchub, Ani Norzom: interviewed in Qinghai, 4–30 June 2011

Thematic Interviews

IN2007/1, IN2007/2, IN2007/3, IN2007/5, IN2007/11, IN2007/12, IN2007/20, IN2007/23, IN2007/24, IN2007/26, IN2007/27, in Xining, Gyegu and Jainca in the PRC, 12.8.–3.11.2007

IN2009/1, in Gyegu, 18.–20.7.2009

N2011/1, IN2011/2, IN2011/3, IN2011/5, IN2011/7, IN2011/8, IN2011/9, IN2011/10, IN2011/11, IN2011/12, IN2011/13, IN2011/14, IN2011/15, IN2011/16, IN2011/19, IN2011/20, in Xining and Kumbum, 30 May to 7 July 2011

Other Interviews

A nun interviewed for the master's thesis in Dharamsala in 2004.

A nun and co-director of the Tibetan Nuns' Project, interviewed for the master's thesis in Dharamsala in 2004.

The interview material and fieldwork notes are in the possession of the author.

Bibliography

Adams, Vincanne (1996). "Karaoke as Modern Lhasa, Tibet: Western Encounters with Cultural Politics." *Cultural Anthropology*, 11 (4): 510–546. https://doi.org/10.1525/can.1996.11.4.02a00040

Ahonen, Johanna & Elina Vuola (2015). "Uskonto ja sukupuoli: konflikteja, vuorovaikutusta ja uusia tuulia." In *Uskonnon ja sukupuolen risteyksiä*, edited by Johanna Ahonen & Elina Vuola. Tietolipas; Vuosikerta 247. Suomalaisen Kirjallisuuden Seura, 7–13.

Allen, Amy (1998). "Rethinking Power." *Hypatia*, 13 (1): 21–40.

Allen, Amy (2011). "Feminist Perspectives on Power." In *The Stanford Encyclopedia of Philosophy (Spring 2011 Edition)*, edited by Edward N. Zalta, http://plato.stanford.edu/archives/spr2011/entries/feminist-power/. Accessed 1.9.2014.

Allione, Tsultrim (1984). *Women of Wisdom*. London: Arkana.

Amara Singham, Lorna Rhodes (1978). "The Misery of the Embodied: Representations of Women in Sinhalese Myth." In *Women in Ritual and Symbolic Roles*, edited by Judith Hoch-Smith and Anita Spring, 101–126. New York: Plenum Press.

Anand, Dibyesh (2000). "(Re)imagining Nationalism: Identity and Representation in the Tibetan Diaspora of South Asia." *Contemporary South Asia* 9 (3): 271–287. https://doi.org/10.1080/713658756

Anderson, Benedict (1991). *Imagined Communities: Reflections on the Origin and Spread of Nationalism*. London: Verso.

Arai, Paula (1999). *Women Living Zen: Japanese Soto Buddhist Nuns*. New York: Oxford University Press.

Aronson, Jodi (1994). "A Pragmatic View of Thematic Analysis." *The Qualitative Report*, 2: 1–3. www.nova.edu/ssss/QR/BackIssues/QR2-1/aronson.html. Accesed 12.1.2015.

Asikainen, Raisa, and Juha Vuori (2005). "Johdanto." In *Kiinan yhteiskunta muutoksessa*, edited by Raisa Asikainen and Juha Vuori, 1–17. Helsinki: Gaudeamus.

Atkinson, Robert (1998). *The Life Story Interview*. Qualitative Research Methods, vol. 44. Thousand Oaks, CA: Sage Publications.

Aziz, Barbara Nimri (1987). "Moving Towards a Sociology of Tibet." In *Feminine Ground. Essays on Women and Tibet*, edited by Janice D. Willis, 76–95. Ithaca: Snow Lion Publications.

Bangsbo, Ellen (2008). "Schooling and 'Quality Education' in the Tibetan Diaspora and Tibet." In *Tibetan Modernities: Notes from the Field on Cultural*

References

and Social Change, edited by Robert Barnett and Ronald Schwartz, 189-212. Leiden: Brill.

Barnett, Robert (2005). "Women and Politics in Contemporary Tibet." In *Women in Tibet*, edited by Janet Gyatso and Hanna Havnevik, 285-366. New York: Columbia University Press.

Barnett, Robert (2008). "Preface." In *Tibetan Modernities: Notes from the Field on Cultural and Social Change*, edited by Robert Barnett and Ronald Schwartz, xii-xxii. Leiden: Brill.

Bartholomeusz, Tessa (1994). *Women under the Bō Tree: Buddhist Nuns in Sri Lanka*. Cambridge: Cambridge University Press.

Bartholomeusz, Tessa (2000). "Women, War, and Peace in Sri Lanka." In *Women's Buddhism, Buddhism's Women: Tradition, Revision, Renewal*, edited by Ellison Banks Findly, 283-296. Boston, MA: Wisdom Publications.

Baumann, Martin (2001). "Global Buddhism: Developmental Periods, Regional Histories, and a New Analytical Perspective." *Journal of Global Buddhism*, 2: 1-43.

Bell, Charles, Sir (1968) [1928]. *The People of Tibet*. Oxford: Clarendon Press.

Bird, Frederick, and Laurie Lamoureux Scholes (2011). "Research Ethics." In *The Routledge Handbook of Research Methods in the Study of Religion*, edited by Michael Stausberg and Steven Engler, 81-105. London: Routledge.

Braun, Virginia, and Victoria Clarke (2006). "Using Thematic Analysis in Psychology." *Qualitative Research in Psychology*, 3 (2): 77-101. https://doi.org/10.1191/1478088706qp063oa

Bruce, Steve (1996). *Religion in the Modern World: From Cathedrals to Cults*. New York: Oxford University Press.

Bruce, Steve (1999). "Modernization, Individualism and Secularization." In *Religion and Social Transitions*, edited by Eila Helander, 15-27. Publications of the Department of Practical Theology, 95. Helsinki: University of Helsinki.

Bruce, Steve (2002). *God is Dead: Secularization in the West*. Oxford: Blackwell.

Bunnag, Jane (1973). *Buddhist Monk, Buddhist Layman: A Study of Urban Monastic Organization in Central Thailand*. Cambridge: University Press.

Butler, Alex (2003). *Feminism, Nationalism and Exiled Tibetan Women*. New Delhi: Kali for Women.

Butler, Judith (1999). *Gender Trouble: Feminism and the Subversion of Identity*. New York: Routledge.

Campbell, June (2002). *Gender, Identity and Tibetan Buddhism*. Delhi: Motilal Banarsidass Publishers.

Carbonnel, Laure (2009). "On the Ambivalence of Female Monasticism in Theravāda Buddhism: A Contribution to the Study of the Monastic System in Myanmar." *Asian Ethnology* 68 (2): 265–282.

Casanova, José (1994). *Public Religions in the Modern World*. Chicago, IL: University of Chicago Press.

Castelli, Elizabeth A. (2001). "Introduction." In *Women, Gender, Religion: A Reader*, edited by Elizabeth A. Castelli, 3–25. New York: Palgrave.

Chertow, Jennifer Marie (2008). "Embodying the Nation: Childbirth in Contemporary Tibet." In *Tibetan Modernities: Notes from the Field on Cultural and Social Change*, edited by Robert Barnett and Ronald Schwartz, 139–162. Leiden: Brill.

Cho, Sumi, Kimberlé Williams Crenshaw and Leslie McCall (2013). "Toward a Field of Intersectionality Studies: Theory, Applications, and Praxis." *Signs*, 38 (4): 785–810. https://doi.org/10.1086/669608

Cho, Yasmin (2015). *Politics of Tranquility: Religious Mobilities and Material Engagements of Tibetan Buddhist Nuns in Post-Mao China*. Department of Cultural Anthropology, Duke University. PhD dissertation.

Coleman, Simon, and Pauline von Hellermann (2011). "Introduction: Queries, Collaborations, Calibrations." In *Multi-sited Ethnography: Problems and Possibilities in the Translocation of Research Methods*, edited by Simon Coleman and Pauline von Hellermann, 1–15. New York: Routledge.

Collins, Patricia Hill (2000). *Black Feminist Thought: Knowledge, Consciousness, and the Politics of Empowerment*. New York: Routledge.

Collins, Patricia Hill (2015). "Intersectionality's Definitional Dilemmas." *Annual Review of Sociology*, 41: 1–20. https://doi.org/10.1146/annurev-soc-073014-112142

Costello, Susan (2008). "The Flow of Wealth in Golok Pastoralist Society: Towards an Assessment of Local Financial Resources for Economic Development." In *Tibetan Modernities: Notes from the Field on Cultural and Social Change*, edited by Robert Barnett and Ronald Schwartz, 73–112. Leiden: Brill.

Crenshaw, Kimberlé Williams (1991). "Mapping the Margins: Intersectionality, Identity Politics, and Violence against Women of Color." *Stanford Law Review*, 43 (6): 1241–1299. https://doi.org/10.2307/1229039

Davidsson Bremborg, Anna (2011). Interviewing. In *The Routledge Handbook of Research Methods in the Study of Religion*, edited by Michael Stausberg and Steven Engler, Routledge, 310–322.

Davis, Kathy (2014). "Intersectionality as Critical Methodology." In *Writing Academic Texts Differently: Intersectional Feminist Methodologies and the Playful Art of Writing*, edited by Nina Lykke, 17–29. New York: Routledge.

References

Dawa Norbu (2003). "The Settlements: Participation and Integration." In *Exile as Challenge: The Tibetan Diaspora*, edited by Dagmar Bernstorff and Hubertus von Weck, 186–212. New Delhi: Orient Longman.

Denwood, Philip (1999). *Tibetan*. Amsterdam: John Benjamins Publishing.

Delanty, Gerard, and Krishan Kumar (2006). "Introduction." In *The Sage Handbook of Nations and Nationalism*, edited by Gerard Delanty and Krishan Kumar, 1–4. London: Sage Publications.

Dhamoon, Rita Kaur (2011). "Considerations of Mainstreaming Intersectionality." *Political Research Quarterly*, 64 (1): 230–243. https://doi.org/10.1177/1065912910379227

Dreyfus, Georges (2003). *The Sound of Two Hands Clapping: The Education of a Tibetan Buddhist Monk*. Berkeley, CA: University of California Press.

Dubisch, Jill (2016). "Can There Be Religion Without Gender?" In *Contemporary Encounters in Gender and Religion: European Perspectives*, edited by Lena Gemzöe, Marja-Liisa Keinänen and Avril Maddrell, 31–51. Palgrave Macmillan.

Eichman, Jennifer (2011). "Prominent Nuns: Influential Taiwanese Voices." *Cross Currents* 61 (3): 345–373. https://doi.org/10.1111/j.1939-3881.2011.00187.x

Eriksen, Thomas Hylland (2001). *Small Places, Large Issues: An Introduction to Social and Cultural Anthropology*. London: Pluto Press.

Falk, Nancy Auer (1980). "The Case of the Vanishing Nuns: The Fruits of Ambivalence in Ancient Indian Buddhism." In *Unspoken Worlds: Women's Religious Lives in Non-Western Cultures*, edited by Nancy Falk and Rita M. Gross, 206–224. San Francisco: Harper & Row.

Falk Lindberg, Monica (2000). "Women in Between: Becoming Religious Persons in Thailand." In *Women's Buddhism, Buddhism's Women: Tradition, Revision, Renewal*, edited by Ellison Banks Findly, 37–57. Boston, MA: Wisdom Publications.

Falzon, Mark-Anthony (2012). "Introduction to Multi-Sited Ethnography: Theory, Praxis and Locality in Contemporary Research." In *Multi-Sited Ethnography: Theory, Praxis and Locality in Contemporary Research*, edited by Mark-Anthony Falzon, 1–23. Farnham: Ashgate.

Ferguson, James (2011). "Novelty and Method. Reflections on Global Fieldwork." In *Multi-sited Ethnography: Problems and Possibilities in the Translocation of Research Methods*, edited by Simon Coleman and Pauline von Hellermann, 194–208. New York: Routledge.

Fjeld, Heidi (2008). "Pollution and Social Networks in Contemporary Rural Tibet." In *Tibetan Modernities: Notes from the Field on Cultural and Social Change*, edited by Robert Barnett and Ronald Schwartz, 113–138. Leiden: Brill.

Florida, Robert (2000). "Buddhism and Abortion." In *Contemporary Buddhist Ethics*, edited by Damien Keown, 137-168. New York: Routledge Curzon.

Gemzöe, Lena, Marja-Liisa Keinänen and Avril Maddrell (2016). "Contemporary Encounters in Gender and Religion: Introduction." In *Contemporary Encounters in Gender and Religion European Perspectives*, edited by Lena Gemzöe, Marja-Liisa Keinänen and Avril Maddrell, 1-28.

Goldstein, Melvyn C. (1989). *A History of Modern Tibet, Volume 1: 1913-1951: The Demise of the Lamaist State*. Berkeley, CA: University of California Press.

Goldstein, Melvyn C. (1997). *A History of Modern Tibet, Volume 2: The Calm Before the Storm: 1951-1955*. Berkeley, CA: University of California Press.

Goldstein, Melvyn C. (1998a). "Introduction." In *Buddhism in Contemporary Tibet: Religious Revival and Cultural Identity*, edited by Melvyn Goldstein and Matthew Kapstein, 1-14. Berkeley, CA: University of California Press.

Goldstein, Melvyn C. (1998b). "The Revival of Monastic Life in Drepung Monastery." In *Buddhism in Contemporary Tibet: Religious Revival and Cultural Identity*, edited by Melvyn Goldstein and Matthew Kapstein, 15-52. Berkeley, CA: University of California Press.

Goldstein, Melvyn C., Ben Jiao, Cynthia Beall & Phuntsog Tsering (2003). "Development and Change in Rural Tibet: Problems and Adaptations." *Asian Survey*, 43(5), 758-779. https://doi.org/10.1525/as.2003.43.5.758

Goldstein, Melvyn C., Ben Jiao, Cynthia M. Beall and Phuntsog Tsering (2002). "Fertility and Family Planning in Rural Tibet." *The China Journal*, 47: 19-39. https://doi.org/10.2307/3182072

Goldstein, Melvyn C., and Cynthia M. Beall (1990). *Nomads of Western Tibet: The Survival of a Way of Life*. Hong Kong: Serindia Publications.

Goldstein, Melvyn, and Paljor Tsarong (1985). "Tibetan Buddhist Monasticism: Social, Psychological and Cultural Implications." *The Tibet Journal*, 10 (1): 14-31.

Graham, Gordon (1988). *Contemporary Social Philosophy*. Oxford: Basil Blackwell.

Grimshaw, Anna (1994). *Servants of the Buddha: Winter in a Himalayan Convent*. Cleveland: The Pilgrim Press.

Gross, Rita M. (1993). *Buddhism after Patriarchy: A Feminist History, Analysis, and Reconstruction of Buddhism*. Albany: State University of New York Press.

Gross, Rita M. (2005). "Gender and Religion: Gender and Buddhism." In *Encyclopedia of Religion*, edited by Lindsay Jones. 2nd ed. Vol. 5. Detroit, MI: Macmillan Reference, 3330-3335.

Gruschke, Andreas (2001). *The Cultural Monuments of Tibet's Outer Provinces: Amdo. Volume 1. The Qinghai Part of Amdo*. Bangkok: White Lotus Press.

References

Gupta, Akhil, and James Ferguson (1997). "Beyond 'Culture': Space, Identity, and the Politics of Difference." In *Culture, Power and Place: Explorations in Critical Anthropology*, edited by Akhil Gupta and James Ferguson, 33–51. Durham, NC: Duke University Press.

Gutschow, Kim (1997). "Unfocussed Merit-Making in Zangskar: A Socio-Economic Account of Karsha Nunnery." *The Tibetan Journal*, 22 (2): 30–58.

Gutschow, Kim (2000). "Novice Ordination for Nuns: The Rhetoric and Reality of Female Monasticism in Northwest India." In *Women's Buddhism, Buddhism's Women: Tradition, Revision, Renewal*, edited by Ellison Banks Findly, 103–118. Boston, MA: Wisdom Publication.

Gutschow, Kim (2001). "What Makes a Nun? Apprenticeship and Ritual Passage in Zanskar, North India." *JIABS Journal of the International Association of Buddhist Studies*, 24 (2), 187–216.

Gutschow, Kim (2004). *Being a Buddhist Nun: The Struggle for Enlightenment in the Himalayas*. Cambridge, MA: Harvard University Press.

Gyatso, Janet (1987). "Down With the Demoness: Reflections on a Feminine Ground in Tibet." In *Feminine Ground: Essays on Women and Tibet*, edited by Janice D. Willis, 33–51. Ithaca, NY: Snow Lion Publications.

Gyatso, Janet, and Hanna Havnevik (2005). "Introduction." In *Women in Tibet*, edited by Janet Gyatso and Hanna Havnevik, 1–25. New York: Columbia University Press.

Haas, Michaela (2013). *Dakini Power: Twelve Extraordinary Women Shaping the Transmission of Tibetan Buddhism in the West*. Boston & London: Snow Lion.

Hae-ju Sunim (1999). "Can Women Achieve Enlightenment? A Critique of Sexual Transformation for Enlightenment." In *Buddhist Women Across Cultures: Realizations*, edited by Karma Lekshe Tsomo, 123–141. Delhi: Sri Satguru Publications.

Hallisey, Charles (2015). *Therīgāthā: Poems of the First Buddhist Women*. Cambridge, MA: Harvard University Press.

Hammersley, Martyn, and Paul Atkinson (2007). *Ethnography: Principles in Practice*. London: Routledge.

Hannerz, Ulf (2003). "Being There ... and There ... and There! Reflections on Multi-site ethnography." *Ethnography*, 4 (2): 201–216. https://doi.org/10.1177/14661381030042003

Härkönen, Mitra (2005). *Myötätunnosta autuaan: Nunnien asema ja sukupuolten ero tiibetinbuddhalaisessa luostari-instituutiossa Pohjois-Intiassa*. Helsinki: University of Helsinki. Master's thesis.

Härkönen, Mitra (2008). "Tibetan Refugee Communities and Tibetan Buddhism in the West." In *Tibet. A Culture in Transition*, edited by Marjo-Riitta

Saloniemi and Tiina Hyytiäinen, 86–107. Tampere: Tampere Museum's Publications.

Härkönen, Mitra (2009). "The Changing Place of Religion and the Question of Secularization in the 'Modernization' of Tibet." In *Local and Global Encounters: Norms, Identities and Representations in Formation*, edited by Tuija Veintie and Pirjo Kristiina Virtanen, 43–60. Helsinki: University of Helsinki.

Härkönen, Mitra (2010). "(Com)passionate Enlightenment: On the Soteriological Significance of Tibetan Monasticism." In *Pilgrimage of Life: Studies in Honour of Professor René Gothóni*, edited by Riku Hämäläinen, Heikki Pesonen, Mari Rahkala and Tuula Sakaranaho, 371–384. Helsinki: Maahenki.

Härkönen, Mitra (2013). "Tibetan Nuns: Gender as a Force in a Culture under 'Threat'." In *Ex Oriente Lumina: Historiae variae multiethnicae*, Studia Orientalia, 113, edited by Tiina Hyytiäinen, Lotta Jalava, Janne Saarikivi and Erika Sandman, 27–38. Helsinki: University of Helsinki.

Härkönen, Mitra (2016). "Tiibetiläisnunnat: ikuisia noviiseja ja isänmaallisia aktivisteja." In *Enemmän kuin puoli taivasta: Kiinalainen nainen historiassa, yhteiskunnassa ja kulttuurissa*, edited by Tiina Airaksinen, Elina Sinkkonen and Minna Valjakka, 281–284. Tallinn: Arthouse.

Harris, Elisabeth (1999). "The Female in Buddhism." In *Buddhist Women Across Cultures: Realizations*, edited by Karma Lekshe Tsomo, 49–65. Delhi: Sri Satguru Publications.

Harvey, Peter (2005). *An Introduction to Buddhism: Teachings, History and Practices*. Cambridge University Press.

Havnevik, Hanna (1989). *Tibetan Buddhist Nuns: History, Cultural Norms and Social Reality*. Oslo: Norwegian University Press.

Havnevik, Hanna (1994). "The Role of Nuns in Contemporary Tibet." In *Resistance and Reform in Tibet*, edited by Robert Barnett, 259–266. London: Hurst & Company.

Heirman, Ann (2011). "Buddhist Nuns: Between Past and Present." *Numen* 58, 603–631. https://doi.org/10.1163/156852711X593278

Horner, I. B. (1975) [1930]. *Women Under Primitive Buddhism: Laywomen and Almswomen*. Delhi: Motilal Banarsidass.

Huber, Toni (2002). "Introduction: Amdo and Its Modern Transition." In *Amdo Tibetans in Transition. Society and Culture in the Post-Mao Era*, edited by Toni Huber, xi–xxiii. Leiden: Brill.

Huttunen, Laura (2010). "Tiheä kontekstointi: Haastattelu osana etnografista tutkimusta." In *Haastattelun analyysi*, edited by Johanna Ruusuvuori, Pirjo Nikander and Matti Hyvärinen, 39–63. Tampere: Vastapaino.

References

Hu Wang, Yujun Cui, Zuyun Wang, Xiaoyi Wang, Zhaobiao Guo, Yanfeng Yan, Chao Li, Baizhong Cui, Xiao Xiao, Yonghai Yang, Zhizhen Qi, Guojun Wang, Baiqing Wei, Shouhong Yu, Duolong He, Hongjian Chen, Gang Chen, Yajun Song, and Ruifu Yang (2011). "A Dog-Associated Primary Pneumonic Plague in Qinghai Province, China." *Clinical Infectious Diseases.* https://doi.org/10.1093/cid/ciq107

Hyytiäinen, Tiina (2008). "Between Kitchen Stove and Monastery: Facets of Amdo Tibetan Women." In *Tibet: A Culture in Transition*, edited by Marjo-Riitta Saloniemi and Tiina Hyytiäinen, 108–136. Tampere: Tampere Museum's Publications.

Jacobsen, Christine M. (2011). "Troublesome Threesome: Feminism, Anthropology and Muslim Women's Piety." *Feminist Review* 98, 65–82. https://doi.org/10.1057/fr.2011.10

Jacoby, Sarah (2015). "Relational Autonomy in the Life of a Contemporary Tibetan Dākinī." In *Women as Visionaries, Healers and Agents of Social Transformation in the Himalayas, Tibet and Mongolia*, Revue d'Etudes Tibétaines, 34, edited by Mona Schrempf and Nicola Schneider, 79–113.

Janhunen, Juha (2008). "Tibet: A Land of Ancient Dreams and Modern Realities." In *Tibet: A Culture in Transition*, edited by Marjo-Riitta Saloniemi and Tiina Hyytiäinen, 10–39. Tampere: Tampere Museum's Publications.

Jayawardena, Kumari (1986). *Feminism and Nationalism in the Third World*. London: Zed Books.

Jones, Katherine Castiello, Joya Misra, and K. McCurley (2013). "Intersectionality in Sociology." *SWS Fact Sheet.* Sociologists for Women in Society. https://socwomen.org/about/current-officers-and-chairs-2/.

Kallio, Jyrki (2005). "Onko Kiinassa keskiluokkaa?" In *Kiinan yhteiskunta muutoksessa*, edited by Raisa Asikainen and Juha Vuori, 73–88. Helsinki: Gaudeamus.

Kalsang Gyamtso (2008). "Modern Challenges in Tibet." In *Tibet: A Culture in Transition*, edited by Marjo-Riitta Saloniemi and Tiina Hyytiäinen, 138–155. Tampere: Tampere Museum's Publications.

Kapstein, Matthew T. (1998). "Concluding Reflections." In *Buddhism in Contemporary Tibet: Religious Revival and Cultural Identity*, edited by Melvyn Goldstein and Matthew Kapstein, 139–150. Berkeley, CA: University of California Press.

Keown, Damien (2005). *Buddhist Ethics: A Very Short Introduction*. Oxford: Oxford University Press.

King, Ursula (1995). "Introduction: Gender and the Study of Religion." In *Religion & Gender*, edited by Ursula King, 1–38. Oxford: Blackwell.

Kolås, Åshild (1996). "Tibetan Nationalism: The Politics of Religion." *Journal of Peace Research*, 33(1):51–66. https://doi.org/10.1177/0022343396033001004

Kragh, Ulrich Timme (2011). "Appropriation and Assertion of the Female Self: Materials for the Study of the Female Tantric Master Lakṣmī Uḍḍiyāna." *Journal of Feminist Studies in Religion*, 27 (2): 85–108. https://doi.org/10.2979/jfemistudreli.27.2.85

Kupari, Helena, and Salome Tuomaala (2015). "Toimijuus ja muutoksen mahdollisuus. Esimerkkinä vanhoillislestadiolaisuuden tutkimus." In *Uskonnon ja sukupuolen risteyksiä*, edited by Johanna Ahonen and Elina Vuola, 161–187. Helsinki: Suomalaisen Kirjallisuuden Seura.

Kvaerne, Per (1984). "Tibet: the Rise and Fall of a Monastic Tradition." In *The World of Buddhism. Buddhist Monks and Nuns in Society and Culture*, edited by Heinz Bechert, and Richard Gombrich, 253–270. London: Thames and Hudson.

LaFever, Kathryn (2017). "Buddhist Nuns in Nepal and Women's Empowerment: A Biographical Approach." *Women's Studies International Forum* 64, 41–50. https://doi.org/10.1016/j.wsif.2017.08.002

Lahtinen, Anja (2010). *Governance Matters: China's Developing Western Region with a Focus on Qinghai Province*. Publications of the Institute for Asian and African Studies 11. Helsinki: University of Helsinki. PhD Dissertation.

Lam, Willy (2006). "The Qinghai-Tibet Railway: China's New Instrument for Assimilation." *China Brief. A Journal of Analysis and Information*, 6 (14):1–3.

LaMacchia, Linda (2001). *Songs And Lives of The Jomo (Nuns) Of Kinnaur, Northwest India: Women's Religious Expression in Tibetan Buddhism*. University of Wisconsin-Madison. PhD Dissertation.

LaMacchia, Linda (2016). "Buddhist Women Masters of Kinnaur: Why Don't Nuns Sing about Nuns?" *International Journal of Dharma Studies*, 4:5. https://doi.org/10.1186/s40613-016-0029-5.

Lamotte, Étienne (1984). "The Buddha, His Teachings and His Sangha." In *The World of Buddhism: Buddhist Monks and Nuns in Society and Culture*, edited by Heinz Bechert and Richard Gombrich, 41–59. London: Thames and Hudson.

LeClear, McKenna (2013). "Bhikshunis and Breaking Barriers: The Changing Status of Women in Monastic Life." *Independent Study Project (ISP) Collection*. 1565. https://digitalcollections.sit.edu/isp_collection/1565

Leshkowich, Ann Marie (2006). "Woman, Buddhist, Entrepreneur: Gender, Moral Values, and Class Anxiety in Late Socialist Vietnam." *Journal of Vietnamese Studies*, 1: 277–313. https://doi.org/10.1525/vs.2006.1.1-2.277

Lhundrub Dorji (2010). "Tibetan Buddhist Nuns. Damcho Pema's Prostrating Pilgrimage to Lhasa." In *Pilgrims and Travellers in the Search of the Holy*, edited by René Gothóni, 259–272. Oxford: Peter Lang.

References

Lopez, Donald S. Jr. (1998). *Prisoners of Shangri-La: Tibetan Buddhism and the West*. Chicago, IL: University of Chicago Press.

Luova, Outi (1999). "Kiinan reuna-alueet 1990-luvulla: Taloudellista ja poliittista tasapainoilua Kiinan ja Aasian muuttuessa." In *Kiinan modernisaatio: Kiinalaisia ominaispiirteitä*, Turun yliopiston poliittisen historian tutkimuksia, 16, edited by Marita Siika, 135–150. Turku: University of Turku.

Luova, Outi (2005). "Työvoiman muuttoliikkeet Kiinassa: kohti vaurautta ja eriarvoisuutta." In *Kiinan yhteiskunta muutoksessa*, edited by Raisa Asikainen and Juha Vuori, 52–72. Helsinki: Gaudeamus.

Mahmood, Saba (2005). *Politics of Piety: The Islamic Revival and the Feminist Subject*. Princeton, NJ: Princeton University Press.

Makley, Charlene (1997). "The Meaning of Liberation: Representations of Tibetan Women." *The Tibetan Journal*, 22 (2): 4–29.

Makley, Charlene (1999). *Embodying the Sacred: Gender and Monastic Revitalization in China's Tibet*. The University of Michigan. PhD Dissertation.

Makley, Charlene (2002a). "Sexuality and Identity in Post-Mao Amdo." In *Amdo Tibetans in Transition: Society and Culture in the Post-Mao Era*, edited by Toni Huber, 53–98. Leiden: Brill's Tibetan Studies Library.

Makley, Charlene (2002b). "On the Edge of Respectability: Sexual Politics in China's Tibet." *Positions: East Asia Cultures Critique*, 10 (3): 575–630. https://doi.org/10.1215/10679847-10-3-575

Makley, Charlene (2005). "The Body of a Nun: Nunhood and Gender in Contemporary Amdo." In *Women in Tibet*, edited by Janet Gyatso and Hanna Havnevik, 259–284. New York: Columbia University Press.

Mann, Amy L. (2009). Anis of Dolma Ling: Buddhist Doctrine and Social Praxis Through the Monasticism of Tibetan Nuns in Exile. *Scripps Senior Theses*. Paper 13. http://scholarship.claremont.edu/scripps_theses/13

Marcus, George E. (1995). "Ethnography in/of the World System: The Emergence of Multi-Sited Ethnography." *Annual Review of Anthropology*, 24: 95–117. https://doi.org/10.1146/annurev.an.24.100195.000523

Marcus, George E. (1999). "What is at Stake – and is Not – in the Idea and Practices of Multi-sited Ethnography." *Canberra Anthropology*, 22 (2): 6–14. https://doi.org/10.1080/03149099909508344

Marcus, George E. (2005). "Multi-sited Ethnography: Five of Six Things I Know About it Now." Problems and Possibilities in Multi-sited Ethnography Workshop, 27–28 June 2005, University of Sussex. (Unpublished paper.)

Martin, Dan (2005). "The Woman Illusion? Research into the Lives of Spiritually Accomplished Women Leaders of the 11th and 12th Centuries." In *Women in Tibet*, edited by Janet Gyatso and Hanna Havnevik, 49–82. New York: Columbia University Press.

May, Vivian M. (2012). "Intersectionality." In *Rethinking Women's and Gender Studies*, edited by Catherine M. Orr, Ann Braithwaite and Diane Lichtenstein, 155–172. New York: Routledge.

McCall, Leslie (2005). "The Complexity of Intersectionality." *Signs*, 30 (3): 1771–1800. https://doi.org/10.1086/426800

Miller, Tina (2013). Messy Ethics. Negotiating the Terrain between Ethics Approval and Ethical Practice. In *Ethics in the Field: Contemporary Challenges*, edited by Jeremy MacClancy and Agustín Fuentes, 140–155. Oxford: Berghahn Books.

Mills, Martin (2000). "*Vajra* Brother, *Vajra* Sister: Renunciation, Individualism and Household in Tibetan Buddhist Monasticism." *Journal of the Royal Anthropological Institute*, 6 (1): 17–34. https://doi.org/10.1111/1467-9655.t01-1-00002

Mills, Martin (2003). *Identity, Ritual and State in Tibetan Buddhism. The Foundations of Authority in Gelukpa Monasticism*. London: RoutledgeCurzon.

Mrozik, Susanne (2009). "A Robed Revolution: The Contemporary Buddhist Nun's (*Bhikṣuṇī*) Movement." *Religion Compass* 3/3: 360–378. https://doi.org/10.1111/j.1749-8171.2009.00136.x

Nadai, Eva, and Christoph Maeder (2005). "Fuzzy Fields: Multi-Sited Ethnography in Sociological Research." *Forum Qualitative Sozialforschung / Forum: Qualitative Social Research*, 6 (3), [24 paragraphs]. Art. 28, http://nbn-resolving.de/urn:nbn:de:0114-fqs0503288. Accessed 15.3.2015.

Neitz, Mary Jo (2011). "Feminist Methodology." In *The Routledge Handbook of Research Methods in the Study of Religion*, edited by Michael Stausberg and Steven Engler, 54–67. New York: Routledge.

Ortner, Sherry (1978). *Sherpas Through Their Rituals*. Cambridge: Cambridge University Press.

Ortner, Sherry (1996). *Making Gender: The Politics and Erotics of Culture*. Boston, MA: Beacon Press.

Pachen, Ani, and Adelaide Donnelley (2000). *Sorrow Mountain: The Journey of a Tibetan Warrior Nun*. New York: Kodansha International.

Padma'tsho (Baimacuo), and Sarah Jacoby (2020). Gender Equality in and on Tibetan Buddhist Nuns' Terms. *Religions* 11: 543. https://doi.org/10.3390/rel11100543.

Palmer, Jane, Dena Fam, Tanzi Smith and Sarina Kilham (2014). Ethics in Fieldwork: Reflections on the Unexpected. *The Qualitative Report*, 19 (28), 1–13. https://doi.org/10.46743/2160-3715/2014.1136.

References

Paul, Diana (1979). *Women in Buddhism: Images of the Feminine in Mahāyāna Tradition*. Berkeley, CA: Asian Humanities Press.

Pelak, Cynthia Fabrizio (2007). "Intersectionality." In *Blackwell Encyclopedia of Sociology*, edited by George Ritzer. Blackwell Publishing, www.blackwell reference.com/subscriber/tocnode.html?id=g9781405124331_chunk_g978140512433115_ss1-67. Accessed 15.10.2015.

Powers, John (1995). *Introduction to Tibetan Buddhism*. Ithaca, NY: Snow Lion Publications.

Powers, John (2006). *A Concise Encyclopedia of Buddhism*. Oxford: Oneworld.

Rajan, Kaushik Sunder (2011). "Teaching with George Marcus (and Learning from Michael Fischer). Pedagogy as Multi-sited Ethnography." In *Multi-sited Ethnography: Problems and Possibilities in the Translocation of Research Methods*, edited by Simon Coleman and Pauline von Hellermann, 174–193. New York: Routledge.

Ramsay, Nancy (2014). "Intersectionality: A Model for Addressing the Complexity of Oppression and Privilege." *Pastoral Psychology*, 63: 453–469. https://doi.org/10.1007/s11089-013-0570-4

Rastas, Anna (2010). "Haastatteluaineistojen monet tehtävät etnografisessa tutkimuksessa." In *Haastattelun analyysi*, edited by Johanna Ruusuvuori, Pirjo Nikander and Matti Hyvärinen, 64–89. Tampere: Vastapaino.

Ray, Reginald (1980). "Accomplished Women in Tantric Buddhism of Medieval India and Tibet." In *Unspoken Worlds: Women's Religious Lives in Non-Western Cultures*, edited by Nancy Falk and Rita M. Gross, 227–242. San Francisco, CA: Harper & Row.

Ruusuvuori, Johanna, and Liisa Tiittula (2005). "Johdanto." In *Haastattelu: Tutkimus, tilanteet ja vuorovaikutus*, edited by Johanna Ruusuvuori and Liisa Tiittula, 1–21. Tampere: Vastapaino.

Ryen, Anne (2011). "Ethics and Qualitative Research." In *Qualitative Research: Issues of Theory, Method and Practice*, edited by David Silverman, 416–435. Los Angeles, CA: Sage.

Said, Edward (1978). *Orientalism*. New York: Pantheon Books.

Samuel, Geoffrey (1993). *Civilized Shamans: Buddhism in Tibetan Societies*. Washington, DC: Smithsonian Institution Press.

Samuels, Jonathan (2014). *Colloquial Tibetan. The Complete Course for Beginners*. London: Routledge.

Saresma, Tuija (2010). "Kokemuksen houkutus." In *Käsikirja sukupuoleen*, edited by Tuija Saresma, Leena-Maija Rossi and Tuula Juvonen, 59–74. Tampere: Vastapaino.

Schaeffer, Kurtis R. (2004). *Himalayan Hermitess: The Life of a Tibetan Buddhist Nun.* Oxford: Oxford University Press.

Schaeffer, Kurtis R. (2005). "The Autobiography of a Medieval Hermitess: Orgyan Chokyi (1675-1729)." In *Women in Tibet*, edited by Janet Gyatso and Hanna Havnevik, 83-109. New York: Columbia University Press.

Schneider, Nicola (2011). "The Third Dragkar Lama: An Important Figure for Female Monasticism in the Beginning of the Twentieth Century Kham." In *Revisiting Tibetan Culture and History*, Vol. 1, Revue d'Etudes Tibétaines, 21, edited by Nicola Schneider, Alice Travers, Tim Myatt and Kalsang Norbu Gurung, 45-60.

Schrempf, Mona, and Nicola Schneider (2015). "Editorial: Female Specialists between Autonomy and Ambivalence." In *Women as Visionaries, Healers and Agents of Social Transformation in the Himalayas, Tibet and Mongolia*, Revue d'Etudes Tibétaines, 34, edited by Mona Schrempf and Nicola Schneider, i-viii.

Schwartz, Ronald (1994). "The Anti-Splittist Campaign and Tibetan Political Consciousness." In *Resistance and Reform in Tibet*, edited by Robert Barnett and Shirin Akiner, 207-237. London: Hurst & Company.

Schwartz, Ronald (2008). "Introduction: Tibet and Modernity." In *Tibetan Modernities: Notes from the Field on Cultural and Social Change*, edited by Robert Barnett and Ronald Schwartz, 1-34. Leiden: Brill.

Shaw, Miranda (1994). *Passionate Enlightenment: Women in Tantric Buddhism.* Princeton, NJ: Princeton University Press.

Shields, Stephanie A. (2008). "Gender: An Intersectionality Perspective." *Sex Roles*, 59: 301-311. https://doi.org/10.1007/s11199-008-9501-8

Shneiderman, Sara (1999). "Appropriate Treasure? Reflections on Women, Buddhism, and Cross-Cultural Exchange." In *Buddhist Women Across Cultures*, edited by Karma Lekshe Tsomo, 221-238. Delhi: Sri Satguru Publications.

Simien, Evelyn M., and Ange-Marie Hancock (2011). "Mini-Symposium: Intersectionality Research." *Political Research Quarterly*, 64 (1): 185-186. https://doi.org/10.1177/1065912910393647

Slobodník, Martin (2004). "Destruction and Revival: The Fate of the Tibetan Buddhist Monastery Labrang in the Peoples' Republic of China." *Religion, State & Society*, 32 (1): 7-19. https://doi.org/10.1080/0963749042000182104

Smith, Warren (1994). "The Nationalities Policy of the Chinese Communist Party and the Socialist Transformation of Tibet." In *Resistance and Reform in Tibet*, edited by Robert Barnett and Shirin Akiner, 51-75. London: Hurst and Company.

References

Smith, Warren (1996). *Tibetan Nation: A History of Tibetan Nationalism and Sino-Tibetan Relations*. Boulder, CO: Westview.

Sonam Wangmo and Juli Edo (2016). "Empowerment through Monastic Education: A Case Study of Buddhist Nuns in Bhutan." *Sarjana*, 31 (1), 29–44.

Spiro, Melford. (1970). *Buddhism and Society: A Great Tradition and its Burmese Vicissitudes*. New York: Harper & Row.

Sponberg, Alan (1992). "Attitudes toward Women and the Feminine in Early Buddhism." In *Buddhism, Sexuality, and Gender*, edited by José Ignacio Cabezón, 3–36. New York: State University of New York Press.

Swanepoel, Elizabeth (2014). "Blossoms of the Dharma: The Contribution of Western Nuns in Transforming Gender Bias in Tibetan Buddhism." *Journal of Buddhist Ethics*, 21, 569–599.

Swanepoel, Elizabeth (2016). "The Startling Phenomenon of the Western Tibetan Buddhist Nun: The Challenges Faced by Western Nuns in the Tibetan Buddhist Tradition Living Outside the Traditional Tibetan Buddhist Regions." *Journal for the Study of Religion*, 29 (1) 127–149.

Thonsur, Tsering Norzom (2003). "Women: Emancipation in Exile." In *Exile as Challenge: The Tibetan Diaspora*, edited by Dagmar Bernstorff and Hubertus von Weck, 322–341. New Delhi: Orient Longman.

Tobler, Judy (2006). "Tibetan Buddhist Nuns in Exile: Creating A Sacred Space to be at Home." *Journal for the Study of Religion*, 19 (1), 41–62. https://doi.org/10.4314/jsr.v19i1.6175

Tsering Chotso (1997). "A Drop from an Ocean: The Status of Women in Tibetan Society." *The Tibet Journal*, 22 (2): 59–68.

Tsomo, Karma Lekshe (1987). "Tibetan Nuns and Nunneries." In *Feminine Ground. Essays on Women and Tibet*, edited by Janice D. Willis, 118–134. Ithaca, NY: Snow Lion Publications.

Tsomo, Karma Lekshe (ed.) (1988). *Sakyadhītā: Daughters of the Buddha*. Ithaca, NY: Snow Lion Publications.

Tsomo, Karma Lekshe (1996). *Sisters in Solitude: Two Traditions of Buddhist Monastic Ethics for Women: A Comparative Analysis of the Chinese Dharmagupta and the Tibetan Mūlasarvāstivada Bhikṣuṇī Prātimokṣa Sūtras*. Delhi: Sri Satguru Publications.

Tsomo, Karma Lekshe (1999a). "Change in Consciousness: Women's Religious Identity in Himalayan Buddhist Cultures." In *Buddhist Women Across Cultures: Realizations*, edited by Karma Lekshe Tsomo, 169–189. Delhi: Sri Satguru Publications.

Tsomo, Karma Lekshe (1999b). "Mahāprajāpatī's Legacy: The Buddhist Women's Movement: An Introduction." In *Buddhist Women Across Cultures: Realizations*, edited by Karma Lekshe Tsomo, 1–44. Delhi: Sri Satguru Publications.

Tsomo, Karma Lekshe (2003). "Tibetan Nuns: New Roles and Possibilities." In *Exile as Challenge: The Tibetan Diaspora*, edited by Dagmar Bernstorff and Hubertus von Welck, 342–366. New Delhi: Orient Longman.

Tuomi, Jouni, and Anneli Sarajärvi (2009). *Laadullinen tutkimus ja sisällönanalyysi*. Helsinki: Tammi.

Urban, Greg (1996). *Metaphysical Community: The Interplay of the Senses and the Intellect*. Austin, TX: University of Texas Press.

Van Ede, Yolanda (1999). *House of Birds: A Historical Ethnography of a Tibetan Buddhist Nunnery in Nepal*. Faculteit der Maatschappij- en Gedragswetenschappen. Amsterdam: University of Amsterdam. PhD Dissertation.

Van Ede, Yolanda (2000). "Of Birds and Wings: Tibetan Nuns and their Encounters with Knowledge." In *Innovative Buddhist Women: Swimming against the Stream*, edited by Karma Lekshe Tsomo, 201–211. Richmond: Curzon.

Van Esterik, Penny (1982). "Laywomen in Theravāda Buddhism." In *Women of Southeast Asia*, edited by Penny van Esterik, 55–78. DeKalb, IL: Northern Illinois University, Center for Southeast Asian Studies.

Von Fürer-Haimendorf (1964). *Sherpas of Nepal: Buddhist Highlanders*. Berkeley, CA: University of California Press.

Von Fürer-Haimendorf (1989). *The Renaissance of Tibetan Civilization*. Delhi: Oxford University Press.

Vuola, Elina (2010). "Feministinen uskonnontutkimus." In *Käsikirja sukupuoleen*, edited by Tuija Saresmaa, Leena-Maija Rossi and Tuula Juvonen, 170–182. Tampere: Vastapaino.

Vuola, Elina (2017). "Religion, Intersectionality, and Epistemic Habits of Academic Feminism: Perspectives from Global Feminist Theology." *Feminist Encounters: A Journal of Critical Studies in Culture and Politics*, 1(1), 1–15. https://doi.org/10.20897/femenc.201704

Walby, Sylvia (2006). Gender Approaches to Nation and Nationalism. In *The SAGE Handbook of NATIONS and NATIONALISM*, edited by Gerard Delanty & Kumar Krishan. London: SAGE Publications, 118–128.

Wang Lixiong (2002). "Reflections on Tibet." *New Left Review*, 14: 79–111.

Wang Shiyong (2009). *Tibetan Market Participation in China*. Institute of Development Studies. Helsinki: University of Helsinki. PhD Dissertation.

References

Warren, Carol A. B. (2001). "Qualitative Interviewing." In *Handbook of Interview Research*, edited by Jaber F. Gubrium and James A. Holstein, 83–101. Sage: Thousand Oaks.

Weber, Lynn (1998). "A Conceptual Framework for Understanding Race, Class, Gender, and Sexuality." *Psychology of Women Quarterly*, 22: 13–32. https://doi.org/10.1111/j.1471-6402.1998.tb00139.x

Wiesner-Hanks, Merry (2002). "Women, Gender, and Church History." *Church History* 71 (3), 600–620. https://doi.org/10.1017/S000964070013029X

Williams, Paul. 1989. *Mahāyāna Buddhism. The Doctrinal Foundations*. London: Routledge.

Willis, Janice (1987). "Tibetan Ani-s: The Nun's Life in Tibet." In *Feminine Ground: Essays on Women and Tibet*, edited by Janice Willis, 96–117. Ithaca, NY: Snow Lion Publications.

Wilson, Liz (2001). "Seeing Through the Gendered 'I'. The Self-Scrutiny and Self-Disclosure of Nuns in Post-Asokan Buddhist Hagiographic Literature." *Journal of Feminist Studies in Religion*, 11 (1): 41–80.

Wu Qi (2013). *Tradition and Modernity. Cultural Continuum and Transition among Tibetans in Amdo*. Publications of the Institute for Asian and African Studies, 14. Helsinki: University of Helsinki. PhD Dissertation.

Yeh, Emily (2007). "Exile Meets Homeland: Politics, Performance, and Authenticity in the Tibetan Diaspora." *Environment and Planning D. Society and Space*, 25 (1), 648–667. https://doi.org/10.1068/d2805

Young, Serenity (2000). "Women Changing Tibet, Activism Changing Women." In *Women's Buddhism, Buddhism's Women: Tradition, Revision, Renewal*, edited by Ellison Banks Findly, 229–242. Boston, MA: Wisdom Publications.

Yu, David C. (1971). Buddhist in Communist China: Demise or Co-Existence? *Journal of the American Academy of Religion*, 39 (1): 48–61. https://doi.org/10.1093/jaarel/XXXIX.1.48

Yuval-Davis, Nira, & Floya Anthias (1989). "Introduction." In *Woman - Nation - State*, edited by Nira Yuval-Davis and Floya Anthias, 1–15. New York: Palgrave Macmillan.

Zheng, George G. (2010). "Culture, Development, and Regional Ethnic Autonomy: Tibet Issue in China's Constitutional Framework." https://doi.org/10.2139/ssrn.1634570. Accessed 2.5.2016.

Index

Note: page numbers followed by *n* refer to footnotes.

abortion 142, 149
Adams, Vincanne 168
African-American women 5*n*4, 18–19, 20, 21, 22, 23, 166
agency 6, 6*n*7, 14, 16, 17, 24, 173, 174–177, 186, 202–203, 206–207
    ethical/political context of 191–192
    and karma 174*n*1
    as resistance 178
    and social structures 193
agriculture 56, 57, 57*n*6, 59, 110, 132
    and Chinese regime 135
Ahonen, Johanna 24, 204
Allen, Amy 203, 207
Allione, Tsultrim 162
altruism 69, 189, 190–191
Amdo (Qinghai/Sichuan) 12, 26, 27, 28, 29, 33, 35
    lay informants from 70, 113–114, 117–118
    marriage in 140–141
    nunneries/monasteries in 38, 66, 74–75, 85–86, 88, 88–89, 99, 109, 117, 184
    nuns' family background in 48–49, 52, 53, 56, 63, 77–78, 111, 137
    Tibetan nationalism in 179, 182
    women in 165
animal husbandry 57–58, 65, 132, 132–133*n*2
    and Chinese regime 138
Anthias, Floya 28
anthropology 29–30, 31, 32, 178*n*1
Arya Kshema Gathering 195
asceticism 15, 186*n*1, 187

Atkinson, Paul 39, 42
attachment 54, 118, 158, 187
Aziz, Barbara Nimri 35, 163

Barkham (Tibet) 85
Barkhor (Lhasa) 179, 180
Barnett, Robert 8, 32–33, 180, 196
Bell, Charles 8
bhikṣu saṅgha 80, 194
bhikṣuṇī ordination 10, 144, 194*n*2
hikṣuṇī Prātimokṣa Sūtra 80, 194
bhikṣuṇī saṅgha 10, 80
Bhutan 15, 26*n*3, 27
Bird, Frederick 42
Blue Annals 11
bodhisattvas 154, 155, 156, 159, 188, 190–191
    female 160, 161, 174
Bön school 28, 154*n*2, 157
brothers 60
    death of 54–55, 68, 69, 71, 72
    monk 52, 96
Bruce, Steve 182–183
Buddha 51, 56, 64, 80, 154, 155–156, 183
    and women 158, 162
buddha-nature 155, 156
Buddhism *see* Tibetan Buddhism
Buddhist education 15, 51, 52, 101–104, 133, 195, 207
    and academic degrees 82*n*9, 193
    in exile nunneries 13–14, 102, 103–104, 106, 107–108, 193
    and khenpos 13*n*16, 102, 103
    and monastic obligations 103–104
    and nuns as teachers 52, 87–88, 98

Index

bureaucratic hierarchies 146, 148
Butler, Alex 8

calligraphy 104, 106
Campbell, June 162
Castelli, Elizabeth A. 24, 204
caterpillar fungus 56, 137
celibacy 15, 80, 82, 176n4
cham dances 104
Changchub, Ani 5, 54, 81, 88, 112, 188, 213
chanting master 86
chanting prayers/scriptures 52, 55, 59, 65, 67, 80, 101, 103, 104, 106, 109
chastity 74, 140n11
Chentsa (Qinghai) 34
Chertow, Jennifer Marie 150
children 132n2, 133
    death of 65–66
    see also motherhood
China 6, 8, 25–26, 25n1, 111, 163, 195
    and autonomous regions 147, 147n3, 148
    economy of 135–137
    and ethnic minorities 136–137, 147–148
    ethnic minorities in 136–137, 147–148, 147nn2, 4, 170, 205–206
    and gender equality 168, 195
    migration in 137, 166n13, 167, 205
    and research restrictions 7, 32–33, 37–38
    Tibet viewed as backward by 166, 166n14, 167, 168, 168n17
    and Tibetan nationalism see Tibetan nationalism
    Tibetan regions of 26, 27, 104, 105, 109, 125, 180
    Western Development Policy 135–136, 166n13
    see also specific regions
Chinese occupation of Tibet 4, 40, 118–127, 131–145
    and agricultural reforms 135
    and Chinese police 120, 121, 122, 126–127
    and disciplinary domain of power 147, 152, 205–206
    and domains of power 131–132
    and economic reforms 135–139
    escape from 3, 43, 123–127
    and intersectionality 131
    and modernization 133, 135–136, 136n8, 147, 148, 150–151, 166–168, 179, 183–185, 197, 205, 206
    and nuns/nunneries 3, 12, 80, 98–99, 119, 125, 143–145
    and pastoralism/nomadism 138
    and power relations 147
    resistance to see Tibetan nationalism
    and secularization 167–168, 183, 201
    "strike hard campaign" 125
    and torture/imprisonment 120–123, 127
    and women 132–135, 148–151
Cho, Sumi 19
Cho, Yasmin 12, 94
Choedron, Ani 61–62, 72–73, 87–88, 211
chuba 47, 76
circumambulation 88, 104, 105, 180
class 9, 18, 19, 20, 23, 24, 110, 131, 173
Collins, Patricia Hill 6nn5, 7, 19, 20–21, 23, 131, 146, 166, 169, 204
    and domains of power 173
commune system 135
community 28–29, 183
    imagined 28n6
    see also lay community
compassion 155, 156, 174n3, 188, 191n3
contraception 141–142
CPC (Communist Party of China) 3, 147n3, 148, 166
Crenshaw, Kimberlé 18, 19

Index

Cultural Revolution (1966-1976) 80, 90, 103, 135, 166-167, 179
culture
    and ethnography 31, 32
    and hegemonic domain of power 21, 153
    see also Tibetan culture
cyclic existence (*saṃsāra*) 47-48, 51, 54n4, 154, 190
    and emptiness 155, 156
    and female rebirth 163, 164
    and marriage/motherhood 65, 65n7, 158
    and suffering *see* suffering

ḍākinīs 83n11, 145, 161, 162
Dalai Lama 3, 11, 83, 108
    13th 28, 146, 150n7, 178n2
    14th 141n13, 166, 194-195
    and India 26, 93, 124, 125-126
    and Tibetan nationalism 120, 121, 122
data analysis 38-39
Davidsson Bremborg, Anna 36, 42
Davis, Kathy 22-23
Dawa, Ani 69, 73, 114, 189, 212
Dawa Draba 96-97
death 47-48, 54-55, 56, 57, 97
    of children 65-66
Dechen, Ani 53, 71, 72, 78-79, 93-94, 125-126, 180-181, 209
desire 80, 158, 160
Dhamoon, Rita Kaur 23
Dharamsala (India) 26, 29n7, 93, 125-126
dharma 9, 51, 55, 66, 67, 68, 87, 103, 183, 188-189
dharma camps 12-13
Dikey, Ani 48-49, 50, 59, 76, 98, 109, 212
disciplinary domain of power 20, 21, 146, 148, 153, 169, 173, 197
    and Chinese regime 147, 152, 205-206
discrimination 169-170

disease 34, 49, 55, 76
divination 75-76, 96-97
divorce 64, 66, 82, 139
    and remarriage 141
Dolkar, Ani 92-93, 119, 120-122, 124, 125, 209
Dolma, Ani 52, 78, 93, 103-104, 119-120, 122-125, 209
Dolma/Drolma 49, 114
domestic violence 63, 140-141, 175
domestic work 57, 62, 87, 110, 132-133, 134, 148, 163-164, 175
    done by nuns 105, 106, 111
domination, matrix of 20-21
Domkar Monastery (Gyegu) 91
Dragar Jangchubling monastery (Kham) 101
dreams 50, 51
Dreyfus, Georges 85, 101, 154, 186n1, 188
Drukpa Kagyu lineage 195

Edo, Juli 15
education 15, 58-62, 72-73, 77, 115, 132, 137, 205
    Buddhist *see* Buddhist education
    Chinese patriotic 125, 145
    and Compulsory Education Law (1986) 133, 134
    and gender inequality 9, 60-61, 133, 134, 138-139, 144-145, 163
    and intersectionality 138
    and language of instruction 134, 134n5
    and school enrolment rates 133-134
    and women 9, 59-62, 134-135, 175, 176, 194
Egypt 191-192
Ekvall, Robert 27
employment 61-62, 137, 138
empowerment 18, 20, 156, 173, 202, 203
empowerments 86, 87, 156n6
emptiness 154, 155, 156, 160, 161, 162

233

Index

enlightenment 154, 155, 156, 157, 187
    and women 14–15, 118, 159, 160
ethics, research 39–43
ethnic identity 181, 182, 185
ethnic minorities 136–137, 147–148, 147nn2, 4, 170, 205–206
ethnography 6, 7, 12–14, 15, 191
    criticisms of 31–32
    multi-sited *see* multi-sited ethnography
    see also research approach
exile nunneries/nuns 15, 34, 74n1, 78n4, 93, 99, 119, 193–195
    and Buddhist education 13–14, 102, 108
    and daily schedules 105, 107–108, 109–110
    and escape from persecution 123–127
exiled Tibetans 3n1, 7, 8, 26, 29

Falk, Nancy 159
Falzon, Mark-Anthony 30, 32
families 3, 9, 47, 48, 49, 52–53, 64, 67, 69, 95
    and contraception 141–142
    and death 54–55
    and education 59–61
    escape from, to become nun 75, 77–79
    lineage conventions of 139
    livelihoods of 56–59, 132–133
    middle-class 110
    and poverty 55, 56, 58–59, 65, 82
    in support of nuns 111, 114
    and women's labor 56–62, 58, 59, 66, 71–72, 87, 132–133, 135, 138, 163
    see also marriage; parents
family planning 149–150, 175–176
fasting 104, 109
female body 8, 15, 159, 160–161
    and purity/impurity 158, 163, 165
    see also nuns' bodies
feminine 16, 158, 161, 176n4, 206

feminism 15, 17, 24, 157–158, 195
    African-American 5n4, 18–19, 20, 22, 23, 166
    and agency 191–192, 203
    and intersectionality 5, 6–7, 18, 19
    and religion 203–204
Ferguson, James 28
Finnish Advisory Board on Research Integrity 41
Four Noble Truths 154

Gansu (China) 12, 26, 33, 37, 135
Garze (Sichuan) 91
gelong/gelongma ordination 79, 80, 83, 84, 194–195, 194n2, 202, 208
Geluk school 37, 82–83, 82n9, 85, 89, 91, 117, 145, 154n2
    and education 101, 107
gender 4, 4n2, 12, 15, 16–17, 90, 113, 117–118, 131, 170, 208
    Buddhist origin myth of 158–159
    and Chinese regime 151–152
    and intersectionality 5–6, 5n4, 7n8, 18, 19, 20, 22–23, 24, 173, 202, 204, 207
    performativity of 12n14
    and tantras 161–162
    and Tibetan nationalism 196–197
    transformation 160
gender equality 16, 163, 168, 195, 197, 207
gender inequality 15, 110, 111, 112–113, 114–116, 143, 152
    and education 9, 60–61, 133, 134, 138–139, 144–145, 163, 205
genyen 79, 79n8, 80, 83
geshe exams 82, 193
getsül precepts 79n8, 80, 83
globalization 30, 30n9
Goldstein, Melvyn 26–27, 110, 137, 142, 143, 146, 149–150n6, 150, 187
gompas 85
grandparents 72

Index

Great Prayer Festival 193
Grimshaw, Anna 62, 105, 116
Gross, Rita 16, 161
Gruschke, Andreas 28
Gupta, Akhil 28
Gutschow, Kim 10, 14, 51, 69, 73, 79–80, 83n10, 105, 110–111, 144, 164, 188
Gyaltsen, Ani 59, 98, 211
Gyatso, Janet 9
Gyegu 91, 95, 97
Gyurmey, Ani 55–56, 60, 69, 95, 189, 210

Hae-Ju Sunim 160
Hainan (China) 83, 145
hair 47, 49, 76, 81–82
   and ordination (*rabchung*) 51, 77, 79–80, 82, 83, 88
Hammersley, Martyn 39, 42
Han Chinese 8, 57, 111n9, 137, 147n3, 148, 149, 166, 170, 205
Hannerz, Ulf 31, 32, 35
happiness 3, 47, 48, 52, 57, 58, 62, 63, 65, 67
Harris, Elizabeth J. 158, 159
Havnevik, Hanna 4, 9, 11, 13, 14, 101, 104–105, 110, 112, 165, 185
hegemonic domain of power 21, 153, 168, 173, 197, 206
hegemonies 20, 153, 166, 168, 191
hermitages 85, 188
Himachal Pradesh (India) 13n17, 26, 29n7, 34
Himalayas 10, 14, 16–17, 28
Hinayāna 154
Hortso (Tibet) 85
Huber, Toni 27
human rights 124, 148n5

identity 18, 27–29
   ethnic 181, 182, 185
ideology 153
ignorance 54, 118, 155
impermanence 47, 56, 154, 158

India 10, 26n3, 27, 40, 78n4, 96, 180–181
   Buddhist education in 13–14, 103–104
   daily routines in 105–108
   Dharamsala 26, 29n7, 93–94, 125–126
   escape to 3, 43, 123–127
   Tibetan Nuns' Project in 193
   Tibetan schools in 134n4
   women in 158, 159
interpersonal domain of power 20, 21–22, 153, 169, 173, 197
intersectionality 4–7, 7n8, 18–24, 39, 43, 202, 204n2, 207
   application of 22–24
   and change 24
   and Chinese oppression 131
   and conceptions of women 163
   definitions of 19
   and gender *see under* gender
   as knowledge project 20
   and matrix of domination 20–21
   and power 18, 19, 20–22, 23, 24, 173
   and resistance 22
interviews 33, 34, 35–37, 38, 40, 42

Jacoby, Sarah 12, 66
Jamyang, Ani 63, 89, 210
Jari nunnery 87, 88, 95, 96
Jiegu Monastery (Gyegu) 91
Jokhang temple (Lhasa) 120n12, 179

Kagyu school 34, 83–84, 85, 86, 95, 96, 107, 145, 154n2
Kailash, Mount (Tibet) 124, 126
Kalsang, Ani 60, 67, 81, 87, 94, 211
Kangyur 126, 153
Kapstein, Matthew 27
karma 48, 49, 50–51, 68, 73, 142, 154, 164
Karma, Ani 80–81, 91–92, 109, 210
Karma Kagyu lineage 195
Karnataka (India) 26

Index

Kham (Qinghai) 26, 27, 28, 29, 33, 35, 56n5
   and education 101
   family backgrounds in 56, 57–58, 59, 60–62
   motivations for monasticism in 50–51, 63–64, 66
   nunneries in 85, 86, 87, 89, 90, 93, 94, 111
   and ordination 80–81
   status of nuns in 195
   Tibetan nationalism in 179, 183–184
Khandro Rinpoche 66
khandromas 83, 117, 145
khata 51
khenpos 13n16, 102, 103
King, Ursula 17
kleśas 54
knowledge systems 5, 30
Kongpo (Tibet) 139
Kragh, Ulrich Timme 162
Kumbum monastery (Qinghai) 34, 34n13, 84
Kupari, Helena 203

Lab Monastery (Thrindu) 96
Labrang (Gansu) 12, 37n15, 53, 75, 78, 82, 90, 117
   gender relations in 151
Ladakh (India) 13n17, 14, 27, 28, 62, 105, 187
LaFever, Kathryn 15
Lahtinen, Anja 38
lamas 80, 115
   and education 101
   and exclusion of women 145
   income of 111, 111n9
   and nunneries 33, 38, 86, 89, 92, 93, 95, 97, 100, 101, 145, 195, 202
   and ordination *see* ordination
   prophesies by 75–76, 96–97
Lamotte, Étienne 186
Lamrim 109

Larung Gar Five Sciences Buddhist Academy 12–13, 13n16
lay community 12, 15, 36, 43, 50, 70, 102, 110
   attitudes towards nuns of 73–74, 112–113, 114–116, 157
   and gender 117–118
   and monastics, relationship between 112–114, 187–188
   and status of nuns 112–113, 114–116, 157, 202
   and women *see* Tibetan women
Leshkowich, Ann Marie 35–36
Lhamo, Ani 50, 63, 75, 76, 109, 213
Lhasa (Tibet) 3, 28, 98, 119, 126, 168, 176, 179–180
Lhatso, Ani 60–61, 63, 68, 94, 107, 211
life stories 35–36, 37, 39
literacy/illiteracy 52, 59, 101, 103, 133, 133n3, 134
livelihoods 56–59, 132–133, 137–139
   animal herding 57–58, 65, 132, 132–133n2
   farming 56, 57, 57n6, 59, 110, 132
   of nuns 110, 111–114
living standards 62, 135, 136, 168, 183

McCall, Leslie 18n1, 19, 22
Maeder, Cristoph 31
Mahāyāna 153, 154–156, 154n3, 159–160, 187
Mahmood, Saba 23, 191, 193, 207
Makley, Charlene 8, 12, 12n14, 16, 40, 82, 90, 134, 140–141, 140n11, 141n12, 151, 163
mani walls 37
mantras 37n16, 53, 88n3, 105, 109
Mao Zedong 166
Marcus, George E. 29–30, 32
marriage 47, 50, 57, 58, 62–66, 68, 70, 148–149
   arranged 140, 175, 205
   and Chinese regime 139–143
   and domestic violence 63, 140–141, 175

and dowries 63, 64, 140
and patrilocal residence system 140
and polygyny/polyandry 139, 140
and *saṃsāra* 65, 65n7
see also divorce; motherhood
Martin, Dan 10–11
Marxism 167
masculinity 16, 158, 161
Matsuda, Mari 22
media 21, 124, 194
meditation 89, 103, 104, 106, 188
menstruation 158, 163, 165
merit-making 14
migration 137, 166n13, 167
Mills, Martin 188
modernity 150, 151, 152, 166–167n14, 167
monasteries 11, 12–13, 33, 37, 202
   and Chinese regime 167, 182
   and education 101, 102
   and nationalism 181–182, 183, 184
   types of 85
Mongolia 16, 178n2
morality 32, 72, 152, 154, 165
mother 158, 159, 190, 191
motherhood 62–63, 64–66, 141–143, 175–176
   and contraception 141–142
   and suffering 142, 143, 158, 159, 176
motivation for monasticism 4, 39, 43, 47–49, 50–51, 131, 132, 189–191
   and agency *see* agency
   hardships of lay life 56–62, 70, 175
   helping others 69, 188–189, 207
   and marriage/motherhood 47, 50, 57, 58, 62–66, 68, 70, 139, 142–143, 175
   nuns/monks as inspirations 47, 48, 49, 52–54, 57, 65
   and rebirth 73–74, 187, 190, 191, 192, 207
   religious devotion 66–70
   and suffering 3, 47–48, 51, 54–56, 57
   and Tibetan nationalism 185
multi-sited ethnography 29–31, 35, 208
   aim of 31
   criticisms of 30–31
   and world system 31, 32

Nadai, Eva 31
Namdzong nunnery (Amdo) 75, 77–78, 98
Nangchen 97
nation 28, 28n6, 148, 151, 173, 174, 178
nationalism *see* Tibetan nationalism
Nepal 13, 15, 26, 26n3, 27, 124, 126, 163, 186
Ngawang, Ani 81, 94, 211
ngöndro 88, 97, 102, 104, 107
Nikāyas 158
nirvāṇa 154, 159, 186
nomadism 7, 56, 57–58, 59, 132, 138, 141
non-violence 142, 180, 185, 197
norms, religious 13
Norzom, Ani 65–66, 213
novice (śrāmaṇerī) ordination 79, 80, 83, 144
nunneries 11, 15, 33, 34, 37–38, 85–100
   and accommodation 86, 108
   administration of 86
   caring function of 176
   and Chinese restrictions 98–99, 111n9, 145
   daily schedules in 105–110
   data on, access to 90
   domestic chores in 105, 106
   and education 101–104, 145, 176
   enrolling in 77–79, 98–99
   founding/rebuilding of 86, 89, 92–94, 100, 109–110
   holidays in 108–109
   income of 110, 111, 112
   and lamas 86, 89, 92, 93, 95, 97
   locations/numbers of 85–86

Index

nuns' choice of 96–98
nuns' role in establishing 94, 100
nuns' travel between 11, 89, 95
recent growth of 90–92, 94–95
remoteness of 38
scarcity of 74–75, 76, 87–90, 102, 144
and Tibetan schools 95–96
nuns' bodies 12, 116, 151–152, 159
nuns' communities 86, 88, 94, 98, 100, 109, 112, 145
Nyingma school 85–86, 117, 145, 154n2

offerings 104n4, 106
opportunities 4, 5, 6, 6n6, 16, 21, 24, 173, 186, 206–207
  educational 11, 13
  and inequality 9–10, 15
  and status 17
oppression, systems of 20, 21, 23, 131, 173
ordination 10–11, 14, 14n19, 15, 43, 49, 53, 76, 77, 79–84, 98
  of children 80–81
  and exclusion of laity 79n5
  full (gelongma), denied to nuns 79, 80, 83, 84, 144, 194–195, 194n2, 202, 208
  and haircut 79–80
  levels of 79, 80, 83, 84, 144
  literature on 81, 82–83, 84
  novice (śrāmaṇerī) 79, 80, 83, 144
  of older women 81, 82–83, 83n10
  and rabchung 79, 79n8, 80, 82, 83
  status, of nuns 81–82
Ortner, Serry 187, 188

Padma'tso (Baimacuo) 12
Palden, Ani 52, 60, 78, 211
Pāli Canon 153, 158, 159
Palkyi, Ani 67, 68–69, 71–72, 75–76, 81–82, 94, 99, 103, 110, 176, 211
Palzon, Ani 99, 213
Panchen Lama 122

parents 47, 48, 49, 56, 58, 59, 65, 79, 82, 95
  death of 54
  opposition to monastic life of 71–76, 157
  and preference for sons 163–164
  and reputation of daughters 73–74, 152
  responsibility towards 71–72, 87
Pasang, Ani 53, 83, 212
pastoralism 53, 56, 57, 57n, 58, 60, 62
patriarchy 4, 9, 13, 14, 139
patrilocal residence system 140
Pelak, Cynthia Fabrizio 22, 23
Pema, Ani 64, 82–83, 84, 212–213
philosophical studies 102, 103, 107, 193
Phuntsok, Ani 51, 55, 61, 72, 81, 95, 102, 106–107, 210–211
pilgrimage 26, 27, 105, 176
police 120, 121, 122, 126–127
poverty 55, 56, 58–59, 110, 119, 137, 139, 175, 189, 190
  in China 136
power 5–6, 17, 18, 19, 24, 40, 41, 202–203
  -over/-to/-with 203, 207
  domains of 20–22, 23, 131–132, 146, 169, 173, 197, 204–205
prayer 69, 93, 103, 104, 105, 106, 107, 113–114
prophesies 75–76, 96–97
prostrations 64, 88n3, 104, 106, 107
purification 14

Qinghai (China) 26, 33, 34, 37–38, 83, 134, 135, 189
  Kumbum monastery 34, 34n13, 84
  see also Amdo; Kham; Yushu

rabchung 79, 79n8, 80, 82, 83
race 5n4, 18, 19, 20, 23, 24, 131, 173
Rajan, Kaushik Sunder 32
Ramsay, Nancy 19
Rastas, Anna 40

238

Index

rationalization 21, 43, 146
Ray, Reginald A. 161
realms of existence 69, 73, 189n2
Rebgong (Qnghai) 34, 83, 88
reflexive research 24
reincarnation 152
religion 24, 203–204
    and women 4, 7, 208
religious freedom 49, 50, 120, 125
religious texts 48, 51, 52, 69, 97, 101, 126, 153, 156
    memorizing of 92–93, 109
    and women 158, 159–163
renunciation 77, 79, 82, 158, 186, 188
research approach 29–43
    and administrative data 38
    and Chinese restrictions 32–33, 33n12, 34
    and data analysis 38–39
    and disease/earthquake 34, 35
    and field trips 33, 37–38
    and interviews 33, 34, 35–37, 38, 40, 42–43
    and life stories 35–36, 39
    and positionality/ethics 39–43
    see also multi-sited ethnography
retreats 11, 66, 92, 95, 104, 108
Richardson, Hugh 27
Rinchen, Ani 50–51, 61, 83–84, 93, 96–97, 209–210
rinpoche (head lama) 79, 92, 95, 96, 98, 100
rural Tibet 12, 26, 56–57, 137, 196, 205
    and Chinese reforms 135, 175
    and family planning 149–150
    poverty in 58–59, 110, 119, 137
    schools in 133–134
    women's labor in 132
Ryen, Anne 41

sādhanas 104
Sakya school 34, 85, 95–96, 107, 145, 154n2
Samdup, Ani 63–64, 72, 74, 82, 87, 96, 103, 211

saṃsāra see cyclic existence
Samuel, Geoffrey 27, 28, 85
saṅgha 80, 85, 153n1, 159
Sangmo, Ani 77, 213
Sangye, Ani 95, 212
Schaeffer, Kurtis 10
Schneider, Nicola 16, 101
Scholes, Laurie Lamoureux 42
Schrempf, Mona 16
self-immolation 180
Sershül Monastery (Sichuan) 96
Serta Monastery (Sichuan) 88, 91
sexual intercourse 160–161, 162
sexuality 8, 12, 12n14, 14, 18, 20, 23, 131, 151, 173
Shaw, Miranda 161
Sherab, Ani 5, 77, 99, 104, 107–108, 149, 209
    in escape to India 3, 125, 126–127
Sherab, Thupton 189–190
Sherpa monastics 13, 15, 176, 176n4, 187
Shneiderman, Sara 15, 176–177
Shugsep nunnery (India) 78, 93
Sichuan (China) 12, 26, 37, 61, 99, 135
sickness 34, 49, 55–56, 61, 76, 81
Singham, Lorna Amara 158
Smith, Warren 179
social inequalities 17, 20
social institutions 21, 132, 146, 153, 205
social mobility 15
social organization 20, 21, 146, 169
Sonam, Ani 95, 98–99, 105, 212
Sponberg, Alan 162
śrāmaṇerī ordination 79, 80
structural domain of power 20, 21, 148, 153, 169, 173, 197
stūpas 37, 112
suffering 3, 47–48, 51, 54–56, 54n, 57, 68, 154, 186, 190
    three types of 54n4, 190
    and women 142, 143, 158, 176, 177
surveillance 21, 146, 148, 152, 197, 205
sūtras 153, 156, 157, 158, 160

Index

Taiwan 84, 195
tantras/tantric Buddhism 28, 84, 104, 156–157, 158
   and women 160–162
TAR (Tibet autonomous region) 13, 25–26, 32, 37, 78, 93
   Chinese oppression in 98, 127
   education in 60
   family planning/contraception in 142, 142n4, 149
   motivations for monasticism in 52, 53
   poverty in 136, 137
Tashi, Ani 47–48, 52, 57–58, 59, 64–65, 74, 87, 21096
teachers, nuns as 51, 52, 53
Tenzin, Ani 74–75, 98, 209
Theravāda Buddhism 14n19, 144
Theravāda Pāli Canon 153
Therīgāthā 159
therīs 159
Thonsur, Tsering Norzom 140
Thrangu Monastery 91
Three Precious Jewels 154
Tibet 25–43
   arrival of Buddhism in 181–182
   Chinese migrants in 136–137
   cultural identity in 27–29, 35
   economy of 57n6, 135–136
   ethnic 27, 28
   geography of 25
   modernization of 150–151, 150n7, 166–168
   as political entity 25–26
   rural *see* rural Tibet
   secularization in 167–168
   social strata in 5n4
   Western projection of 7n9, 201
   see also specific regions
Tibet, historical 201
   economy of nunneries in 110
   and gender 163, 168
   number/distribution of nunneries in 85–86
   power relations in 146–147
   status of women in 7–11

Tibetan Buddhism 4, 9–10, 13, 35, 40–41
   and Bön school 28, 154n2, 157
   Chinese restrictions on 80, 98–99, 145, 170
   conceptions of women in 157–163
   and dharma *see* dharma
   and folk beliefs/practices 153, 157
   four doctrinal layers of 153–157
   Geluk school *see* Geluk school
   and *Hinayāna* 154
   and impermanence/suffering 47–48, 51
   Indian influence on 158
   Kagyu school *see* Kagyu school
   and karma 48, 49, 50–51, 68, 73, 142, 154
   and Mahāyāna 153, 154–156, 154n3, 159–160
   Nyingma school 85–86, 117, 145, 154n2
   revival of 179, 183–184, 201
   Sakya school 34, 85, 95–96, 107, 145, 154n2
   and *saṃsāra see* cyclic existence
   and six perfections 155
   and status of women 57–63
   tantric *see* tantras/tantric Buddhism
   and Vajrayāna 104, 153, 156–157, 162n10
Tibetan Canon 153
   see also religious texts
Tibetan culture 26, 27, 35, 52, 79, 182, 207
   and ethnicity 28–29
   and gender 9–10, 13, 16–17, 134, 139, 141, 153
Tibetan language 37, 37n14, 40, 134, 176
Tibetan monasticism 4, 7, 12, 14, 33, 35, 36–37, 100, 117–118, 183, 186–192
   and Christian monasticism, compared 186n1

240

and communal salvation 186, 187, 188–189, 191
as escape from death/rebirth cycle 47–48
and laity *see* lay community
and nationalism 181–182, 183–185
otherworldliness of 186–188
revival of 90, 179, 183–184, 201
and state 146
and types of monasteries 85–86
Tibetan monks 10, 11n13, 15, 33, 50, 96, 104, 146, 187, 189–190
and education 102, 109
and laity 187–188
numbers of 88, 91–92
and nunneries 86, 87–88, 105
and nuns, inequality between 15, 110, 111, 112–113, 114–116, 143, 144–145, 152, 207
and ordination 80, 81, 84
religious activities of 110, 112–113, 114, 186n1
as role models 47, 48, 49, 52
status of 15, 110, 114
Tibetan names 36
Tibetan nationalism 4, 8, 11, 13, 26, 35, 152, 168, 174, 178–185, 195–197
and Buddhism as cultural defense 181–182, 184
and Buddhist revival 179, 183–184, 201
and ethnic identity 181, 182, 185
and gender 196–197
and monasticism 181–182, 183–185, 206–207
and protests 119–120, 123, 179–180
Tibetan nationality 5, 6, 24, 28, 41, 186, 192, 202, 204, 208
Tibetan nuns 3–7, 10
agency of *see* agency
androgyny of 151–152, 159
approach to researching *see* research approach
careers of 104–105
communities 86, 88, 94, 98, 100

dress/appearance of 14, 15, 47, 49, 51, 76
and education 13–14, 15, 52, 87–88, 98, 101–104
empowerment of 15, 173, 202, 203
in exile *see* exile nunneries/nuns
families of *see* families
freedoms of 4, 16, 68, 69, 174, 175–177
in historical Tibet 10–11
and intersectionality *see* intersectionality
and laity *see* lay community
and lay community 12, 15, 36, 43, 102, 110
literature on 10, 12–16, 69, 81, 82–83, 83n10
livelihoods of 110, 111–114
living outside nunneries 87–88, 105, 109, 111, 144
as medical practitioners 61, 113
and monks, compared *see under* Tibetan monks
motivation to become *see* motivation for monasticism
and nationalism *see* Tibetan nationalism
ordination of *see* ordination
religious activities of 43, 87, 101–102, 104, 105, 109, 110, 112–114, 157, 191, 193
and religious hierarchy 13, 117, 143–144, 170
status of 4, 10–11, 13, 15–17, 19, 89, 90, 111, 114–118, 144, 157–158, 194, 202, 208
stories about 54, 79
subordination of 4, 5, 6, 14–15
and surveillance 152
terms for 3n1, 11, 36, 195
wandering lifestyle of 11, 89, 95
Tibetan refugees 13–14, 15, 26
Tibetan studies 6, 7–8, 16
Tibetan women 3–17
and Chinese regime 132, 148–152, 168

and contraception/family
  planning 141–142, 149–150
and education 59–62, 115, 138–139, 175
freedoms of 8, 9
and intersectionality 4–7
and labor 58, 59, 62, 66, 71, 132–133, 138, 148, 175, 205
and modernity 150, 151, 152
and power relations 148–151
professional 135
research gap for 7, 9, 10
restrictions on 9, 10, 14–15
status of 4, 7–11, 115, 117–118, 139, 157–158, 202
and Tibetan nationalism 4, 8
Tobler, Judy 13–14
torture/violence 120–123, 127
trade 27
Trikha (Hainan) 83
Triple Gem 80
Tsarong, Paljor 187
Tsering, Ani 95, 212
Tsering Chotsho 163
Tsewang, Ani 118–119, 212
Tsomo, Ani 54, 55, 88, 188, 213
Tsomo, Karma Lekshe 10, 14–15, 16–17, 111, 144, 193, 194
Tuomaala, Salome 203

Ü-Tsang (Tibet) 26, 28, 77, 85, 92, 143
United States, African-American feminism in 5n4, 18–19, 20, 21, 22, 23
Urban, Greg 29

Vajrayāna 104, 153, 156–157, 162n10
Vajrayāna nuns 15
van Ede, Yolanda 15, 176
vinaya texts 80
violence 120–123, 127
  domestic 63, 140–141, 175
vows 34, 49, 73, 79, 79n5
Vuola, Elina 24, 204

Wang Shiyong 27–28, 134, 136, 136n8, 191

Wangchuk, Ani 52, 59, 73, 212
Wangmo, Sonam 15
wealth, worldly 47, 48, 57, 65, 190
Weber, Lynn 24
Wesel Dorje, Lama 97
Western Development Policy 135–136, 166n13
widows 66
Willis, Janice 10, 11nn12, 13
Wilson, Liz 159
women 157–165
  Buddhist conceptions of 157–163
  cultural conceptions of 163–165
  and education 9, 59–62, 134–135
  and enlightenment 14–15, 118, 159, 160, 161
  and impurity 117, 158, 165
  and power 203
  and religion 4, 7, 157–158
  and reputation 73–74
  status of 92, 115, 157–158, 163–165
  and suffering 142, 143, 158, 163
  and tantras 160–162
Wu Qi 140, 141, 151n9

Xining (Qinghai) 34, 61, 62, 90

Yachen Gar nunnery (Tibet) 12, 33, 88, 94, 96
yoga 88n3, 105, 161
Yongtsen, Ani 58–59, 61, 64, 81, 88, 94–95, 102, 188–189, 210
Yonten, Ani 50, 69, 77–78, 111–112, 189, 212
Yunnan (China) 26, 135
Yushu (Qinghai) 3, 33, 33n11, 34, 37, 176
  Chinese occupation of 119
  earthquake in (2010) 91, 91n4, 103
  education in 60
  motivations for monasticism in 52
  nunneries in 78, 90, 104, 195
Yuval-Davis, Nira 28

Zangskar (India) 13n17, 14, 27

www.ingramcontent.com/pod-product-compliance
Lightning Source LLC
Chambersburg PA
CBHW061244230426
43662CB00020B/2422